The OpenVMS User's Guide

The OpenVMS User's Guide

Second Edition

Patrick J. Holmay

Digital Press

Boston • Oxford • Johannesburg • Melbourne • New Delhi • Singapore

Butterworth–Heinemann supports the efforts of American Forests and the Global ReLeaf program in its campaign for the betterment of trees, forests, and our environment.

Library of Congress Cataloging-in-Publication Data

Holmay, Patrick, 1957–
    The OpenVMS user's guide / Patrick J. Holmay. — 2nd ed.
        p.   cm.
    Includes bibliographical references and index.
    ISBN 1-55558-203-6 (alk. paper)
        1. VAX/VMS.   I. Title.
QA76.76.063H6484   1998
005.4'44—dc21   98-3746
                                                                    CIP

British Library Cataloguing-in-Publication Data

A catalogue record for this book is available from the British Library.

The publisher offers special discounts on bulk orders of this book.
For information, please contact:
Manager of Special Sales
Butterworth–Heinemann
225 Wildwood Avenue
Woburn, MA 01801-2041
Tel: 781-904-2500
Fax: 781-904-2620

For information on all Butterworth–Heinemann publications available, contact our World Wide Web home page at: `http://www.bh.com`

10   9   8   7   6   5   4   3

Printed in the United States of America

Contents

Appendixes

Index   **293**

Preface

In the world of computers, Digital computer systems enjoy celebrity status. They are used widely and have a reputation for being user-friendly. This book is about the OpenVMS operating system from beginning user's point of view. The OpenVMS operating system is the bridge that allows you to use the power of Digital computers. Actually, OpenVMS is a collection of programs that provide an interface between users and a Digital computer system. OpenVMS is responsible for the user-friendliness of Digital computers.

The focus of this book is the Digital command language (DCL), which provides a straightforward means of issuing commands to OpenVMS. DCL is a language that, among other things, makes it possible for users to create, name, store, and edit files. We rely on files to store information that we want to preserve on some storage medium, such as a magnetic tape or a diskette.

In addition to an extensive tour of the basic DCL commands, this book provides an instruction to two commonly used OpenVMS editors: EVE and EDT. An editor is a program used in the preparation of new files or in making corrections and additions to existing files. EVE and EDT provide convenient and varied means of editing OpenVMS files. In addition to a thorough introduction to editing techniques that can be used with EVE and EDT, we provide editing experiments you can try at your terminal.

The experiments given in this book are self-teaching tools. They are designed to show you, step by step, the usage of the features of OpenVMS. This book also provides a variety of other self-teaching tools, such as

▶ Aims at the beginning of every chapter—these single out what you can expect to learn

▶ Chapter summaries

▶ Quizzes at the end of each chapter

▶ Lists of important terms with accompanying definitions

▶ Chapter exercises

▶ Further reading lists

▶ User-defined DCL commands to help you customize your OpenVMS environment

▶ A reference guide to selected DCL commands and utilities

This book has been designed to be useful as a textbook in courses about the OpenVMS environment. It also provides a convenient self-teaching tool for those who want easy access to the essentials of OpenVMS. In addition, it explains how you can customize your OpenVMS environment to fit the way you want to work with OpenVMS.

Acknowledgments

I want to thank and extend my appreciation to the following people:

To my wife, Mary, without whose love and support I could not have found the discipline to complete this project;

To my sons, Dan, Nick, and Eric, for their patience and understanding that Dad was busy working on his book;

To my entire family, who never gave up hope that they would someday see this in print;

To my uncle, Bernard Schultz, who has always been a positive influence on my writing efforts;

To Chris Gawarecki, John Muggli, and Steve Simonett, for their help and guidance during the preparation of this edition of the book;

To the individuals mentioned in the first edition, who reviewed various stages of this book and were very helpful in making the final result better;

To James Peters III, my coauthor on the first edition of this book, whose composure and influence made the first edition possible; and

To Liz McCarthy and Pam Chester, whose enthusiasm and resolve to oversee this project helped guide this edition to its successful completion.

Introduction

This book is designed to give you a solid basis for working with the many features and functions of Digital computer systems using the OpenVMS operating system. It does not cover specific application programs that run on Digital computers but rather concentrates on the capabilities and flexibility of OpenVMS. The book takes a hands-on approach, providing you with experiments and exercises to try at your terminal. It also provides discussions and examples that you can use as a reference when you work with OpenVMS on your own.

The book addresses users new to the OpenVMS environment as well as those with OpenVMS experience who need a reference guide. You may be in an instructor-led college class, in a company-sponsored training session, or working on your own without instructor supervision.

The OpenVMS Landscape

Formerly known as VMS (virtual memory system), OpenVMS was first conceived in 1976 as an operating system for Digital's new VAX (virtual address extension) computers. The new 32-bit, multitasking, multiprocessing virtual memory operating system was developed as the successor to Digital's RSX-11M operating system for the PDP-11.

OpenVMS's official name change came with the release of V6.0 of the operating system. The change occurred primarily to ease the misimpression that OpenVMS was designed solely for the Alpha AXP computer system and to signify the high degree of support for international standards for an open systems environment. The proper names for OpenVMS on the two platforms are now *OpenVMS VAX* and *OpenVMS Alpha,* the latter having superseded *OpenVMS AXP.*

OpenVMS uses virtual memory when processing programs and data. Virtual memory is composed of computer memory, or storage, that is not physically present in the computer system. When a computer uses virtual memory, it processes programs and data in segments. Only the segments currently needed are in the computer's memory; the rest are stored on disk or other storage device. The computer retrieves different stored segments as needed, returning unneeded segments to storage to free memory space for newly retrieved segments. The use of virtual memory allows OpenVMS systems to support more users or larger programs than physical memory limitations would permit.

The implementation of this virtual memory scheme is made possible by a collection of software programs (or images) that control computing operations. The base operating system is made up of core components and an array of services, routines, utilities, and related software. The OpenVMS operating system serves as the foundation from which all optional software products and applications operate. The services and utilities in the base OpenVMS operating system support functions such as system management, data management, and program development.

An important feature of the OpenVMS operating system, in addition to its use of virtual memory, is its interactive mode of communication. Because it can schedule system resources efficiently, many users can use a Digital computer system at the same time and yet feel that each has exclusive use of the system. In fact, each user's tasks are being swiftly executed one at a time, with the order of processing based on need and priority.

As a user, you communicate with OpenVMS using an interface called DCL, or the Digital command language. You enter into a dialogue with OpenVMS by issuing various DCL commands. These commands are the basis for your work with OpenVMS, and so the discussion in this book focuses on their use.

Important Considerations

Users can access the OpenVMS operating system from a wide variety of devices, ranging from desktop devices to terminals connected to large computer complexes. Depending on the configuration, OpenVMS users can share in the full capabilities of OpenVMS VAX, OpenVMS Alpha, and VAXcluster systems and can access resources on other computers throughout a worldwide multivendor network.

The means by which you communicate with an OpenVMS system may vary, depending on the user interface (keyboard, windowing, or forms based). For example, you may find that your keyboard is slightly different from those illustrated in Chapter 1. (If this is the case, you can refer to your documentation or Help facility or check with system manager to learn about key equivalents for your specific keyboard.) Although the system configuration may differ, Digital computers running OpenVMS all function basically the same way.

The experiments and examples shown in this book are current through Version 7.0 of OpenVMS. If you are working with an earlier version of OpenVMS, there may be some slight variations in your results, although there should be no major differences. Also, because the setup of each system is site specific, you may encounter slight variations in experiment results or in the availability of certain utilities.

In general, if your results differ greatly from the book's or if you encounter problems in using features discussed in the book, check with your system manager. He or she will know the specifics of your system and be able to advise you on using the features available to you.

About This Book

This book is designed to help OpenVMS users who are in a class or working on their own. Each chapter contains discussions, examples, experiments that demonstrate the concepts and commands, and other learning aids.

Users new to OpenVMS will find it invaluable to work through each experiment, step by step, while at their keyboards. More experienced users may find the discussions and examples sufficient for understanding the material or they may choose to follow the experiments. Because the experiments build on each other within the chapter, it is important to work through them from the beginning of the chapter.

In addition to the examples and experiments, each chapter contains the following learning aids and self-teaching tools:

▶ The summaries at the end of each chapter review important information and contain tables of the commands, symbols, special characters, and key terms used in the chapter. These tables are useful references for review or reinforcement of the material.

▶ Chapter exercises appear after the summaries. They reinforce the chapter's content and suggest further exploration of the capabilities of OpenVMS.

▶ Each chapter contains a review quiz, which will help you to gauge how well you understand the material.

▶ Finally, at the end of each chapter is a list of readings designed to expand your study of OpenVMS, DCL, and the uses of Digital computers.

The Structure of This Book

This book contains seven chapters and eight appendixes. Although the chapters follow a logical progression in presenting the material, it is not necessary to read them in order, particularly if you have some experience with OpenVMS.

Chapter 1 explains the basics of logging in and out of the computer and getting help through the extensive OpenVMS Help facility. It then introduces a series of concepts, all of which are explored in detail in the chapters that follow.

Chapter 2 details the system files and directories that OpenVMS uses to store your information. You learn to create and manage files and work with the directory structure that helps you organize your files.

Chapter 3 introduces one of the OpenVMS editors, EVE, which allows you to enter and edit text in files. This editor provides many features similar to those of EDT as well as some unique capabilities, such as using two windows at a time.

Chapter 4 introduces a second OpenVMS text editor, EDT. Although not a complete word-processing application, EDT provides the commands necessary for easy text entry and manipulation.

Chapter 5 covers the Phone and Mail utilities, which allow you to communicate with other users on the system.

Chapter 6 continues with an examination of files, showing you alternative ways to create and manipulate files, sort records, merge files, and print files. In addition, it covers the creation of library files, which you use to store groups of related files.

Chapter 7 discusses the creation and use of command procedures. These procedures help you customize OpenVMS for maximum efficiency by allowing you to automate routine tasks.

Appendixes A through H present a guide to selected DCL commands, file protection, information on EDT line mode commands, remote host access, program development, an ASCII table and DCL characters, ANSI mode control sequences, and DECTPU Programming.

Conventions Used in This Book

Throughout the book, certain conventions are used for presenting information and representing commands and keys:

Ctrl/X	A key sequence such as Ctrl/X indicates that you must hold down the key labeled Ctrl while pressing another key or a pointing device button.
Gold x	A sequence such as Gold x indicates that you must first press and release the key labeled Gold and then press and release another key or a pointing device button
`Return`	In examples, a key name enclosed in a box indicates that you press a key on the keyboard. (In text, a key name is not enclosed in a box.)
`Exit`	In examples, shaded text indicates that a command or application has been canceled or interrupted.
. . .	Vertical ellipsis points indicate the omission of items from a example or command format.
[ ]	Optional parameters in command lines are enclosed in brackets, for example, directory [*filespec*].
[,...]	To indicate an unspecified number of optional parameters, a comma with horizontal ellipsis points enclosed in brackets are used.
UPPERCASE TEXT	In text, user-typed entries—like commands, names of routines, names of files, parameters, or the abbreviation for a system privilege—appear in uppercase font; for instance, the DIRECTORY command. (You may use either uppercase or lowercase letters to type in command lines at the keyboard.)
lowercase boldface text	In examples, experiments, and command syntax illustrations, user-typed entries are shown in lowercase boldface **typewriter** font so that you can distinguish them from the information that Open-VMS displays; for example, the **show** command. (You may use either uppercase or lowercase letters to type in command lines at the keyboard.)
`nonbold text`	Information displayed by OpenVMS in examples and experiments appear in nonboldface `typewriter` font.
Italic text	Complete titles of manuals or books, important information, and generic names that accompany commands, for instance, print *filespec,* are shown in italics, indicating that the user is to substitute an actual file specification for the italicized word.

I

Discovering OpenVMS

> *Intelligence . . . is the faculty of making artificial objects, especially tools*
> *to make tools, and varying the fabrication indefinitely.*
>
> —Henri Bergson, *Creative Evolution*, 1907

This chapter provides an overview of the commands, procedures, and capabilities of OpenVMS. In doing so, it also introduces you to the topics discussed in the remaining chapters of this book. In this chapter, you will

▶ Explore the fundamentals of using DCL commands

▶ Become familiar with commonly used commands

▶ Explore the uses of various control keys

▶ Begin creating files

▶ Start exploring your login directory

▶ Experiment with the Recall, Type-Ahead, and EVE buffers

▶ Create and implement a LOGIN.COM file

1.1   Introducing the Digital Command Language

The OpenVMS operating system is an interactive, virtual memory operating system. When a user logs on the system, OpenVMS creates an environment from which you can enter commands and run programs. Within this environment you and the system conduct a dialogue using the Digital command language (DCL).

DCL is a traditional and consistent user interface to OpenVMS that supports batch and interactive operations. You enter a DCL command by typing it from your keyboard and pressing the Return key. OpenVMS will respond by executing the command or by displaying an error message on the screen if it cannot interpret what you entered.

The DCL command language is a set of Englishlike instructions that tell the OpenVMS operating system to perform specific actions or tasks. Table 1.1 lists examples of computing tasks and some of the DCL commands that perform those tasks.

DCL provides over 200 commands and functions that offer an easy-to-use interface between users and the many OpenVMS services. When you enter a DCL command, it is read and translated by the DCL interpreter. The type of command entered determines how the command interpreter responds to a command. Table 1.2 lists some commonly used DCL commands, or command verbs. As you can see from the table, the results describe the actions attributable to the command.

Like a spoken language, DCL is made up of words (vocabulary) and word order (syntax or format). The vocabulary consists of commands, parameters, and qualifiers, that are combined to form what is known as the *command line*. Just as a spoken language depends on the order of words to create meaning, DCL requires that you put the correct elements of the command line in a specific word order or format. This is referred to as the *command line syntax*.

The syntax or format of a DCL command is shown in Figure 1.1.

Each DCL command operates on a parameter or parameters. For example, to display information about a specific user, you enter the SHOW USERS command with the *username* parameter. If *username* is Curry, you would type the following command line and press the Return key to enter it:

```
$ show user curry  Return
```

Table 1.1 *Types of Tasks Performed by Commonly Used DCL Commands*

Task Type	Examples of DCL Commands
General session control and environmental control	HELP, SHOW, SET, ASSIGN, DEFINE, PHONE, MAIL, LOGOUT
Program development and execution control	LIBRARY, LINK, RUN, DEBUG, SPAWN, SUBMIT, WAIT, CANCEL, STOP
File manipulation control	DIRECTORY, CREATE, EDIT, DELETE, PURGE, RENAME, COPY, APPEND, SORT, PRINT, TYPE

Table 1.2 *Commonly Used DCL Commands*

Command	Result
CREATE	Creates a new file
DELETE	Deletes a file in the specified directory
DIRECTORY	Displays (or lists) the contents (or files) of a specified directory
EDIT	Displays and allows the user to change the contents of a text file
LOGOUT	Ends your user session
MAIL	Activates the Mail utility, which allows you to send and receive messages from users on your system or any other computer connected to your system
PHONE	Activates the Phone utility, which allows users to *talk* to each other via their terminals, workstations, computers, or computer networks
RENAME	Changes the name or the location of a specified file
SET	Controls how you see the system on the screen
SHOW	Displays information about your system, such as users, quota, and time
TYPE	Displays the contents of a specified file on the screen

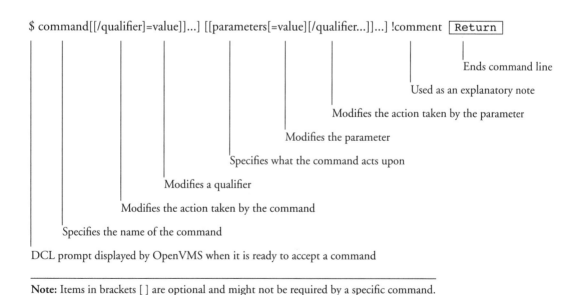

$ command[[/qualifier]=value]]...] [[parameters[=value][/qualifier...]]...] !comment ⎡Return⎤

Ends command line

Used as an explanatory note

Modifies the action taken by the parameter

Modifies the parameter

Specifies what the command acts upon

Modifies a qualifier

Modifies the action taken by the command

Specifies the name of the command

DCL prompt displayed by OpenVMS when it is ready to accept a command

Note: Items in brackets [ ] are optional and might not be required by a specific command.

Figure 1.1 *Command Line Syntax*

The parameter indicates what you want shown, in this case, information about the user Curry.

Some commands assume a default (preset) parameter if you do not specify a parameter in the command line. Other commands accept or require multiple parameters. You must separate each parameter from the command verb, parameter, or qualifier before it with space(s) or tab(s).

A command qualifier may be used to further control or modify the command and parameters. Qualifiers narrow or broaden the scope of the requested processing. For example, to log out and, at the same time, see how much time has elapsed while you have been using the system, you would type the command line

`$ logout/full` [Return]

The /FULL qualifier displays a summary of accounting statistics for the current terminal session.

Qualifiers usually are optional in DCL commands. Many commands allow you to use multiple qualifiers for a command verb or parameter. You must separate each qualifier from the command verb, parameter, or qualifier before it with a slash (/).

You can add comments to a command line by typing an exclamation point (!) and then the comment. The comment can explain what the command does or supply other useful information. DCL ignores any characters to the right of the exclamation point, so

`$ show users` [Return]

does the same thing as

`$ show users !display current users` [Return]

If you are working with a hard-copy terminal, commented command lines provide you a permanent record of explanations of new commands you have used.

When you type a DCL command line, you may use any combination of uppercase and lowercase letters, because DCL is not case sensitive.

With its many commands, parameters, and qualifiers, DCL provides a rich selection of tools that let you use the resources of your computer system efficiently. The trick is to learn how to use these tools to fashion new tools tailor-made to your own needs. The sections that follow introduce the topics covered in the other chapters of this book. They include the basics of working with DCL and some of the possibilities for customizing your OpenVMS system.

1.2   The First Steps with OpenVMS

Users can access the OpenVMS operating system from a wide variety of devices, ranging from desktop devices to character-based terminals. If you are accessing OpenVMS with a windowing device such as a personal computer (using UNIX, MS Windows, OS/2, or Macintosh), it is recommended that you familiarize yourself with the keyboard functions associated with the terminal emulation software in use before proceeding. In this book we focus on two principal character-based terminal types: the VT100 and VT200. Before you begin, take a minute to familiarize yourself with your keyboard. Figure 1.2 illustrates the two common character-based keyboard layouts.

The main keyboard contains standard typewriter keys as well as some special keys like the Ctrl (control) key. The auxiliary, or numeric, keypad contains special function keys—<PF1 through PF4>—and keys for entering numeric data. In some applications, these keys are used for special commands; for

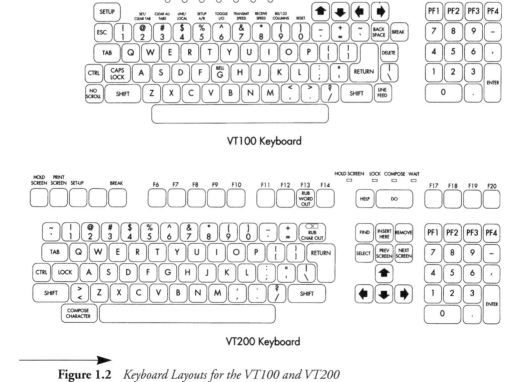

VT100 Keyboard

VT200 Keyboard

Figure 1.2   *Keyboard Layouts for the VT100 and VT200*

example, the EVE editor uses them for entering editing commands. On the VT100 keyboard, arrow keys, which you use to move the cursor, and indicators appear across the top of the keyboard. The VT200 keyboard has special keys, function keys, and indicators across the top. The editing keypad contains the arrow keys and special editing keys.

The Return key on the main keyboard is particularly important. You use it to enter a line of text that you have typed and to advance the cursor to the beginning of the next line.

Pressing the Return key tells the OpenVMS command interpreter to start doing something with the current line you have typed. Be sure to press the Return key at the end of each command line to enter the command.

Also press Return key to move to the login prompt when you first turn on a terminal connected to an OpenVMS system. After you turn on your terminal and press the Return key one or more times, the screen displays the login prompt:

```
Username:
```

Your system manager supplies your user name, which often is your last name. When you enter your user name and press the Return key, the password prompt appears:

```
Username: PHOLMAY  Return
Password:
```

Your system manager also supplies your assigned password. For security reasons, your password is not displayed, or echoed. When you enter your password and press the Return key, the system displays the DCL prompt (a dollar sign, $, by default) in the left margin of your screen.

If you make a mistake in entering either your user name or password, the system denies you access and displays a message. For example, if pholmay's correct password is *digital* and he enters *digits* instead, the results would be

```
Username: PHOLMAY  Return
Password: digits  Return
User authorization failure
```

If you make a mistake and you receive this message, you can restart the login procedure by pressing the Return key again.

Try logging in on your terminal, following the steps in Experiment 1.1.

Experiment 1.1 *Logging In*

1. Turn on your terminal or workstation and use the appropriate command sequence to connect to the OpenVMS system. When you see the login prompt, enter your user name and press Return:

```
Username: your-username  Return
Password:
```

2. At the password prompt, enter your password and press Return.

```
Username: PHOLMAY
Password: your-password  Return
   Welcome to OpenVMS Operating System on node TINY
   Last interactive login on Monday, 4-AUG-1997 20:43:59.35
   Last non-interactive login on Monday, 4-AUG-1997 19:34:58.32
$
```

Once you have typed your user name and password correctly, the system displays the systems DCL prompt ($). You can respond to the prompt with any DCL command. For example, you might want to type the LOGOUT command to tell OpenVMS to end the current session. Log out, following the steps in Experiment 1.2.

Experiment 1.2 *Logging Out*

1. End the session by typing the LOGOUT command.

```
$ logout  Return
PHOLMAY logged out at 4-AUG-1997 20:48:41.95
```

2. The system displays the logout message, assuring you that the session has terminated properly. Because you want to explore other DCL commands, log in again.

```
Username: your-username  Return
Password: your-password  Return
```

It is important to log out properly at the end of each terminal session. If you fail to log out, you run the risk of someone else using your account. In addition, if you are on a pay-by-time-logged-in system, charges against your account will continue to accumulate until you log out.

1.2.1   Other Forms of Logging In and Out

The procedures for logging in and logging out that you have just explored are the most common ones. You can use qualifiers to create many useful variations on these procedures, however.

For example, when you log in, you can specify that instead of using the default working disk you want to use a different working disk. You accomplish this by appending the /DISK qualifier to your user name when you log

> *prompt is*
> *MYDISK$* ?

...se a disk called MYDISK$ instead of the

...sk$ `Return`

Because of the /DISK qualifier, MYDISK$ would become the default working disk for your session.

When you log out, you may find it helpful to display the accounting statistics for the terminal session you have just completed by using the /FULL qualifier. The /FULL qualifier tells you how long your terminal session lasted, how much CPU (central processor unit) time you used, and so on. For example,

```
$ logout/full  Return
  PHOLMAY logged out at 4-AUG-1997 14:23:11.89

  Accounting information:
  Buffered I/O count:        117   Peak working set size: 1824
  Direct I/O count:           22   Peak page file size:  17040
  Page faults:               361   Mounted volumes:          0
  Charged CPU time: 0 00:00:00.27 Elapsed time: 0 00:07:40.03
```

You can get a list of the various forms of logging in, with examples, by using the HELP command. At the $ prompt, type

```
$ help login  Return
```

You can also use the HELP command to list the various forms of the LOGOUT command by typing

```
$ help logout  Return
```

1.2.2   Changing Your Password

For security reasons, OpenVMS does not echo your password when you log in. You may be wondering if any DCL command makes it possible for you to display your password. Again, for security reasons, the answer is no. In fact, if you forget your password, you will not be able to log in without your system manager's help.

Once you have logged in, it is possible to change your password by typing

```
$ set password  Return
Old password: your-current-password  Return
New password: your-new-password  Return
Verification: your-new-password  Return
$
```

The passwords entered in response to the password prompts will not be echoed on your screen.

Passwords may contain from 1 to 31 characters. It is common for system managers to set the minimum number of characters for a password at 6 or 7, in which case your password must contain at least that many characters. The following characters may be used when creating passwords:

A through Z (uppercase or lowercase)

0 through 9

$ (dollar sign)

_(underscore)

For example, Pascal, popcorn, catch22, catch_22, and too_much_$ are valid passwords. It is wise to change your password regularly.

Note: From this point on, the Return key at the end of command lines in examples and experiments is omitted and should be understood.

1.3   Exploring Your System's Characteristics

Your system has a variety of characteristics, and after you have logged in, you can display these characteristics using various SHOW commands (see Table 1.3). Each SHOW command lists a particular type of information about the system. For example, to see the characteristics of your terminal, you would type

```
$ show terminal
Terminal: _NTY7926: Device_Type: VT200_Series Owner: PHOLMAY
Input:  9600     LFfill: 0    Width: 132     Parity: None
Output: 9600     CRfill: 0    Page:    29
```

Table 1.3 *Commonly Used SHOW Commands*

Command	Result
SHOW DEFAULT	Displays the current default device and directory
SHOW KEY	Displays the definitions of keys created with the DEFINE/KEY command
SHOW QUOTA	Displays the disk quota currently authorized and currently used
SHOW SYMBOL	Displays the current symbol definitions
SHOW TERMINAL	Displays the characteristics of the terminal
SHOW TIME	Displays the current date and time
SHOW USERS	Displays information about the users currently logged into the system

```
Terminal Characteristics:
Interactive      Echo            Type_ahead       No Escape
No Hostsync      TTsync          Lowercase        Tab
Wrap             Scope           Remote           Eightbit
Broadcast        No Readsync     No Form          Fulldup
No Modem         No Local_echo   Autobaud         Hangup
No Brdcstmbx     No DMA          No Altypeahd     Set_speed
       .              .               .                .
       .              .               .                .
       .              .               .                .
$
```

To get a list of users currently logged into the system, you would type

```
$ show users
        OpenVMS User Processes at 4-AUG-1997 14:12:06.43
     Total number of users = 4, number of processes = 5

 Username           Interactive Subprocess Batch
 JMUGGLI                1
 YOU                    1
 PHOLMAY                1
 SYSTEM                 -           -         2
$
```

This listing tells you that three other people besides you are currently logged into the system.

In addition, like most DCL commands, many SHOW commands have a variety of qualifiers. For instance, the SHOW USERS command line has the following syntax:

```
show users [username] [/output=output-filespec][/nooutput]
```

In this command, *username* is an optional parameter. It is the name of a user about whom you want information. If you omit a specific user name, a list of all interactive users is displayed. SHOW USERS has the two optional qualifiers /OUTPUT and /NOOUTPUT. /OUTPUT specifies where the output from SHOW USERS (the list of logged-in users) is sent. By default, the output is written to the screen or hard-copy terminal. By including a file specification with /OUTPUT, you can direct the output to that file. /NOOUTPUT inhibits the output; it is not displayed, printed, or sent to a file.

Thus, to check on the availability of a particular user, you could use a specific user name with the SHOW USERS command:

```
$ show users pholmay
      OpenVMS User Processes at 4-AUG-1997 14:06:54.09
      Total number of users = 1, number of processes = 1
```

```
        Username        Interactive     Subprocess      Batch
        PHOLMAY             1
    $
```

Some of the other show commands also have qualifiers, allowing you to view exactly the information you need.

In addition to viewing the system characteristics, you can use the SET commands to change some of them. You have already seen that SET PASS-WORD can be used to change your password. Table 1.4 lists several SET commands.

For example, by default, OpenVMS assigns your user name to your process name. You could change your process name by using the SET PROCESS command with the /NAME qualifier. The syntax is

set process/name=*new-name*

The process name can be any string, so, for example, you could use your telephone extension or another useful string:

```
$ set process/name=ext.2788
$
```

Because the process name is displayed in the SHOW USERS listing, changing your process name in this way can convey useful information to other users.

You can modify the width of your display by using the SET TERMINAL command with the /WIDTH qualifier. For example, to change your screen width to 132 columns, you would type

```
$ set terminal/width=132
$
```

You can explore your system and practice using the SHOW and SET commands by following Experiment 1.3. Other SHOW and SET commands are introduced throughout the rest of the chapter.

Table 1.4 *Commonly Used SET Commands*

Command	Result
SET PASSWORD	Changes the user's password
SET PROMPT	Personalizes the OpenVMS prompt
SET PROCESS	Defines the execution characteristics of the current process
SET TERMINAL	Defines the operational characteristics of a terminal

Experiment 1.3 *Using SHOW and SET Commands*

1. To see the current date and time, use the SHOW TIME command:

```
$ show time
4-AUG-1997 00:05:21
```

2. The default system prompt is $. You can change this prompt and personalize your working environment by using the SET PROMPT command:

```
$ set prompt=":-)"
:-)
```

If you turn your head sideways, you can see that your system prompt now is a smile.

3. Use the SET PROMPT command to return to the default system prompt:

```
$ set prompt
$
```

1.4   Getting Help

At any point during an OpenVMS session, you can use the HELP command to get information about working with your system and with DCL commands, qualifiers, and parameters. The HELP command accesses the Help library, which contains information about various topics and subtopics. The command syntax is

```
help [keyword]
```

The optional keyword parameter is any Help topic.

If you enter the HELP command without a parameter, a list of topics appears along with the Topic? prompt. You then can type the name of a topic and press the Return key to see information about that topic and a list of subtopics (if any exist). You can enter a subtopic to see information about the subtopic and, possibly, a list of sub-subtopics. You can enter another subtopic or a sub-subtopic.

If you press the Return key without entering a subtopic, you return to the previous Help level (unless you are at the first level; in which case, you exit Help). Alternatively, you can type HELP INSTRUCTIONS or HELP HINTS at the $ prompt to see instructions on using Help or hints about possible commands or topics.

If you want to see the previous screen of text, type a question mark, ?. Press the Ctrl and the letter Z simultaneously, or Ctrl/Z, to exit Help, or press the Return key to back out of the Subtopic? and Topic? prompts. If you enter an unknown topic or subtopic, an appropriate list of topics or subtopics is displayed.

If you know the topic about which you want help, you can enter it as a parameter in the HELP command line. For example, to get help about the SET PROCESS command, type

```
$ help set process

SET

  PROCESS

      Changes the execution characteristics associated with the
      specified process for the current terminal session or job. If
      .
      .
      .

  Parameter Qualifiers
    /AUTO_UNSHELVE  /DUMP        /IDENTIFICATION  /NAME
    /PRIORITY       /PRIVILEGES  /RESOURCE_WAIT   /RESUME
    /SUSPEND        /SWAPPING
    Examples

SET PROCESS Subtopic?
```

1.5   A First Look at Files and Directories

Many DCL commands identify one or more files to be processed. A *file* is a named collection of information. Files are stored permanently on an auxiliary storage device such as a magnetic disk, diskette, tape, or CD-ROM.

Each time you log in, OpenVMS provides you with a login directory that lists files you own. A *directory* is a file that contains information about other files. Chapter 2 discusses files and directories in more detail.

1.5.1   Getting a List of Files

The DIRECTORY command displays a list of the files in the specified directory. To see a list of files in the current directory, type

```
$ directory

Directory PACK2:[YOURGROUP.YOU]

LOGIN.COM;1

Total of 1 file.
$
```

This form of the DIRECTORY command elicits the file names, file types, and version numbers of the files in the current directory. For example, for the file LOGIN.COM;1, the file name is LOGIN, the file type is .COM, and the version number is 1. This information is part of the file specification. If no files are in your directory, a message appears to that effect.

The /FULL qualifier may be used to see more information about the files, such as the number of blocks used, number of blocks allocated, date of creation, date of last backup, file protection, and so on for the specified file or files. For example, to see full information about the LOGIN.COM file, you would type

```
$ directory/full login.com

Directory PACK2:[YOURGROUP.YOU]

LOGIN.COM;1                     File ID:  (38657,93,256)
Size:              1/9          Owner:    [GROUP,YOU]
Created:           4-AUG-1997 16:09:48.82
Revised:           4-AUG-1997 16:10:00.06 (1)
Expires:           None specified>
Backup:            <5-AUG-1997 02:51:43.43
Effective:         <None specified>
Recording:         <None specified>
File organization: Sequential
Shelved state:     Online
File attributes:   Allocation: 9, Extend: 0,
                   Global buffer count: 0, Version limit: 3
Record format:     Variable length, maximum 0 bytes, longest 7 bytes
Record attributes: Carriage return carriage control
RMS attributes:    None
Journaling enabled: None
File protection:   System:RWED, Owner:RWED, Group:RE,
                   World:
Access Cntrl List: None

Total of 1 file, 1/9 blocks.
$
```

You can manipulate files and the information in them in many ways. For example, you can create a file using the CREATE command or by sending the results of a command line to a file. The next two sections explore these two methods of file creation.

1.5.2   Saving Command Line Output as a File

Many DCL commands that display information on the screen let you redirect that output to a file using the /OUTPUT qualifier. For example, SHOW

USERS displays the list of people currently logged in. If you wanted to save that list in a file for future reference, you would type

```
$ show users/output=users.now
$
```

In this example, the file specification is USERS.NOW. The output from SHOW USERS is redirected to the file called USERS.NOW. You can create a file in this way by following Experiment 1.4.

Experiment 1.4 *Saving Command Line Output*

1. First use the DIRECTORY command to get a listing of the current files:

```
$ directory

Directory PACK2:[YOURGROUP.YOU]

LOGIN.COM;1

Total of 1 file.
$
```

If no files are in the directory, a message to that effect appears.

2. Save the output from a SHOW USERS command by directing it to a file called USERS.NOW:

```
$ show users/output=users.now
$
```

3. The /OUTPUT qualifier caused the output from the SHOW USERS command to be written to the USERS.NOW file. To verify this, use the DIRECTORY command again. You could type just the DIRECTORY command to get the listing of all files. Instead, use the DIRECTORY command with the file specification and the /FULL qualifier to see the characteristics of the new USERS.NOW file:

```
$ directory users.now/full

Directory PACK2:[YOURGROUP.YOU]

USERS.NOW;1 File ID: (16030,13,512)
Size: 3/9    Owner: [GROUP,YOU]
Created: 4-AUG-1997 14:45:26.90
     .
     .
     .
Total of 1 file, 3/9 blocks.
$
```

4. You also can verify the file's existence by using the TYPE command. TYPE displays the contents of the specified file. If you do not specify a version number, OpenVMS displays the most recent version of the file:

```
$ type users.now
    OpenVMS User Processes at 25-SEP-1997 15:00:32.48
    Total number of users = 2, number of processes = 2
    Username    Interactive    Subprocess    Batch
    PHOLMAY         1
    YOU             1
    $
```

Many DCL commands have an /OUTPUT qualifier. Chapter 6 explores more uses of this qualifier. You can also consult Appendix A or another list of DCL commands, parameters, and qualifiers to see which commands have an /OUTPUT qualifier.

1.5.3   Creating a File

Although saving command line output as a file can be useful, you often want to create a file by typing in information. You can use the CREATE command to create a file of text entered from the keyboard. The CREATE command requires a file name as a parameter. For example, to create a file called NOTE.TXT, type

```
$ create note.txt
```

After you press Return at the end of the command line, the next text you enter becomes the contents of the file. Everything you input, in fact, is entered in the file until you press Ctrl/Z.

With OpenVMS, the Control key is used together with a second key to change the meaning of the second key and tell OpenVMS to perform a control sequence. Pressing Ctrl/Z ends a CREATE session and returns you to the DCL prompt. (Other control sequences are explored in Section 1.6.)

To enter information in the NOTE.TXT file and complete its creation, type

```
$ create note.txt
Check the date for the poem
Jabberwocky in Lewis Carroll's
Through the Looking-Glass
Ctrl/z
Exit
$
```

When entering the information in the file, press Return to move to a new line, Spacebar to enter a space, and Shift to use alternative key characters such as uppercase letters. If you need to erase a character after you have typed it, use the DELETE command by pressing the ⟨ × ⟩ key on the VT200 or the Delete key on the VT100 to delete the last character entered.

Explore creating a file and entering text using these keys. Experiment 1.5 creates a file containing lines from "Jabberwocky," a poem from Lewis Carroll's *Through the Looking-Glass* (1872).

Experiment 1.5   *Creating a Sample File*

1. Use the CREATE command to start creating a file called AI.TXT:

```
$ create ai.txt
```

2. Now enter the lines of the poem, pressing the Return key to move down to the next line, as necessary. Complete the process by pressing Ctrl/Z.

```
'Twas brillig, and the slithy toves
      Did gyre and gimble in the wabe:
All mimsy were the borogoves,
      And the mome raths outgrabe.
"Beware the Jabberwock, my son!
      The jaws that bite, the claws that catch!
Beware the Jubjub bird, and shun
      The frumious Bandersnatch!"
He took his vorpal sword in hand:
      Long time the manxome foe he sought—
So rested he by the Tumtum tree,
      and stood awhile in thought.
Ctrl/z
Exit
$
```

3. Thanks to the CREATE command, the poem is written to a file called AI.TXT. The Ctrl/z terminates the input to AI.TXT, and the system responds with Exit and the DCL prompt. You can verify that you now have a file AI.TXT by using the DIRECTORY command:

```
$ directory

Directory PACK2:[YOURGROUP.YOU]

AI.TXT;1        USERS.NOW;1        LOGIN.COM;1

Total of 3 files.
$
```

4. Notice that the version number, 1, indicates that this is version 1 of the AI.TXT file. At this point, there are no other versions of the file. You can view the contents of the AI.TXT file by using the TYPE command:

How modify ?
Can not !

```
                                    slithy toves
                                 ble in the wabe:
                                 ogoves,
                      •
                      •
                      •
                      $
```

As you work with OpenVMS files, remember that OpenVMS file names are not case sensitive. For example, ai.txt and AI.TXT identify the same file. Also, remember that, if you do not specify a version number for a file when entering a command line, OpenVMS will select the most recent version of the file.

1.6   Exploring Control Keys

The Ctrl/Z key sequence is one among a variety of useful control keys. The next two sections explore some of these control keys and their functions.

1.6.1   Control Keys That Control Output to the Terminal

Table 1.5 lists control keys that you can use to manage output to the terminal.

You should become comfortable with the key that suspends and resumes the flow of output to your terminal. On the VT200, this key is the Hold Screen key; on the VT100, this key is the No Scroll key. If you press either of these keys while output is being displayed or printed, the display is frozen on the screen or hard-copy terminal. This gives you a chance to read a screenful of information before resuming the program or command execution and the display of new output. To resume the execution, press the Hold Screen or No Scroll key again. You can press the key repeatedly, toggling it on and off.

Ctrl/O provides another way to control the display. Pressing this key sequence stops the display of the output flowing to the terminal; that is, the

Table 1.5   *Keys Used to Control Output to the Terminal*

Key	*Result*
Ctrl/O	Stops and starts the echoing of output to the terminal
Ctrl/S	Suspends output to the terminal
Ctrl/Q	Resumes output to the terminal
Hold Screen or No Scroll	Suspends and resumes output to the terminal

output does not echo on the screen. Unlike Hold Screen or No Scroll, Ctrl/O does not suspend the flow of output. Even though it does not appear on the screen, the output continues flowing to the terminal. When you press Ctrl/O a second time, a display of the *current* portion of the output appears. In other words, Ctrl/O makes it possible to skip past portions of output from a program or command.

Follow Experiment 1.6 to explore the Hold Screen or No Scroll key and Ctrl/O.

Experiment 1.6 *Suspending and Resuming Output and the Echoing of Output*

1. Enter a TYPE command to see the contents of the file AI.TXT. As the output appears, press the Hold Screen or No Scroll key to suspend output:

```
$ type ai.txt
'Twas brillig, and the slithy toves
      Did gyre and gimble in the wabe:
 No Scroll
```

2. Resume output by pressing the Hold Screen or No Scroll key again. Then press it again to suspend output:

```
 No Scroll
All mimsy were the borogoves,
      And the mome raths outgrabe.
 No Scroll
```

3. Resume output again. Then use Ctrl/C to cancel the execution of the command:

```
 No Scroll
"Beware the Jabberwock, my son!
 No Scroll
 Ctrl/c
 Interrupt
```

4. Next experiment with Ctrl/O. Enter a TYPE command again and press Ctrl/O to turn off the echoing of the output. Then press Ctrl/O again to resume echoing of the output:

```
$ type ai.txt
'Twas brillig, and the slithy toves
 Ctrl/o
 Output Off
 Ctrl/o
 Output On
```

```
        Did gyre and gimble in the wabe:
    So rested he by the Tumtum tree,
        and stood awhile in thought.
    $
```

1.6.2   Control Keys Used When Editing Command Lines

Some control keys are particularly useful when you are entering and editing command lines (see Table 1.6). When entering or editing a command line, use Ctrl/A to toggle between the Insert and Overstrike modes inside the command line. Use the Ctrl/E, Ctrl/H, Left Arrow, and Right Arrow keys to move through the command line. Using Ctrl/J deletes the previous word from the command line. Ctrl/U deletes what is to the left of the cursor; so if the cursor is at the end of a command line and you want to discard the command line entirely, use Ctrl/U. You can explore these control keys by following Experiment 1.7.

Experiment 1.7 *Editing a Command Line*

1. Type the DIRECTORY command line with the /FULL qualifier, but leave the *i* out of *drectory.* Do not press Return:

   ```
   $ drectory/full
   ```

2. Press Ctrl/A and use the Left Arrow key to move the cursor over the first *r.* Type in an *i* to correct the command line:

   ```
   $ directory/full
   ```

3. To position the cursor at the end of this command line, press Ctrl/E.

Table 1.6 *Control Keys Used to Edit Command Lines*

Key	*Result*
Ctrl/A	Switches between the overstrike and insert modes anywhere in the current command line
Ctrl/E	Positions the cursor at the end of the current line
Ctrl/H	Positions the cursor at the beginning of the current line or at the beginning of the preceding line if the cursor is already at the beginning of the line
Ctrl/J	Deletes backward from the cursor position to the beginning of a word, or if the cursor is at the first character of a word, deletes the previous word
Ctrl/U	Deletes characters from cursor to the beginning of the line

4. To delete /FULL from this command line, press Ctrl/J twice.

5. To position the cursor at the beginning of this command line, press Ctrl/H.

6. Now use Ctrl/E to position the cursor at the end of this line, and purge the current command line by pressing Ctrl/U.

1.7   Recalling Command Lines Using the Recall Buffer

You have just used the editing control keys to edit a command line before you pressed Return to execute it. Many times, however, you will find that you want to edit command lines after you have executed them—to correct a mistake or add qualifiers, for instance. DCL provides you a way to recall previous command lines so that you can edit them.

DCL saves the last several commands (up to 20 and 254 on OpenVMS VAX and OpenVMS Alpha systems, respectively) you have entered during the session in a place in memory called the *Recall buffer*. The Recall buffer stores the command lines as a stack, with the most recent command line on top. You can retrieve command lines from this buffer in several ways.

You can press either Ctrl/B or the Up Arrow key to see the most recently entered command line. For example, suppose the last command you entered was DIRECTORY/FULL. To display that command line again, you would press Ctrl/B or the Up Arrow keys. Both keys achieve the same result: The last command line is redisplayed. Once the command line is displayed, you can edit it.

If you wanted to see the command line that preceded DIRECTORY/FULL, you could press Ctrl/B or the Up Arrow again. By repeatedly pressing either of these keys, you can redisplay the last several command lines, which are stored in the Recall buffer, one at a time. Pressing the Down Arrow key displays the next, or more recent, command line. For example, pressing Up Arrow three times would display

```
$ directory/full
$ show users
$ type ai.txt
```

on the same line as the previous command. Pressing Down Arrow once would display:

```
$ show users
```

A better way to see all the command lines stored in the Recall buffer, however, is to use the RECALL command with the /ALL qualifier. The RECALL command without a qualifier redisplays the most recent command line. With the /ALL qualifier, it displays all the previous command lines, listing the more recent command lines first. For example,

```
$ recall/all
1 directory/full
2 show users
3 type ai.txt
4 directory
5 create ai.txt
  .
  .
  .
```

The RECALL/ALL command provides you a history of your most recent activity. It numbers the command lines, with the most recent labeled as 1.

You also can use the RECALL command to select a particular command line for display. Specify the command line by referring to its number in the RECALL/ALL list. For example, to display the third line in the list, you would type

```
$ recall 3
$ type ai.txt
```

Thus, you can get a list of the previous command lines, select the one you need to edit, and then display just that line for editing. Also, if you then need to move to the previous command line in the buffer, pressing Up Arrow will display that line.

Experiment 1.8 gives you practice in recalling command lines. As you follow the steps in the experiment, notice that the one command the Recall buffer does not store is the RECALL command.

Experiment 1.8 *Recalling Command Lines*

1. First, use RECALL/ALL to see the contents of the Recall buffer if you have just logged in, you should execute five or six commands so that the buffer contains some command lines:

```
$ recall/all
1 type ai.txt
  .
  .
  .
  $
```

2. Use Ctrl/B, the Up Arrow, and the Down Arrow keys to recall and redisplay the previous and next command lines. You can check your location in the buffer from the RECALL/ALL list. For example, pressing the Up Arrow twice displays

```
$ type ai.txt
$ directory
```

Pressing Ctrl/B displays

```
Ctrl/B
$ create ai.txt
```

Last, pressing the Down Arrow twice displays

```
$ directory
$ type ai.txt
```

3. Next, experiment with recalling a specific command line and then moving to the previous line. For example,

```
$ recall 4
$ type users.now
```

Press the Up Arrow twice:

```
$ create ai.txt
$ directory
```

4. Use RECALL/ALL again to see the list of command lines. Then execute a DIRECTORY command and use RECALL/ALL again:

```
$ recall/all
1 type ai.txt
.
.
.
$ directory
$ recall/all
1 directory
2 type ai.txt
.
.
.
```

There is yet another method for recalling a command line. You can type the RECALL command followed by one or more of the leading characters of a previous command. For example, to see the most recent command line that begins with *sh*, you would type

```
$ recall sh
$ show users
```

These techniques offer various ways to retrieve and move backward and forward among the old command lines saved in the Recall buffer. Once you get used to retrieving old command lines, you will probably find that the Recall buffer is a time-saver.

1.8   Using the Type-Ahead Buffer

In addition to a Recall buffer, OpenVMS has the Type-Ahead buffer. Perhaps you noticed that you can enter new commands while OpenVMS is doing something else—printing a directory or listing users logged in, for example. The Type-Ahead buffer stores the new keystrokes while OpenVMS executes the other command. When OpenVMS is finished, it acts on the new keystrokes. For example, you can enter a TYPE command. While OpenVMS is displaying the lines of the specified file, you can enter a DIRECTORY command. As soon as OpenVMS finishes the TYPE command, it executes the DIRECTORY command, which was stored in the Type-Ahead buffer. If you know you made a typing mistake when entering commands into the Type-Ahead buffer, you can clear the Type-Ahead buffer by pressing Ctrl/X . Follow Experiment 1.9 to see how this buffer works.

Experiment 1.9   *Using the Type-Ahead Buffer*

1. Enter a DIRECTORY/FULL command. While the list of file characteristics is being displayed, enter a SHOW USERS command and then a TYPE AI.TXT command:

```
$ directory/full

Directory PACK2:[YOURGROUP.YOU]

AI.TXT;1                        File ID: (38657,93,256)
  .
  .
  .
```

2. Repeat step 1, but this time press Ctrl/X after entering the TYPE command. In the experiment, the output from DIRECTORY/FULL continued to be displayed while you entered the new command lines. The entered command lines were saved in the Type-Ahead buffer. When the DIRECTORY/FULL command finished processing, DCL fetched and executed the commands in the Type-Ahead buffer. In step 2, the Ctrl/X discards the current input line and clears the Type-Ahead buffer. The size of the Type-Ahead buffer varies depending on what your system administrator decided at the time your OpenVMS system was installed.

1.9   Defining Keys

Because you will use some DCL commands repeatedly, you might want to assign them to a key so that you can execute them with a single keystroke.

The DCL DEFINE/KEY command makes it possible to define the function of many of your keys. You enter the command, then the name of a valid key, such as PF1, and then the command string of the command you want to assign to the key. This command string, known as an *equivalence string*, must be enclosed in quotation marks. The syntax for this command line is

define/key *key-name "equivalence-string"*

For example, to define the PF4 key on a VT100 or VT200 keyboard, you would type

```
$ define/key pf4 "show users"
%DCL-I-DEFKEY, DEFAULT key PF4 has been defined
```

This DEFINE/KEY command associates the equivalence string *show users* with the PF4 key. If you press the PF4 key, the following line appears on the screen:

```
$ show users
```

The cursor appears immediately after the last character of the equivalence string displayed by pressing the PF4 key. You must press Return to tell DCL to begin processing this command line.

To increase the usefulness of the defined key, you can use the /TERMINATE qualifier with the DEFINE/KEY command. This qualifier tells DCL to process the equivalence string command when the defined key is pressed, rather than wait for you to press Return. In effect, the /TERMINATE qualifier *embeds* a Return at the end of the string associated with a key. Try defining a key by following Experiment 1.10.

Experiment 1.10 *Defining a Key*

1. Use the DEFINE/KEY command to define the PF1 key so that it executes the SHOW TIME command.

```
$ define/key pf4 "show time"
%DCL-I-DEFKEY, DEFAULT key PF4 has been defined
```

2. Now press PF1 followed by Return:

```
PF1
$ show time Return
04-AUG-1997 15:23:14
```

3. By using the /TERMINATE qualifier in defining a PF key, you can eliminate the need to press Return after pressing a defined PF key. Use

the DEFINE/KEY with the /TERMINATE qualifier to define PF2 so that it executes the SHOW TIME command:

```
$ define/key/terminate pf2 "show time"
%DCL-I-DEFKEY, DEFAULT key PF2 has been defined
```

4. Now press PF2 to compare the performance of this newly defined key with that of the PF1 key from step 1:

```
 PF2 
$ show time
04-AUG-1997 15:26:19
```

Thus, you can define a key so that it immediately processes the command assigned to it or so that you control execution and can add parameters or qualifiers to the command line and then press Return. You cannot define every key on your keyboard. On VT100 and VT200 terminals, the PF1 through PF4 keys can be defined in this way. You also can define the numeric keypad keys 0 through 9 (use KP0, KP1, . . ., KP9 as the key names), the Left Arrow and Right Arrow keys (use LEFT and RIGHT as the key names), and the Period, Comma, Minus, and Enter keys on the numeric keypad (use these names in uppercase as the key names). In addition, VT200 terminals allow you to define the F6 through F20 keys, the editing keypad keys, and Help and Do. If you want to see a list of the key assignments you have made with the DEFINE/KEY command, you can use the SHOW KEY command with the /ALL qualifier. For example,

```
$ show key/all
DEFAULT key definitions:
  PF3 = "directory/full"
  PF4 = "show users"
```

If you want to check the definition for only a specific key, you can specify just that key. For example,

```
$ show key pf4
DEFAULT keypad definitions:
  PF4 = "show users"
```

1.10   A First Look at Using a Text Editor

You have seen that you can use the CREATE command to create a short file of text. You cannot use CREATE to edit or add to the text, however. In general, when you are writing a text file or you want to edit text in a file, you use a text editor. Text editors are programs that provide specific commands and procedures for editing, manipulating, and moving around the text within a new or existing file. OpenVMS provides several text editors, among them EVE and

EDT. Chapters 3 and 4 discuss EVE and EDT in detail. This section provides a brief introduction to working with a text editor, focusing on EVE.

The EDIT command with the editor's qualifier is used to access a text editor. The syntax for the EDIT command that accesses EVE is

edit/tpu *filespec*

The file specification can be for a new or existing file. For example, to begin using the EVE editor to change the contents of the existing file AI.TXT, you would type

$ **edit/tpu ai.txt**

EVE displays the following results:

```
'Twas brillig, and the slithy toves
      Did gyre and gimble in the wabe:
All mimsy were the borogoves,
      And the mome raths outgrabe.
"Beware the Jabberwock, my son!
      The jaws that bite, the claws that catch!
Beware the Jubjub bird, and shun
      The frumious Bandersnatch!"
He took his vorpal sword in hand:
      Long time the manxome foe he sought
So rested he by the Tumtum tree,
      and stood awhile in thought.
[End of File]
 .
 .
 .

Buffer: AI.TXT                      | Write | Insert | Forward
12 lines read from file PACK2:[YOURGROUP.YOU]AI.TXT;1
```

Whatever you type on the keyboard is entered into the file being edited, and you can use the numeric keypad on the right-hand side of the keyboard to perform a variety of editing functions. The [End of file] printed at the end of the file being edited marks the end of an EVE buffer. Behind the scenes, OpenVMS has transferred a copy of the file being edited to a buffer, or temporary storage area, in memory.

You can move around the lines of the file using the arrow keys. To add a new line, move to the beginning or end of a line and press Return. Once you finish editing the file, press Ctrl/Z to terminate the editing session.

Try using the EVE editor by following Experiment 1.11. In this experiment, you create and edit a LOGIN.COM file. Each time you log in, OpenVMS checks for a LOGIN.COM file and, if it finds one, executes any commands in that file. In the experiment, you add several commands to LOGIN.COM.

Experiment 1.11 *Editing with EVE*

1. Although you can use EVE to create a new file, in this experiment first use CREATE to create a LOGIN.COM file, if one does not exist, with a single comment line:

```
$ create login.com
$ ! commands executed each time you log in
 Ctrl/z
 Exit
$
```

Notice that $ is the first character you enter in the newly created LOGIN.COM file.

2. Move to the EVE editor, specifying LOGIN.COM as the file to edit.

```
$ edit/tpu login.com
```

EVE displays the following:

```
$ ! commands executed each time you log in
[End of file]
 .
 .
 .

 Buffer: LOGIN.COM                    | Write | Insert | Forward

1 line read from file PACK2:[YOURGROUP.YOU]LOGIN.COM;1
```

3. Use the Down Arrow key to move the cursor down to the [End of File] line. Open up a blank line by pressing Return:

```
$ ! commands executed each time you log in
 Return
[End of file]
```

4. Use the Up Arrow key to move the cursor up to the blank line and add two command lines, SHOW USERS and SHOW QUOTA. Remember to include a $ at the beginning of each line:

```
$ ! commands executed each time you log in
$ show users
```

```
$ show quota
[End of file]
```

5. You are finished editing the file, so press Ctrl/Z and leave the editor:

```
Ctrl/z
Buffer: LOGIN.COM                      | Write | Insert | Forward
2 lines written to file PACK2:[STAFF.PHOLMAY]LOGIN.COM;2
$
```

6. To see the results of this sample editing session, use the TYPE command:

```
$ type login.com
$ ! commands executed each time you log in
$ show users
$ show quota
$
```

7. You now have two versions of your LOGIN.COM file. Use the DIRECTORY command to verify this:

```
$ directory
Directory PACK2:[YOURGROUP.YOU]
AI.TXT;1    LOGIN.COM;2        LOGIN.COM;1      USERS.NOW;1
Total of 4 files.
$
```

When you log in, OpenVMS uses the most recent version of LOGIN.COM. Each time you exit from the editor with Ctrl/Z, a new version of the file you are working on is created. You may not want this to happen. For instance, if you have made mistakes, you may not want to save the edited file. You can press the Do key, type the QUIT command, and press Return to exit from the editor without saving the changes to the file. In effect, QUIT aborts an editing session.

Challenge Problem

Try using the EVE editor to add the following additional command lines to your LOGIN.COM file:

```
$ show time
$ directory/full
```

1.11   Logging in with the New LOGIN.COM File

A bonus is derived from the sample editing session in the previous section. The LOGIN.COM file you built has a special purpose. Each time you log in, OpenVMS executes the commands in the LOGIN.COM file; so now, more information will appear during the login procedure, as Experiment 1.12 demonstrates.

Experiment 1.12   *Using the New LOGIN.COM File*

1. First, log out of the system:

   $ **logout**

2. Now log back in:

   Username: *your-username*
   Password: *your-password*

   At this point, OpenVMS executes the commands in your LOGIN.COM file.

Summary

A user communicates with OpenVMS through the system command language interpreter, or CLI. A CLI is a program that provides an interface between the various operating system programs and system users. The most commonly used OpenVMS command language interpreter is DCL, the Digital command language.

Command lines begin with command verbs and can include parameters and qualifiers. A command verb identifies an OpenVMS service and, once executed, performs a task according to your specifications. You can enter, recall, and edit command lines.

A file is a named collection of information. Much of what you do with OpenVMS involves some form of file handling. OpenVMS provides a wide variety of tools for managing files. Tables 1.7-1.9 give an overview of the commands, special characters, and important terms used in this chapter.

Table 1.7   *DCL Commands*

Command	Result
CREATE	Establishes a new file
DEFINE/KEY	Defines the function of a key
DIRECTO	... or directories
/FULL	... about the files
EDIT	... edit a file
/EDT	... editor
/TPU	Activates the EVE editor. By default the EVE editor is activated by simply typing the EDIT command

Table 1.7 *DCL Commands (Continued)*

Command	Result
HELP	Displays information about commands and procedures
LOGOUT	Logs out of the system
/FULL	Displays a summary of accounting statistics when logging out
RECALL	Displays old command lines stacked in the recall buffer
/ALL	Displays the last several command lines (up to 20 and 254 on Open-VMS VAX and OpenVMS Alpha systems, respectively)
SET PASSWORD	Changes your password
SET PROCESS	Changes the characteristics associated with a process
/NAME	Changes the process name
SET TERMINAL	Changes the characteristics of the terminal
/WIDTH	Changes the width of the display
SHOW KEY	Displays the function of the specified defined key
/ALL	Displays the functions of all defined keys
SHOW TERMINAL	Displays the characteristics of the terminal
SHOW USERS	Displays information about the users currently logged in to the system
/OUTPUT	Redirects the information to a file
TYPE	Displays the contents of specified file(s)

Table 1.8 *Special Characters*

Character	Meaning
Ctrl	Control key
[End of file]	End-of-file marker for the EVE editor
Space	Delimits the parts of a command line
$	DCL prompt
!	Begins a command line comment
" "	Encloses a character string
/	Precedes a command qualifier

Table 1.9 *Important Terms*

Term	Definition
Buffer	Temporary storage area
CLI	Command language interpreter, a program that processes command lines
Command	Instruction specifying an action for the system to perform
Command line	Instruction consisting of a verb plus optional parameters and qualifiers
Current directory	Directory currently being used
DCL	Digital command language
Directory	File containing the names of files
Editor	Program that makes it possible to modify the contents of a file
File	Named collection of information
Login directory	Directory assigned by OpenVMS to you when you log in
Recall buffer	Buffer used to store previously entered command lines (up to 20 and 254 on OpenVMS VAX and OpenVMS Alpha systems, respectively)
Type-Ahead buffer	Buffer used for temporary storage of command lines typed during execution of other commands

Exercises

1. Make a list of the uses of optional qualifiers for the following commands: DIRECTORY, RECALL.

2. Which key is used most often? Why?

3. Give a command line that would cause *Happy New Year!* to be printed on your screen.

4. Perform the following steps:
   a. Create a JOHN.LTR file that contains the first line of a letter.
   b. Repeat step a, but type in the next line of the same letter. The preceding line of the letter will be in the earlier version of the JOHN.LTR file.
   c. Execute a DIRECTORY command to check on the number of versions of the JOHN.LTR file in your current directory.
   d. Repeat steps b and c at least ten times. Explain what you find.

5. Give the command lines to define the following keys:
   a. PF1 to print a list of current users
   b. PF2 to list the contents of your login directory
   c. PF3 to print the date and time
   d. PF4 to recall all the command lines in the Recall buffer

6. List three ways to retrieve a previous command line.

7. How does the Type-Ahead buffer differ from the Recall buffer?

8. Execute a RECALL/ALL command and use Ctrl/B and RECALL instead of the Up Arrow and Down Arrow keys to recall command lines.

9. Give a listing of the new LOGIN.COM file that was created in the Challenge Problem at the end of Section 1.10.

Review Quiz

Indicate whether the following statements are true or false:

1. The Recall and Type-Ahead buffers both are used to hold command lines.

2. You can flush out your Recall buffer by pressing Ctrl/X.

3. The Ctrl/B and Up Arrow keys both can be used to recall a previous command line.

4. A directory is a file.

5. Pressing Ctrl/O and pressing Hold Screen or No Scroll do the same thing during the execution of a program that is sending output to the screen.

6. DCL is an interpreter.

7. Your CLI is a program.

Further Reading

VMS User's Guide. Austin, Texas: Academic Computing and Instructional Technology Services; The University of Texas at Austin, l996. URL: http://www.utexas.edu/docs/ccug2.

Kenah, L. J., R. E. Goldenberg, and S. F. Bate. *VAX/VMS Internals and Data Structures.* Bedford, Mass.: Digital Press, 1988.

Levy, H. M., and R. H. Eckhouse. *Computer Programming and Architecture: The VAX.* Bedford, Mass.: Digital Press, 1989.

Peters, J. F. *The Art of Assembly Language Programming VAX-11.* Englewood Cliffs, N. J.: Reston Publishing Co., 1985.

Sawey, R. M., and T. T. Stokes. *A Beginner's Guide to VAX/VMS Utilities and Applications.* Maynard, Mass.: Digital Press, 1992.

Digital Equipment Corporation, POB CS2008, Nashua, NH 03061:

Printed Documentation   *OpenVMS DCL Dictionary: A–M*
                                 OpenVMS DCL Dictionary: N–Z
                                 OpenVMS Software Overview
                                 OpenVMS User's Manual
On-Line Documentation   OpenVMS On-Line Help Facility
                                 OpenVMS Bookreader
                                 http://www.openvms.digital.com

2

A Beginner's Guide to OpenVMS File Management

Information reaching long-term memory must be filed, and this process depends on the context.

—James L. Adams, *Conceptual Blockbusting,*1979

OpenVMS provides several methods for creating, manipulating, and organizing files. In this chapter, you will

▶ Obtain an overview of OpenVMS files

▶ Become familiar with various forms of file specifications

▶ Begin using wildcards in file specifications

▶ Survey commonly used file management tools

▶ Explore the uses of the /LOG qualifier with various file-handling commands

▶ Distinguish between purging and deleting files

▶ Experiment with the /CONFIRM qualifier when purging and deleting files

▶ Begin exploring the OpenVMS directory system

▶ Begin creating and using subdirectories

2.1   Files and Directories

Many OpenVMS command lines identify one or more files to be processed. A file is a named, organized collection of components stored on a hard drive or on media such as magnetic disks and tapes, diskettes, cassettes, or a CD-ROM. Files are comparable to the file folders in a filing cabinet, as shown in Figure 2.1. Each holds a collection of related information.

Files are useful because they allow you to permanently store and manage information. For example, you can type

```
$! See Kenah, Goldenberg, & Bate, p. 625, on logical names
```

This information would be lost, however, when you press the Return key. To make a permanent record of this reference, you would type

```
$create logical.nms
See Kenah, Goldenberg, & Bate, p. 625, on logical names
 Ctrl/z
```

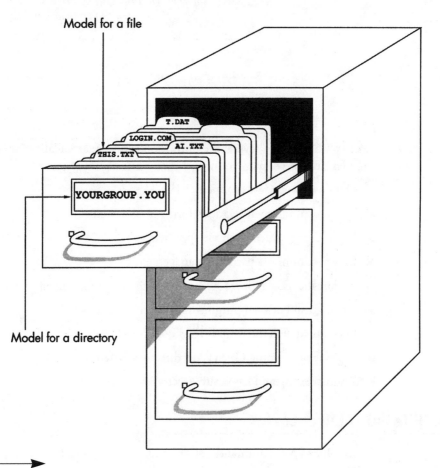

Figure 2.1 *A Model for Files and Directories*

```
Exit
$
```

This stores the information in a file.

Once the information is in a file, you can retrieve it in a variety of ways. For example, you can use the TYPE command to display the file's contents. It also is easy to update a file, refining an old piece of information or adding new information, using an editor like EVE or EDT.

In addition, files make information sharing possible. Files can be exchanged between users on the same system or across computer networks. For example, OpenVMS has a Mail utility that you can use to send files to other users. For instance, you could send the file LOGICAL.NMS to another person on your system by typing

```
$ mail logical.nms jmuggli
```

In this case, jmuggli is the other person's user name. When you press the Return key at the end of this command line, a copy of the LOGICAL.NMS file is sent to jmuggli.

Files make it possible to work with massive segments of information that are too large to be brought into primary memory at one time but that you want to keep together as a single logical entity. For example, suppose the system on which you are working limits your workspace to 4 million bytes, and you need to save birth records for a large city, which requires 20 million bytes. You can take advantage of the typically large capacities of storage volumes to build these large files. Then OpenVMS will bring chunks of the large files into memory when you need that information.

Every file you own is listed in a directory. A directory is a file containing information about other files and has a file type of .DIR. When you log in, OpenVMS makes your default, or login, directory available to you. The names of the files you created are maintained by OpenVMS in this login directory and possibly in other directories and subdirectories.

To check the directories you have available to you, type

```
$ directory *.dir
```

This command line uses the wildcard * to specify all files with a .DIR extension, which is the file type of directory files. Wildcards are discussed in Section 2.1.2.

If you wanted to see only the name of your login directory, which is the default directory unless you have changed the default, you would type

```
$ show default
```

Using directories helps you to organize and keep track of your files. Directories also provide an enormously valuable means of information sharing. Section 2.3 discusses directories in detail.

2.1.1   OpenVMS File Specifications

Each file on a OpenVMS system has a file specification that uniquely identifies the file to the system. The complete specification for a file has the following syntax:

```
pathname filename.filetype;version
```

For example, Figure 2.2 shows the file specification for a file on an MIT network, and Figure 2.3 breaks down the pathname for this file. The sample pathname consists of a network node name, a device name, and directory and subdirectory names.

The network node name identifies the specific computer system in the network. Network node names have from one to six characters and end with a double colon (::). If the system is not a node on a network, the file specification does not have a node name.

The device name indicates the physical device (such as a disk drive) that contains the files and directories. Device names can have up to 15 alphanumeric characters, and they end with a single colon (:).

Directory names are listed in hierarchical order. They are separated by a period (.) and enclosed in brackets ([ ]) or angle brackets (< >). In the exam-

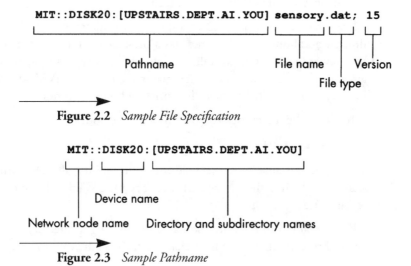

Figure 2.2 *Sample File Specification*

Figure 2.3 *Sample Pathname*

ple in Figure 2.3, the UPSTAIRS directory is a directory for the system and contains the DEPT directory. The DEPT directory is a directory for all departments and contains the AI directory. The AI directory contains all files and directories for the AI department including the YOU directory. The YOU directory contains your files and directories. In effect, this sample file specification identifies the hierarchy of directories shown in Figure 2.4.

For the sake of simplicity, you can identify a file in your current default directory by referring to only its file name and file type. For example, to see the contents of the file specified in Figure 2.2, you would type

```
$ type sensory.dat
```

A file name can have up to 39 alphanumeric characters. It generally is best to use a file name that helps you remember the contents of the file. The file name is separated from the file type by a period (.).

The file type indicates the type of information in the file. The file type also can consist of up to 39 alphanumeric characters, but certain three-character file types are commonly used, such as .DAT for data files, .COM for command procedure files, and so on. Table 2.1 lists some of the more common default file types used by DCL commands.

File version numbers assigned by OpenVMS range from 1 to 32767. Each time you change the file or create another version of it, the file version number increases by 1. You may specify a specific version number if you do not want OpenVMS to automatically assign the next higher version.

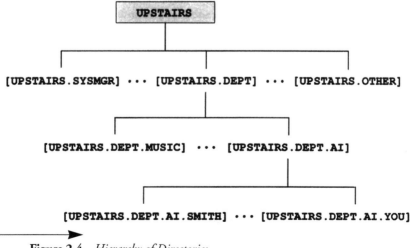

Figure 2.4   *Hierarchy of Directories*

Table 2.1 *Default File Types Used by DCL Commands*

File Type	Contents
.COM	Command procedure file
.DAT	Data file
.DIR	Directory file
.DIS	Distribution list file for the Mail utility
.EXE	Executable program image file created by the linker
.INI	Initialization file
.JOU	Journal file created by the EDT editor
.LOG	Batch job output file
.TJL	Journal file created by DECTPU and ACL editors
.TMP	Temporary file
.TPU	Command file for the EVE editor
.TPU$JOURNAL	Journal file created by the EVE editor
.TXT	Input file for text libraries or Mail utility output files

You can use file version numbers to select earlier versions of a file—after various editing sessions, for example. For instance, instead of version 15, you can inspect version 14 (if you still have it) by typing

```
$ type sensory.dat;14
```

To economize on the use of disk space, system managers typically limit the number of versions of a file that are kept.

If you want to see the pathname for your files, and their file names, file types, and version numbers, use the DIRECTORY command. For example,

```
$ directory

Directory PACK2:[YOURGROUP.YOU]

AI.TXT;1        LOGIN.COM;2        LOGIN.COM;1        USERS.NOW;1

Total of 4 files.
$
```

The pathname for the files in your default directory is the first line displayed by the DIRECTORY command. In this example, PACK2 identifies the disk drive being used to store the files. If your OpenVMS system is part of a network, the pathname will include its network node name. The files are listed in the next line.

To see the pathname of a specific file and a list of all the file's versions, enter the file name and file type after the DIRECTORY command. For example, to see the pathname of the LOGIN.COM file, you would type

```
$ directory
Directory PACK2:[YOURGROUP.YOU]
LOGIN.COM;2    LOGIN.COM;1
Total of 2 files. $
```

The pathname for LOGIN.COM appears in the first line of the output, and the two versions of LOGIN.COM are listed below it.

There are many ways to select collections of files with the DIRECTORY command and with other commands. Before you explore further, create some new files by following Experiment 2.1.

Experiment 2.1   *Creating Some New Files*

1. Use the CREATE command to create four new files with the file type .DAT. These files will contain information about various books:

```
$ create sfbks.dat
Isaac Asimov, I, Robot
 Ctrl/z
 Exit

$ create csbks.dat
Brinch Hansen, P. The Architecture of Concurrent Programs.
Englewood Cliffs, NJ: Prentice-Hall, 1977.

Stroustrop, B. The C++ Programming Language. Reading,
MA: Addison-Wesley, 1997.
 Ctrl/z
 Exit

$ create openvmsbks.dat
Goldenberg, R.E. Kenah, L.J. Dumas, D.D. VAX/VMS
Internals and Data Structures: version 5.2 Bedford, MA:
Digital Press, 1991.
 Ctrl/z
 Exit

$ create openvmsman.dat
OpenVMS User's Manual.
Maynard, MA: Digital Equipment Corporation, December, 1995.
 Ctrl/z
 Exit
$
```

2. Now create a file with definitions of some OpenVMS terms. The file type should be .TXT:

```
$ create openvmsdef.txt
A wildcard char. can specify more than one file.
DCL stands for Digital Command Language.
A file is a named piece of information.
Ctrl/z
Exit
*.*;* specifies all files in your default directory.
$
```

3. Finally, create two files containing very simple Pascal programs. The file type should be .PAS:

```
$ create doesnothing.pas
program doesnothing;
begin
end.
Ctrl/z
Exit

$ create sayshello.pas
program sayshello (output);
begin
writeln('Hello, world!')
end.
Ctrl/z
Exit
$
```

4. In addition to these files, you might have the single version of AI.TXT and USERS.NOW and two versions of the LOGIN.COM files created in Chapter 1. Get a directory listing of your current files:

```
$ directory

Directory PACK2:[YOURGROUP.YOU]

AI.TXT;1              CSBKS.DAT;1         DOESNOTHING.PAS;1
LOGIN.COM;2           LOGIN.COM;1         SAYSHELLO.PAS;1
SFBKS.DAT;1           USERS.NOW;1         OPENVMSBKS.DAT;1
OPENVMSDEF.TXT;1      OPENVMSMAN.DAT;1

Total of 11 files.
$
```

2.1.2 Using Wildcards to Specify Files

Wildcards are special characters used in the file specifications in command lines to identify zero or more files. Wildcards save you time and keystrokes because they let you enter a single command to process multiple files. Two types of wildcards are used to specify file names, file types, and versions:

▶ Use an asterisk (*) to match 0 to 39 characters in the file name, file type, or version number.

▶ Use a percent sign (%) to match exactly one character in the file name or file type.

The * and % wildcards can be used in a variety of ways to specify groups of files. You can explore some of the possibilities in Experiments 2.2 and 2.3.

Experiment 2.2   *Using * to Select Files*

1. Use the DIRECTORY command and a * wildcard to display the names of all files of type .DAT in your current directory. To do this, enter * instead of a specific file name:

```
$ directory *.dat

Directory PACK2:[YOURGROUP.YOU]

CSBKS.DAT;1        SFBKS.DAT;1         OPENVMSBKS.DAT;1
OPENVMSMAN.DAT;1

Total of 4 files.
$
```

2. Next, to select all your version 2 files, use * in place of both the file name and file type:

```
$ directory *.*;2

Directory PACK2:[YOURGROUP.YOU]

LOGIN.COM;2

Total of 1 file.
$
```

3. Finally, list all versions of your files of type .COM:

```
$ directory *.com;*

Directory PACK2:[YOURGROUP.YOU]

LOGIN.COM;2    LOGIN.COM;1

Total of 2 files.
$
```

Another, more concise, way to accomplish step 3 is

```
$ directory *.com
```

In this command line, all versions of your files of type .COM are selected by *.COM by default. Similarly, you can specify all your files in the default directory by entering either of the following command lines:

```
$ directory *.*;*
```

or

```
$ directory
```

When you want to match a single character, use the % wildcard. For example, you could specify all files with names beginning with OPEN-VMS followed by a single letter by entering

```
$ directory openvms%
```

If you have no files that meet this specification, no list of files appears. To specify files with names beginning with OPENVMS by three letters, you would type

```
$ directory openvms%%%

Directory PACK2:[YOURGROUP.YOU]

OPENVMSBKS.DAT;1  OPENVMSDEF.TXT;1  OPENVMSMAN.DAT;1

Total of 3 files.
$
```

Because * matches multiple characters, you could specify all files with file names beginning with OPENVMS by entering

```
$ directory openvms*

Directory PACK2:[YOURGROUP.YOU]

OPENVMSBKS.DAT;1  OPENVMSDEF.TXT;1  OPENVMSMAN.DAT;1

Total of 3 files.
$
```

Try using the % wildcard by performing Experiment 2.3.

Experiment 2.3 *Using % to Select Files*

1. First create two new files, OPENVMS1.TXT and A.TXT:

```
$ create openvms1.txt
Operating Systems: OpenVMS VAX; OpenVMS Alpha
 Ctrl/z 
 Exit 

$ create a.txt
rhyming words: aha, amoeba, amnesia
```

```
Ctrl/z
Exit
```

2. Now get a directory listing of the .TXT files with four letter names beginning with OPENVMS:

```
$ directory openvms%.txt

Directory PACK2:[YOURGROUP.YOU]

OPENVMS1.TXT;1

Total of 1 file.
$
```

3. Get a directory listing of the .TXT files with single-letter names:

```
$ directory %.txt

Directory PACK2:[YOURGROUP.YOU]

A.TXT;1

Total of 1 file.
$
```

In this last step, notice that %.TXT does not include AI.TXT in its specification. Can you see why?

So far, you have used the * and % wildcards only with the DIRECTORY command, but you can use them with many DCL commands. As you continue exploring, you will see just how widespread the use of wildcards can be in a typical working session on a OpenVMS system. For example, you might want to display the contents of files of type .TXT and so would enter

```
$ type *.txt
```

Or perhaps you want to print copies of your files with names beginning with OPENVMS using the PRINT command, which queues specified files for printing. Then you would type

```
$ print openvms*
```

2.2   Managing Files

As you have seen, you can use the DIRECTORY command to obtain information about OpenVMS files. OpenVMS also provides other commands that help you manage files. Table 2.2 presents some commonly used file management commands. The following sections discuss these commands.

Table 2.2 *Selected File Management Commands*

Command	Result
APPEND	Appends the contents of one file to another file
COPY	Copies the contents of a file to a new file
CREATE	Creates a new file
DELETE	Removes a file
DIFFERENCES	Compares files, flagging any differences
PRINT	Sends a copy of the file to the printer queue
PURGE	Removes all but the latest version of a file or files
RENAME	Gives a file a new name
TYPE	Lists the contents of a file or files

2.2.1 Copying Files

The COPY command makes it possible to duplicate the information in a file. You can copy a file into a new file, thus creating the new file; or you can copy a file into an existing file, adding the copied file's contents to those of the existing file. This file management command has the following syntax:

```
copy input-filespec[,...] output-filespec
```

The *input-filespec* is the file to be copied, [,...] represents optional additional input file specifications, and the *output-filespec* is the copy's destination file. Experiment with the COPY command by following Experiment 2.4.

Experiment 2.4 *Using the COPY Command*

1. Make a copy of the SFBKS.DAT file to begin a new, separate file containing a list of Isaac Asimov's books. Call the new file SFASIMOV.DAT:

```
$ copy sfbks.dat sfasimov.dat
$
```

2. Use the DIRECTORY command to verify that the new file was created:

```
$ directory sf*.dat

Directory PACK2:[YOURGROUP.YOU]

SFASIMOV.DAT;1 SFBKS.DAT;1
```

```
Total of 2 files.
$
```

You can use the COPY command to concatenate, or string together, several input files that you want copied to a specified output file. When specifying more than one input file with the COPY command, place a comma (,) between the input file names. For example, to copy two files into a third file, you could type

`$ copy openvmsbks.dat,openvmsman.dat openvmspubs.dat`

This form of the COPY command copies the first specified input file, OPENVMSBKS.DAT, to the new file named OPENVMSPUBS.DAT and then appends the remaining input file(s) you have specified (OPENVMS-MAN.DAT, in this example) to the output file. You could use the TYPE command to see the contents of the new file created by the example:

```
$ type openvmspubs.dat
Goldenberg, R.E. Kenah, L.J. Dumas, D.D. VAX/VMS
Internals and Data Structures:version 5.2. Bedford, MA:
Digital Press, 1991.

OpenVMS User's Manual.
Maynard, MA: Digital Equipment Corporation, December 1995.
$
```

You also can use wildcards in the input file specification of a COPY command line. For instance, to collect all your files of type .DAT inside a single output file, you would type

`$ copy *.dat all.dat`

specifying multiple output files to be created by copy all your files of type .TXT in new files of type es, you could enter

msdef.txt;1 *.ltr

To see the results of this form of the COPY command, type

`$ directory *.ltr`

```
Directory PACK2:[YOURGROUP.YOU]

AI.LTR;1  OPENVMSDEF.LTR;1

Total of 2 files.
$
```

Challenge Problem

What new files would be created by the following uses of the COPY command when used with the following files: SFBKS.DAT, CSBKS.DAT,

OPENVMSBKS.DAT,   OPENVMSMAN.DAT,   OPENVMSDEF.TXT,
DOESNOTHING.PAS, SAYSHELLO.PAS, and LOGIN.COM?

1. `$ copy *.dat;1 *.ltr`

2. `$ copy login.com;1 *.old`

The COPY command has a variety of qualifiers. You can find out more
about the COPY command by entering

`$ help copy`

Of the many available qualifiers for the COPY command, you will probably find the /LOG qualifier most helpful right away. The /LOG qualifier
causes the COPY command to describe each of its actions line by line. For
example,

```
$ copy/log login.com;1 login.old
%COPY-S-COPIED, PACK2:[YOURGROUP.YOU]LOGIN.COM;1 copied to
PACK2:[YOURGROUP.YOU]LOGIN.OLD;1 (1 block)
$
```

In this example, the /LOG qualifier displays a line indicating that
LOGIN.COM;1 was copied to LOGIN.OLD;1. You can try this form of the
COPY command to verify your answers to the challenge problem.

2.2.2 Appending Files

The APPEND command makes it possible to attach the contents of one or
more files to another file. You can append a file to an existing file or a new
file, thus creating the new file. The APPEND command has the following
syntax:

append *input-filespec[,...] output-filespec*

The *input-filespec* is the file to be appended, [,...] represents optional additional input file specifications, and the *output-filespec* is the file to which the
input files are appended. The APPEND command is a time-saver because you
can add information from one file to another quickly. Experiment 2.5 shows
how the APPEND command is used in its simplest form.

Experiment 2.5 *Using the APPEND Command*

1. Create a file containing a short letter. Call the file MAX.LTR:

```
$ create max.ltr
Hi, Max!
I've appended to this letter the list of books I told you
about earlier.
Sue
```

```
Ctrl/z
Exit
$
```

2. Append the OPENVMSBKS.DAT file to MAX.LTR:

```
$ append openvmsbks.dat max.ltr $
```

3. Now the MAX.LTR file has the contents of the OPENVMSBKS.DAT file appended to it. Use the DIRECTORY command, asking to see all versions of both MAX.LTR and OPENVMSBKS.DAT:

```
$ directory max.ltr, openvmsbks.dat

Directory PACK2:[YOURCROUP.YOU]

MAX.LTR;1      OPENVMSBKS.DAT;1

Total of 2 files.
$
```

Notice that, by default, the version number of a file does not change as a result of an append operation. Like the COPY command, the APPEND command has a /LOG qualifier, which allows you to trace the actions performed by the APPEND command. For example, to see the actions just performed, type

```
$ append/log openvmsbks.dat max.ltr
%APPEND-S-APPENDED, PACK2:[YOURGROUP.YOU]OPENVMSBKS.DAT;1
appended to PACK2:[YOURGROUP.YOU]MAX.LTR;1 (2 records)
$
```

If the output file you specify in an APPEND command line does not exist, you must use the /NEW_VERSION qualifier with the APPEND command to create a new file. So, for example, if you do not have a LETTER.BOX file in your default directory, the following command line will create a new file with that name and append the contents of MAX.LTR to it:

```
$ append/new_version/log max.ltr letter.box
%APPEND-I-CREATED, PACK2:[YOURGROUP.YOU]MAX.LTR;1 created
%APPEND-S-COPIED, PACK2:[YOURGROUP.YOU]LETTER.BOX;1
copied to PACK2:[STAFF.PHOLMAY]LETTER.BOX;1 (1 block)
$
```

In addition to helping you with file management, the APPEND command is useful for many routine tasks. For example, suppose you have a file you want to mail to someone else on your system. You can create a short letter explaining the file you are mailing, append the file to the letter, and then use the OpenVMS Mail utility to send the letter with the appended file.

2.2.3 Purging Files

You have started to accumulate quite a few files, some of which you may no longer need. OpenVMS has DELETE and PURGE commands, which make it possible to eliminate files. The PURGE command completely erases the files from the disk. It is useful if you have multiple versions of the same file and you need to keep only selected versions. The PURGE command has the following syntax:

purge [*filespec*[,...]]

The *filespec* specifies one or more files to be purged. The simplest form of this command eliminates all but the most recent version of every file in your current directory:

`$ purge`

You also can use the PURGE command more selectively, by specifying particular files in the command line. For example, you may have more than one version of the LOGIN.COM file and need only the most recent version of this file. To purge all but the most recent version of this file, you would type

`$ purge login.com`

You can use wildcards in the directory, file name, and file type fields with the PURGE command. For example, to purge all but the most recent versions of files of type .DAT in your default directory, you would type

`$ purge *.dat`

You cannot specify version numbers when entering file specifications in the PURGE command line. If you want to keep more than the most recent version of a file, you must use the /KEEP qualifier, specifying the number of versions to be retained. This form of the PURGE command has the following syntax:

purge/keep=*number-of-versions* [*filespec*[,...]]

For example, suppose you have been editing the LOGIN.COM file repeatedly and have accumulated five versions of it. To keep the two most recent versions of the LOGIN.COM file, you would type

`$ purge/keep=2 login.com`

To explore using the PURGE command, try Experiment 2.6.

Experiment 2.6   *Using the PURGE Command with the /KEEP Qualifier*

1. Create four new versions of the MAX.LTR file using EVE. Add to the file the bold faced text in the following examples. Remember to use the arrow keys to move around the file and the Return key to add a new line. Invoke EVE to edit the existing file MAX.LTR:

```
$ edit/tpu max.ltr
```

```
Hi Maxwell!
I've appended to this letter the list of books I told you
about earlier.
Sue
Goldenberg, R. E. Kenah, L. J. Dumas, D.D. VAX/VMS
Internals and Data Structures: Version 5.2. Bedford, MA:
Digital Press, 1991.
[End of file]
.
.
.
```

| Buffer: MAX.LTR | Write | Insert | Forward |

```
6 lines read from file PACK2:[YOURGROUP.YOU]MAX.LTR;1
```

Remember to press Ctrl/Z to exit and save your changes. Once you have saved the changes, edit MAX.LTR a second time:

```
Hi Maxwell!
I've appended to this letter the list of books I told you
about earlier.
Hope this is helpful.
Sue
Goldenberg, R. E. Kenah, L. J. Dumas, D.D. VAX/VMS Inter-
nals and Data Structures: Version 5.2. Bedford, MA: Digi-
tal Press, 1991.
[End of file]
.
.
.
```

| Buffer: MAX.LTR | Write | Insert | Forward |

```
6 lines read from file PACK2:[YOURGROUP.YOU]MAX.LTR;2
```

Notice that each time you invoke EVE the version number increases by 1. Exit your editing session and invoke EVE for a third time:

```
Hi Maxwell!
I've appended to this letter the list of books I told you
about earlier.
Hope this is helpful. Call me if you need more info.
Sue
Goldenberg, R. E. Kenah, L. J. Dumas, D.D. VAX/VMS
Internals and Data Structures: Version 5.2. Bedford, MA:
Digital Press, 1991.
[End of file]
 .
 .
 .
Buffer: MAX.LTR                      | Write | Insert | Forward

7 lines read from file PACK2:[YOURGROUP.YOU]MAX.LTR;3
```

Invoke EVE a fourth time and save any changes to MAX.LTR:

```
Hi Maxwell!
I've appended to this letter the list of books I told you
about earlier.
Hope this is helpful. Call me if you need more info.
Sue Reed
Goldenberg, R. E. Kenah, L. J. Dumas, D.D. VAX/VMS
Internals and Data Structures: Version 5.2. Bedford, MA:
Digital Press, 1991.
[End of file]
 .
 .
 .
Buffer: MAX.LTR                      | Write | Insert | Forward

7 lines read from file PACK2:[YOURGROUP.YOU]MAX.LTR;4
```

2. Check how many versions of MAX.LTR you have:

```
$ directory max.ltr

Directory PACK2:[YOURGROUP.YOU]
```

```
MAX.LTR;5    MAX.LTR;4    MAX.LTR;3    MAX.LTR;2
MAX.LTR;1

Total of 5 files.
$
```

3. Now purge all but the last four versions:

```
$ purge/keep=4 max.ltr
$
```

4. Check the versions you have:

```
$ directory max.ltr

Directory PACK2:[YOURGROUP.YOU]

MAX.LTR;5    MAX.LTR;4    MAX.LTR;3    MAX.LTR;2

Total of 4 files.
$
```

5. Purge all but the last two versions. This time use the /LOG qualifier to
see the file specifications of the files as they are purged:

```
$ purge/keep=2/log max.ltr
%PURGE-I-FILPURG, PACK2:[YOURGROUP.YOU]MAX.LTR;2 deleted
(3 blocks)
%PURGE-I-FILPURG, PACK2:[YOURGROUP.YOU]MAX.LTR;3 deleted
(3 blocks)
$
```

One useful application of the PURGE command is to enter it in your
LOGIN.COM file, specifying the number of versions you want kept.
Then, each time you log in, OpenVMS will purge all but that many versions of each file or of the specified files. For example, if you enter the following command line in your LOGIN.COM file, all but the two most
recent versions of your files of type .COM will be purged:

```
$ purge/keep=2 *.com
```

You probably have guessed that it may be dangerous to use the PURGE command with a file specification containing a wildcard. For example, you might
not want to purge all but the most recent version of all your files of type .COM.
In such a case, you will find the /CONFIRM qualifier useful. This qualifier
causes the PURGE command to check whether you want a file purged. You
respond with either *y* (*es*) to confirm, *n* (*o*) to stop the purging of that file, *a* (*ll*)
to purge all files having the specified name and type, or *q* (*uit*) to stop the processing at that point. Here is the syntax for this form of the PURGE command:

purge/confirm [*filespec*[,...]]

For example, you can confirm the purging of all files of type .COM and type .DAT by entering

```
$ purge/confirm *.com, *.dat
```

```
DELETE PACK2:[YOURGROUP.YOU]LOGIN.COM;1? [N]
```

Then, if you want the file purged, type *y* at the prompt. To keep the file from being purged, type *n*. OpenVMS will ask about each file before the file is purged.

2.2.4   Deleting Files

You can selectively delete unwanted files by using the DELETE command. DELETE differs from PURGE because it requires you to specify file version numbers as well as the directory, file name, and file type. This command has the following syntax:

```
delete filespec[,...]
```

You must always specify a version number for the files you want to delete. For example, to delete version 1 of your MAX.LTR, you would enter

```
$ delete max.ltr;1
$
```

You also can use a wildcard in place of a specific version number or in the directory, file name, and file type fields when using the DELETE command. Experiment 2.7 explores using the * wildcard to delete all versions of a file.

Experiment 2.7 *Deleting All Versions of a File*

1. Because this experiment deletes all versions of the MAX.LTR file, you should first make a copy of the most recent version of this file, giving the copy a new name:

```
$ copy max.ltr copymax.ltr
```

2. Now use the * wildcard to delete all versions of MAX.LTR:

```
$ delete max.ltr;*
```

3. You can use * to delete all files of a certain type, too. Because DELETE requires a version number, you must specify a number or use a wildcard as a version number. Try deleting all .LTR files:

```
$ delete *.ltr;*
```

It is easy to accidentally delete files you need to keep. Remember the danger in using the DELETE command with a file specification that has a wildcard.

Unlike other operating systems, once a file is deleted or purged, the contents may be unrecoverable on an OpenVMS system unless a backup was made.

Like the other file management commands, the DELETE command has several useful qualifiers. You can see the effects of executing the DELETE command by using the /LOG qualifier. For example,

```
$ delete/log *.ltr;*
%DELETE-I-FILDEL, PACK2:[YOURGROUP.YOU]MAX.LTR;5 deleted (3
blocks)
%DELETE-I-FILDEL, PACK2;[YOURGROUP.YOU]COPYMAX.LTR;1 deleted
(3 blocks)
%DELETE-I-TOTAL, 2 FILES DELETED (6 BLOCKS)
$
```

With the /LOG qualifier, at least you can see which files are deleted. Better still, the DELETE command also has a /CONFIRM qualifier, which lets you control which files are deleted by typing *y* or *n* at the prompt before the file is deleted. For example,

```
$ delete/confirm *.txt;*
DELETE PACK2:[YOURGROUP.YOU]AI.TXT;1? [N]: y
DELETE PACK2:[YOURGROUP.YOU]OPENVMSDEF.TXT;1? [N]: n
.
.
.
```

In this example, only AI.TXT was deleted; entering *n* at the prompt retained OPENVMSDEF.TXT. Get used to using the /CONFIRM qualifier with the DELETE command to avoid unintentional losses of valued files.

2.2.5   Renaming Files

At times, you may need to change a file's name. You can give new names to existing files using the RENAME command. This command has the following syntax:

rename *input-filespec[,...]* *output-filespec*

The *input-filespec* is the current file name or names and the *output-filespec* is the new name of the files.

The RENAME command is both versatile and easy to use. For example, to rename the OPENVMSDEF.TXT file, enter

```
$ rename openvmsdef.txt decdefs
$
```

The OPENVMSDEF.TXT;1 file now is renamed DECDEFS;1. After being renamed, OPENVMSDEF.TXT;1 no longer exists in the directory.

As with other file management commands, the /LOG qualifier lets you trace the results of the RENAME command. Experiment 2.8 uses the RENAME command with /LOG at the same time as it explores another feature of all DCL commands, automatic prompts.

When you are entering a command line, you might forget all the required specifications. If you press the Return key before entering all the required information, DCL prompts you for the missing information. These automatic prompts guide you through the requirements of the command.

Experiment 2.8   *Using the RENAME Command and Exploring DCL Automatic Prompts*

1. Begin by entering the RENAME command with the /LOG qualifier. Instead of specifying the file to be renamed, press the Return key:

```
$ rename/log
_From:
```

2. DCL prompts you for the name of the input file. Fill in the name and press the Return key again:

```
_From: sayshello.pas
_To:
```

3. Now you are prompted for the new name of the file. When you enter the name, the RENAME command completes its task. Because of the /LOG qualifier, you can trace the results of the command:

```
_To: hello
%RENAME-I-RENAMED, PACK2:[YOURGROUP.YOU]SAYSHELLO PAS;1
renamed to PACK2:[{CC}YOURGROUP.YOU]HELLO.PAS;1
$
```

2.2.6   Checking the Differences Between Files

The DIFFERENCES command compares the contents of two files and lists the nonmatching portions of the compared files. It has the following syntax:

differences *input1-filespec* [*input2-filespec*]

This command lists the differences between the first and the second input files. If you do not specify a second input file, the DIFFERENCES command compares the first input file with the next lower version of that file. For example, to compare the two highest versions of your LOGIN.COM file, you would type

```
$ differences login.com
************
File PACK2:[YOURGROUP.YOU]LOGIN.COM;2
2 $ show users
3 $ show quota
******
File PACK2:[YOURGROUP.YOU]LOGIN.COM;1
************

Number of difference sections found: 1
Number of difference records found: 2

DIFFERENCES /IGNORE=()/MERGED=1-
  PACK2:[YOURGROUP.YOU]LOGIN.COM;2
  PACK2:[YOURGROUP.YOU]LOGIN.COM;1

$
```

To compare versions 5 and 1 of your LOGIN.COM file, you would type

```
$ differences login.com;5 login.com;1
```

You cannot use wildcards in either of the file specifications in a DIFFER-ENCES command line. Try Experiment 2.9 to see how the DIFFERENCES command works.

Experiment 2.9   *Comparing the Differences Between Two Files*

1. First use the EVE editor to edit the HELLO.PAS file to create two new versions of the file. Change the lines of the file as indicated by the bold text. The first change produces HELLO.PAS;2, and the second change produces HELLO.PAS;3. Use the arrow keys to move through the text and the Delete key or the ⟨ ✕ ⟩ key to erase text as necessary.

```
$ edit/tpu hello.pas
```

```
program sayshello(output);
begin
writeln ('Hello, Your name!')
end.
[End of file]
.
.
.
Buffer: HELLO.PAS                        | Write | Insert | Forward

4 lines read from file PACK2:[YOURGROUP.YOU]HELLO.PAS;1
```

Remember to press Ctrl/Z to exit and save your changes. Invoke EVE a second time and change the text as follows:

```
program sayshello(output);
begin
writeln ('Hello, Your name!')
end.
[End of file]
  .
  .
  .
Buffer: HELLO.PAS                      | Write | Insert | Forward
4 lines read from file PACK2:[YOURGROUP.YOU]HELLO.PAS;2
```

2. Now use the DIFFERENCES command to compare the two most recent versions of HELLO.PAS:

```
$ differences hello.pas
************
File PACK2:[YOURGROUP.YOU]HELLO.PAS;3
3 writeln ('Hello, world, again!')
4 end.
******
File PACK2:[YOURGROUP.YOU]HELLO.PAS;2
3 writeln('Hello, Your name!')
4 end.
************

Number of difference sections found:1
Number of difference records found:1

DIFFERENCES /IGNORE=()/MERGED=1
  PACK2:[YOURGROUP.YOU]HELLO.PAS;3
  PACK2:[YOURGROUP.YOU]HELLO.PAS;2
```

3. Finally, compare versions 3 and 1 of HELLO.PAS:

```
$ differences hello.pas.;3 hello.pas;1
************
File PACK2:[YOURGROUP.YOU]HELLO.PAS;3
3 writeln('Hello, world, again!')
4 end.
******
File PACK2:[YOURGROUP.YOU]HELLO.PAS;1
3 writeln('Hello, world!')
4 end.
************
```

```
Number of difference sections found: 1
Number of difference records found: 1

DIFFERENCES /IGNORE = <>/MERGED = 1
    PACK2:[YOURGROUP.YOU]HELLO.PAS;3
    PACK2:[YOURGROUP.YOU]HELLO.PAS;1
```

2.3   Working with Directories and Subdirectories

When you examined the pathname of the file specification, you saw how the directory names are listed in hierarchical order. A subdirectory is a directory cataloged in another, higher-level directory. In specifications, the different directory levels are separated by a period (.).

For example, so far the experiments have assumed that your login directory, YOU, is a subdirectory of a group or department's directory, YOURGROUP. The directory specification for your files, then, is [YOURGROUP.YOU]. Another directory specification might be PACK2:[UPSTAIRS.AI.YOU]. In this imaginary situation, YOU is a subdirectory of AI; and the AI directory itself is a subdirectory of the UPSTAIRS directory, which might be a directory of all departments.

When referring to a subdirectory of your working, or default, directory, you can specify either the full directory specification or just the subdirectory. For example, the following both specify the subdirectory OPENVMS:

[.OPENVMS]

[YOURGROUP.YOU.OPENVMS]

Subdirectories, like directories, are files of type .DIR.

2.3.1   Creating a Subdirectory

You use the CREATE command with the /DIRECTORY qualifier to establish a new subdirectory. The CREATE/DIRECTORY command has the following syntax:

create/directory *directory-specification[,...]*

When you create a subdirectory, OpenVMS assigns a .DIR extension to it. To list the files contained in a subdirectory, you must specify the name of that subdirectory. For example, to see the files in the TEXTS subdirectory in your default directory, you would type

$ directory [.texts]

Try Experiment 2.10 to explore working with subdirectories.

Experiment 2.10 *Creating a Subdirectory*

1. Use the CREATE/DIRECTORY command to create a OPENVMS subdirectory:

```
$ create/directory [.openvms]
```

2. To verify that the subdirectory now exists, use the DIRECTORY command to list all subdirectories:

```
$ directory *.dir

Directory PACK2:[YOURGROUP.YOU]

OPENVMS.DIR;1

Total of 1 file.
$
```

3. This OPENVMS subdirectory is empty. Add some files to it by copying files from the default directory:

```
$ copy openvms*.* [.openvms]
```

4. Now get a directory listing for the OPENVMS subdirectory:

```
$ directory [.openvms]

Directory PACK2:[YOURGROUP.YOU.OPENVMS]

OPENVMS1.TXT  OPENVMSBKS.DAT;1  OPENVMSDEF.TXT;1
OPENVMSMAN.DAT;1

Total of 4 files.
$
```

If you wanted to display the contents of the OPENVMSBKS.DAT file in the OPENVMS subdirectory, you could use one of the following versions of the TYPE command:

```
$ type [.openvms]openvmsbks.dat
$ type [yourgroup.you.openvms]openvmsbks.dat
```

By default, OpenVMS considers a file name without a specified directory name to be in the default directory. To get more experience with establishing new subdirectories, perform Experiment 2.11.

Experiment 2.11 *Creating More Subdirectories*

1. Create two new subdirectories: PASCAL and TEXTS. You can use the /LOG qualifier after the /DIRECTORY qualifier to trace the procedure:

```
$ create/directory/log [.pascal]
```

```
%CREATE-I-CREATED, PACK2:[YOURGROUP.YOU.PASCAL] created
$ create/directory/log [.texts]
%CREATE-I-CREATED, PACK2:[YOURGROUP.YOU.TEXTS] created
$
```

2. Now check the size of the subdirectories by using the DIRECTORY command with the /SIZE qualifier:

```
$ directory/size *.dir

Directory PACK2:[YOURGROUP.YOU]

PASCAL.DIR;1      1
TEXTS.DIR;1       1
OPENVMS.DIR;1     1
```

3. Copy the files of type .PAS to the PASCAL subdirectory and the files of type .TXT to the TEXTS subdirectory. Again, use /LOG to trace the procedure:

```
$ copy/log *.pas [.pascal]
%COPY-S-COPIED, PACK2:[YOURGROUP.YOU]DOESNOTHING.PAS;1
copied to PACK2:[YOURGROUP.YOU.PASCAL]DOESNOTHING.PAS;1
(1 block)
%COPY-S-COPIED, PACK2:[YOURGROUP.YOU]HELLO.PAS;3 copied to
PACK2:[YOURGROUP.YOU.PASCAL]HELLO.PAS;3 (1 block)
%COPY-S-NEWFILES, 2 files created
$
```

```
$ copy/log *.txt [.texts]
%COPY-S-COPIED, PACK2:[YOURGROUP.YOU]A.TXT;1 copied to
PACK2:[YOURGROUP.YOU.TEXTS]A.TXT;1 (1 block)
%COPY-S-COPIED, PACK2:[YOURGROUP.YOU]AI.TXT;1 copied to
PACK2:[YOURGROUP.YOU.TEXTS]AI.TXT;1 (1 BLOCK)
%COPY-S-COPIED, PACK2:[YOURGROUP.YOU]OPENVMS1.TXT;1 copied
to PACK2:[YOURGROUP.YOU.TEXTS]DIGITAL1.TXT;1 (1 block)
%COPY-S-COPIED, PACK2:[YOURGROUP.YOU]OPENVMSDEF.TXT;1 copied
to PACK2:[YOURGROUP.YOU.TEXTS]OPENVMSDEF.TXT;1 (1 block)
%COPY-S-NEWFILES, 4 files created
$
```

4. Use the DIRECTORY command to get a listing of the contents of each new directory:

```
$ directory [.pascal]

Directory PACK2:[YOURGROUP.YOU.PASCAL]

DOESNOTHING.PAS;1 HELLO.PAS;3

Total of 2 files.
```

```
$ directory [.texts]

Directory PACK2:[YOURGROUP.YOU.TEXTS]

A.TXT;1 AI.TXT;1 OPENVMS1.TXT;1 OPENVMSDEF.TXT;1

Total of 4 files.
$
```

You can create more than one directory with a single command line by entering the directory names separated by commas. For example,

```
$ create/directory [.pascal],[.texts]
```

2.3.2   Changing the Default Directory

The directory in which you are working is called your *working*, or *default directory*. By default, your login directory is your default directory each time you log into an OpenVMS system. Any files you create automatically become part of your default directory. You can change your default directory with the SET DEFAULT command, which has the following syntax:

set default *directory-specification*

For example, if you are working primarily with the files in the OPENVMS subdirectory, you can make that directory the default directory. To change the default directory from your login directory to the OPENVMS subdirectory, you would type

```
$ set default [.openvms]
$
```

You can check which directory is the default directory with the SHOW DEFAULT command:

```
$ show default
PACK2:[YOURGROUP.YOU.OPENVMS]
$
```

You can change back to your login directory with the SET DEFAULT command and the hyphen (-) directory-searching wildcard character. In general, this wildcard changes you from one directory to the next higher directory. For example, to change from the OPENVMS subdirectory back to the YOU subdirectory (your login directory), you would type

```
$ set default [-]
```

Using SET DEFAULT and the [-] wildcard, you can move up the path of directories above your login directory on your system. To explore moving through the directories, try Experiment 2.12.

Experiment 2.12 *Moving Around Your Directory Tree*

1. Use SHOW DEFAULT to make sure you are in your login directory:

```
$ show default
PACK2:[YOURGROUP.YOU]
```

2. Now move up one level in your directory tree, and check the new default directory with SHOW DEFAULT:

```
$ set default [-]
$ show default
PACK2:[YOURGROUP]
```

This step may produce an error message, depending on how the system manager has set up the directory one level above your login directory. That is, you may not be allowed access to the contents of the directories above your login directory. Check whether this is the case:

```
$ directory
```

3. Finally, move back to your login directory (remember to replace PACK2:[YOURGROUP.YOU] with your directory specification):

```
$ set default pack2:[yourgroup.you]
```

As you move up the directory tree above your login directory, you may find you cannot list the contents of any subdirectories above your login directory because you have not been authorized for access to them. OpenVMS has an elaborate scheme for protecting files against unauthorized access. An explanation of how this protection scheme works is given in Appendix B.

By moving up the directory tree of your system in Experiment 2.12, you can get a feel for the overall directory structure. This movement up and down a directory tree is shown in Figure 2.5.

Notice in Figure 2.5 what you must type to return to the login directory if you are more than two levels above this directory. For example, if your working directory is [UPSTAIRS], then to move down the directory tree to your login directory, you would type

```
$ set default [.ai.you]
```

2.3.3   Organizing Files with Subdirectories

By creating subdirectories, you can organize your files into logically related categories. In effect, a subdirectory is like a drawer in a file cabinet, with each

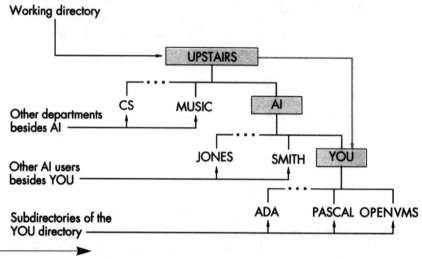

Figure 2.5 *Moving Up and Down a Directory Tree*

file being a file folder. As you work with subdirectories, consider the following tips for setting up a system of subdirectories:

1. Decide how you would like to group the files. For example, for the set of files that you have created so far, the classifications and their corresponding subdirectories might be

Classification	*Subdirectory*	*File Name*
Pascal files	YOU.PASCAL	SAYHELLO.PAS;1
		DONOTHING.PAS;1
Bibliographies	YOU.TEXTS	SFBKS.DAT;1
		OPENVMSBKS.DAT;1
		OPENVMSMAN.DAT;1
Definitions	YOU.DEFS	OPENVMSDEF.DAT;1
OpenVMS ideas	YOU.OPENVMS	OPENVMSBKS.DAT;1
		OPENVMSDEF.TXT;1
		OPENVMSMAN.DAT;1

2. Once you have identified a classification, check for possible categories. These categories can become subdirectories of the classification subdirectory. In the sample classification, here are some possible categories and their corresponding subdirectories:

Classifications	Category	File Name	Sub-subdirectory
Bibliographies	Science Fiction	SFBKS.DAT;1	YOU.TEXTS.SCIFI
	OpenVMS publications	OPENVMSBKS.DAT;1, OPENVMSMAN.DAT;1	YOU.OPENVMS.PUBS
OpenVMS ideas	OpenVMS definitions	OPENVMSDEF.TXT;1	YOU.OPENVMS.DEFS
	OpenVMS books	OPENVMSBKS.DAT;1	YOU.OPENVMS.BOOKS
	OpenVMS manuals	OPENVMSMAN.DAT;1	YOU.OPENVMS.MANUAL

3. When creating subdirectories, it is important to choose meaningful sub-directory names. Then you are less likely to forget what a subdirectory contains. For example, to see how to set up a directory system for the Open-VMS files you have created in this chapter, perform Experiment 2.13.

Experiment 2.13 *Establishing a System of Subdirectories*

1. Use SET DEFAULT to change to your login directory, if necessary.

2. Create a master OpenVMS subdirectory. Use the /LOG qualifier to trace the procedure:

```
$ create/directory/log [.openvmsideas]
%CREATE-I-CREATED, PACK2:[YOURGROUP.YOU.OPENVMSIDEAS] created
$
```

3. Next create three subdirectories of OPENVMSIDEAS:

```
$ create/directory/log [.openvmsideas.books]
%CREATE-I-CREATED, PACK2:[YOURGROUP.YOU.OPENVMSIDEAS.BOOKS]
created
$ create/directory/log [.openvmsideas.manuals]
%CREATE-I-CREATED, PACK2:[YOURGROUP.YOU.OPENVMSIDEAS.MANUALS]
created
$ create/directory/log [.openvmsideas.definitions]
%CREATE-I-CREATED, PACK2:[YOURGROUP.YOU.OPENVMSIDEAS.DEFINITIONS]
created
```

4. Now install the appropriate files in the new subdirectories of your OPENVMSIDEAS subdirectory:

```
$ copy/log openvmsbks.dat [.openvmsideas.books]
%COPY-S-COPIED, PACK2:[YOURGROUP.YOU]OPENVMSBKS.DAT;1
copied to PACK2:[YOURGROUP.YOU.OPENVMSIDEAS.BOOKS]
OPENVMSBKS.DAT;1 (1 block)
```

```
$ copy/log openvmsman.dat [.openvmsideas.manuals]
%COPY-S-COPIED, PACK2:[YOURGROUP.YOU]OPENVMSMAN.DAT;1
copied to PACK2:[YOURGROUP.YOU.OPENVMSIDEAS.MANUALS]
OPENVMSMAN.DAT;1 (1 block)
$ copy/log openvmsdef.txt [.openvmsideas.definitions]
%COPY-S-COPIED, PACK2:[YOURGROUP.YOU]OPENVMSDEF.TXT;1
copied to PACK2:[YOURGROUP.YOU.OPENVMSIDEAS.
DEFINITIONS]OPENVMSDEF.TXT;1 (1 block)
```

2.4   Short Forms for DCL Commands

Most DCL commands have an abbreviated form that you may use rather
than typing the whole command. For example, to use the DIRECTORY
command, you may type DIR rather than DIRECTORY. The short form
of a command usually is its first four characters; you may use fewer
than four characters as long as the abbreviation uniquely identifies the
command.

Because these short forms are composed of fewer characters, they save you
time. As you work with OpenVMS and become familiar with its commands,
you will probably start to use the short forms. Be aware when using abbreviations, however, that an abbreviation unique in one version of OpenVMS
might not be unique in the next version.

Summary

With the OpenVMS file-handling tools you have seen so far, various
approaches to files are possible, as seen in Table 2.3. As you master these file
handling tools, you also will want to consider various means of creating and
organizing your files and directories.

Table 2.3 *Approaches to OpenVMS Files*

Approach	DCL Command	Result
File creation	COPY	Duplicates a file or files
	CREATE	Creates a new file
	EDIT	Creates (and possibly changes) a file
File inspection	DIRECTORY	Displays a list of files
	TYPE	Displays the contents of a file or files

Table 2.3 *Approaches to OpenVMS Files (Continued)*

Approach	DCL Command	Result
File management	APPEND	Appends a copy of a file to a file
	DELETE	Removes a file or files
	DIFFERENCES	Compares a pair of files
	PRINT	Sends a file to the printer queue
	PURGE	Removes a version or versions of a file
	RENAME	Gives a file a new name
Directory management	CREATE/DIRECTORY	Establishes a new subdirectory
	SET DEFAULT	Changes the default directory
	SHOW DEFAULT	Displays the current default directory

Tables 2.4–2.6 give an overview of the commands, special characters, and important terms used in this chapter.

Table 2.4 *DCL Commands*

Command	Result
APPEND	Attaches one or more files to a named file
/LOG	Displays the APPEND command's actions
/NEW_VERSION	Creates a new output file
COPY	Makes a copy of a file
/LOG	Displays the COPY command's actions
CREATE	Establishes a new file
/DIRECTORY	Establishes a new subdirectory
/LOG	Displays the CREATE command's actions
DELETE	Deletes a specified file or files
/CONFIRM	Issues a request to confirm before *each* deletion
/LOG	Displays the DELETE command's actions

Table 2.4 *DCL Commands (Continued)*

Command	Result
DIFFERENCES	Compares the contents of two files
PURGE	Removes the specified versions or all versions of the specified file or files
/CONFIRM	Issues a request to confirm before *each* purge
/KEEP=*n*	Purge all but the *n* most recent file versions
/LOG	Displays the PURGE command's actions
RENAME	Renames a file or files
/LOG	Displays the RENAME command's actions
SET DEFAULT	Changes the default directory to be another directory
SET DEFAULT [-]	Moves the default directory to be the directory up one level
SHOW DEFAULT [-]	Displays the current default directory

Table 2.5 *Special Characters*

Character	Meaning
%	Wildcard representing any single character
*	Wildcard representing one or more characters
[-]	Represents the name of the directory one level above the default directory
[.*subdirectory-name*]	Subdirectory name
[.*subdirectory-name*]*filename*	Subdirectory file's file name

Table 2.6 *Important Terms*

Term	Definition
Default directory	Directory currently being used
Directory	File containing names of files
Login directory	Directory assigned by OpenVMS to you when you log in
Subdirectory	Any directory whose name appears in your default directory and that is *below* your default directory
Wildcard	Special character used in a file name to specify a collection of related files
Working directory	The same as the default directory

Exercises

1. What is the pathname for the files in your login directory?

2. Exercises 2, 3, and 4 reference the following files:

SFBKS.DAT;30	SFBKS.DAT;29	SFBKS.DAT;28
SFASIMOV.DAT;5		
SFHOYLE.DAT;7	SFHOYLE.DAT; 6	
SFDEF.TXT;2	SFDEF.TXT;1	
DIGITALDET.TXT;9	DIGITALDF.TXT;8	
OPENVMSBKS.DAT;9	XENIX.TXT;5	

   List the files in the list that are indicated by the following file specifications:
   a. SF%.DAT;*
   b. SF%%.DAT;*
   c. SF%%%.DAT;*
   d. SF*.*;*
   e. SF*.TXT;*
   f. .*;9
   g. .*;*

3. Give a single file specification for each of the following:
   a. All files whose names begin with OPENVMS
   b. All files of type .TXT
   c. All version 1 files
   d. All files with HOYLE in the file name
   e. All files having a type that begins with *D*
   f. All files with file names having six letters that begin with *V* and end with *S*

4. In terms of the preceding list of files, give command lines that perform the following:
   a. Append all files whose names begin with *SF* to an SFIDEAS.DAT file
   b. Copy all the files to a list of files of type YES

5. Without using wildcards, give four ways to specify a file named OPEN-VMSBKS.DAT in a OPENVMSIDEAS subdirectory of your login directory.

6. For your system, what is the full file specification for the SFBKS.DAT file (created in Experiment 2.1)?

7. Give two ways to specify the directory at the level above your login directory on your system.

8. Give a single command line that tells OpenVMS to display the contents of all your files of type .TXT.

9. Give command lines to do the following:
   a. Create a LETTERS subdirectory of your login directory
   b. Create a sample letter that ends with *PS*
   c. Append all the files of type .TXT to the letter created in part b
   d. Put a copy of the letter from part b into your LETTERS subdirectory

10. Give a single command line that creates three subdirectories named YES1, YES2, and YES3.

11. Using the files created in Experiment 2.1 (Section 2.1.1), give command lines that accomplish the following:
    a. Append the files of type .TXT to ALL.TXT
    b. Create a program subdirectory
    c. Copy all files of type .PAS to the program subdirectory

12. Give a new version of your LOGIN.COM file that produces a list of the subdirectories of your login directory each time you log in.

Review Quiz

Indicate whether the following statements are true or false:

1. The following command line references only version 1 files in your current directory:

   ```
   $ directory *.*;1
   ```

2. The % wildcard can be used in a file specification to specify version numbers.

3. The *.COM file specification specifies *all* versions of your files of type .COM.

4. The *.DAT and *.DAT;* file specifications identify the same group of files.

5. A COPY command line specifies one or more files to be created.

6. The PURGE and DELETE commands both can be used to eliminate files.

7. You must give the version number of a file you wish to delete.

8. It is possible to have version 39 and version 1 of the same file and no other versions of that file.

9. The type specification for a subdirectory is .DIR.

10. The following command line will move down exactly one directory level:

```
$ set default [-]
```

Further Reading

Adams, J. L. *Conceptual Blockbusting: A Guide to Better Ideas.* Reading, Mass.: Addison-Wesley, 1986.

VMS User's Guide. Austin, Texas: Academic Computing and Instructional Technology Services; The University of Texas at Austin, 1996. URL: http://www.utexas.edu/docs/ccug2.

Digital Equipment Corporation, POB CS2008, Nashua, NH 03061:

Printed Documentation:	*OpenVMS DCL Dictionary: A–M*
	OpenVMS DCL Dictionary: N–Z
	OpenVMS Software Overview
	OpenVMS User's Manual
On-Line Documentation:	OpenVMS On-Line Help Facility
	OpenVMS Bookreader
	http://www.openvms.digital.com

3

Full-Screen Editing with EVE

*The form or law of thought . . . is detected when we watch the machine
in operation without attending to the matter operated on.*

—Augustus De Morgan, *On the Syllogism, and
Other Logical Writings,* 1860

OpenVMS provides several different text editors, which you can use to create and edit text files. This chapter introduces the default text editor EVE (extensible versatile editor). In this chapter, you will

▶ Learn how to use EVE keypad mode

▶ Learn how EVE stores a text file

▶ Explore commonly used EVE keypad and line commands

▶ Experiment with various methods of moving the cursor

▶ Explore various ways to locate text

▶ Experiment with multiple editing windows

▶ Examine different ways to recover from system interruptions

3.1   About EVE

As a full-screen editor, EVE incorporates many of the same features that the EDT editor has. What makes EVE unique, however, is its flexibility in allowing you to adapt it for your specific editing needs. EVE can be used to edit or create new files such as letters, memos, or complex computer programs.

EVE is written in DECTPU, which is a high-performance, programmable, text-processing utility. The EVE editor can be activated only on an ANSI standard terminal like the VT100 or VT200. The keyboard on an ANSI standard terminal provides an editing keypad and some additional keys that EVE uses to perform editing functions. The Ctrl key can be used with several main keyboard keys to perform specific editing functions. In addition, EVE uses some of the function keys on the VT200 for editing.

EVE allows you to edit text in one of two ways. The first method is editing in keypad mode. With keypad mode, you use various keypad and function keys on the keyboard. The second method involves typing EVE commands on the EVE command line.

With keypad mode, you can easily manipulate text using simple keystrokes. Using the keys on the numeric keypad (VT100) or the auxiliary keypad (VT200), you can work with characters as well as with larger portions of text. Cursor position determines how text will be affected by the EVE commands, and you can move the cursor through the file in a variety of ways. In keypad mode, EVE keypad commands make it possible to delete, find, insert, substitute, and move text in a file with a single keystroke.

Line commands allow you to manipulate a range of one or more lines of text using any of the EVE line commands. The command line is activated with the Do key (PF4 on the VT100 and Do on the VT200). You type simple commands after the Command: prompt on the command line, which is located at the bottom of your screen.

In addition, EVE provides the following features to make your editing easier:

▶ An on-line Help facility, which you can use at any time during an editing session without interrupting or affecting the work in progress

▶ A fail-safe mechanism, called a *Journal facility*, for retrieving lost files if your system crashes while you are editing

▶ Several methods of searching for text rapidly

▶ A variety of cursor movement functions

▶ Multiple windows in which two files can be viewed and edited on the screen during the current editing session

This chapter concentrates on editing in keypad mode. Occasionally, line commands essential to the editing process are discussed. Before venturing any further, use the DCL CREATE command to set up a file, as explained in Experiment 3.1. You will use this file during the rest of the chapter.

Experiment 3.1 *Creating the Initial File*

1. Use the DCL CREATE command to create the file LETTER.TXT:

   ```
   $ create letter.txt
   ```

2. Type the following text exactly as shown, including the misspelled *Deer*:

   ```
   Deer Mr. Smith:
   Just a brief note to thank you for taking the time to talk
   with me today about the computer programming position you
   are looking to fill. I enjoyed our conversation and found
   your comments very helpful.
   Sincerely,
   ```

   Exit by pressing Ctrl/z:
   ```
   Ctrl/z
   Exit
   ```

   ```
   $
   ```

3.2   Getting Started with EVE

To activate EVE, use the DCL EDIT command with the /TPU qualifier. Its syntax is

```
edit/tpu filespec
```

Because the command to activate EVE may vary somewhat from computer to computer, you may need to check with your system manager to find out how to activate EVE on your system.

Once you have entered the EDIT command with the /TPU qualifier and the file name, you have activated EVE. EVE goes directly into keypad mode, and the first 21 lines of the file appear on the screen. A status line appears at the bottom of the screen and displays information about the current editing buffer. Also, it notifies you of the default editing mode (Insert) and editing direction (Forward), see Figure 3.1.

When EVE is activated, it places a copy of the file in a buffer, a workspace where you can manipulate the text. This buffer is given the same name as the file you are editing. Activate EVE by following Experiment 3.2.

Experiment 3.2 *Activating EVE*

1. First activate EVE by entering the EDIT command with the file name LETTER.TXT:

   ```
   $ edit/tpu letter.txt
   ```

```
Deer Mr. Smith:
Just a brief note to thank you for taking the time
to talk with me today about the computer programming
position you are looking to fill. I enjoyed our
conversation and found your comments very helpful.
Sincerely,
[End of file]




















Buffer: LETTER.TXT                                          Write | Insert | Forward
```

Figure 3.1   *The [End of file] Symbol*

EVE will be in keypad mode and display all six lines of the file and the [End of file] symbol, which signifies the end of the file.

2. Use the Down Arrow key to move the cursor past the [End of file] symbol.

3. Interrupt the EVE session by pressing Ctrl/Y This returns you to the DCL prompt, as shown in Figure 3.2.

4. Activate EVE again by entering the EDIT command with the file name LETTER.TXT.

Once EVE finishes painting the screen with text, the cursor appears in the upper left-hand corner and the [End of file] symbol flags the end of the file, as shown in Figure 3.1.

3.3   An Overview of the EVE Keypads

Many EVE editing commands are assigned to the numeric keypad (PF1–PF4, 0–9, Minus, Period, Comma, Enter) on the VT100 keyboard. For instance,

```
Deer Mr. Smith:
Just a brief note to thank you for taking the time
to talk with me today about the computer programming
position you are looking to fill.  I enjoyed our
conversation and found your comments very helpful.
Sincerely,
    Interrupt

$




Buffer: LETTER.TXT                         Write | Insert | Forward
```

Figure 3.2 *Interrupting an EVE Session*

key number 7 (or KP7) on the numeric keypad is assigned the SELECT command. On the VT200 keyboard, the auxiliary keypad (the eight-key editing keypad with four arrow keys, which is between the main keyboard and the numeric keypad) and the function keys F10 through F14 are assigned many EVE editing commands. The VT200's numeric keypad, by default, is used by EVE only for numerical entries. Figure 3.3 shows the EVE editing commands on the keypads.

3.4   The EVE Command Line

The command line is another way to communicate with EVE. You access the command line with the DO command, which is issued by pressing the Do key on the auxiliary keypad on the VT200 or the PF4 key on the VT100 numeric keypad. After you press the Do key, EVE places the cursor on the line below the status line and prompts you for the command, an Englishlike word or phrase, by displaying Command. Once you type the command, you must press Return to activate the function associated with that command.

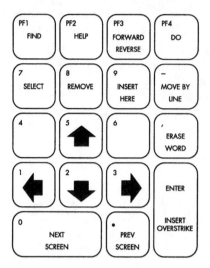

VT100 Terminal

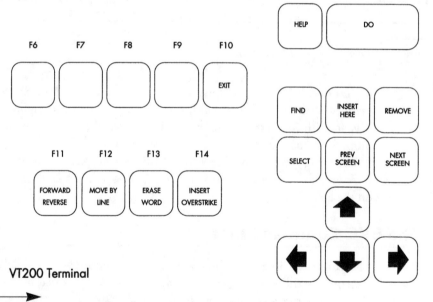

VT200 Terminal

Figure 3.3 *The EVE Keypads*

Some EVE commands require more information than just the command name. If you do not enter all the required information, EVE will prompt you for the needed information in the command line.

You can type line commands in either uppercase or lowercase letters, and you can abbreviate the commands. For example, BOTTOM, bottom, and BOT are all valid ways to type the BOTTOM line command. Command abbreviations must be unique. If not, EVE prompts you with the possible choices.

A line command can be repeated without typing it over each time. If you press the Do key twice in a row, EVE will repeat the last command entered. You can continue this process until you enter a different command.

3.5   Entering and Editing Text

When you work with EVE, you use the commands assigned to the keypad to modify and manipulate text. Some of the commands are used to move the cursor to particular places in the text. You also can use the arrow keys to move the cursor.

3.5.1   Moving Around the File Using Cursor Movement Keys

When you first start an EVE editing session, the cursor is positioned at the beginning of the file. You can move the cursor in any direction through the file using the arrow keys. The Left Arrow and Right Arrow keys move the cursor one character to the left or right, respectively. The Up Arrow and Down Arrow keys move the cursor up or down one line.

A quick way to move to the next line of text is through the MOVE BY LINE command (the F12 function key on the VT200 and Minus on the VT100 numeric keypad). You can use the line command START OF LINE to move to the beginning of the current line and the line command END OF LINE to move to the end of the current line. In addition, you can use the MOVE BY WORD line command to move one word at a time. Experiment with these cursor movement keys and commands by following the steps in Experiment 3.3.

Experiment 3.3   *Exploring Some Cursor Movement Functions*

1. Try using the arrow keys to move around the file.

2. Move to the top of the buffer and then press the Up Arrow key.

3. Try using the MOVE BY LINE command to move to the next line.

4. To move by the word, move to the beginning of a word and activate the command line by pressing Do. Type the MOVE BY WORD line command and press Return. Also try out the line commands START OF LINE and END OF LINE.

5. When you are finished experimenting, move to the top of the buffer with the TOP line command.

Several other ways to move around a file are introduced in later sections of this chapter.

3.5.2 Inserting Text

If need be, text can be added to a file by positioning the cursor where the text should be added and typing that text. The cursor and any text following it will be moved to the right as you type each character. You can insert a single character or many lines of text. The characters always are inserted to the left of the cursor.

Use Return when you want to start a new line. To break a line of text, position the cursor on the character that will be the first character of the new line and press Return.

The text file that you created in Experiment 3.1 is missing the second and third paragraphs. To practice using the EVE editor to make insertions, insert these paragraphs by following the steps in Experiment 3.4.

Experiment 3.4 *Inserting Text*

1. Move the cursor to the letter *S* in *Sincerely* and type the following paragraphs. You can enter blank lines between the paragraphs by pressing Return. This enters an end-of-line character and moves the text that is to the right of the cursor plus the character the cursor is on to the next line:

```
As I told you during the interview, I would like the chance
to show how well I can handle the job. I would be delighted
to discuss the matter further with you at your convenience.

I look forward to hearing from you. Thank you again for
your time and encouragement.
```

2. Notice the word *Sincerely* does not appear on a line by itself. Move it down two lines by pressing Return twice. The completed letter should appear as shown in Figure 3.4.

3.5.3 Deleting Text

Deleting text in EVE is a simple operation handled by a single keystroke or command. You can delete text by the character, the word, or the line. To

```
╭─────────────────────────────────────────────────────────────────────╮
│ Dear Mr. Smith:                                                       │
│                                                                       │
│ Just a brief note to thank you for taking the time                    │
│ to talk with me today about the computer programming                  │
│ position you are looking to fill.  I enjoyed our                      │
│ conversation and found your comments very helpful.                    │
│                                                                       │
│ As I told you during the interview, I would like                      │
│ the chance to show how well I can handle the job.                     │
│ I would be delighted to discuss the matter further                    │
│ with you at your convenience.                                         │
│                                                                       │
│ I look forward to hearing from you.  Thank you again                  │
│ for your time and encouragement.                                      │
│                                                                       │
│ Sincerely,                                                            │
│ [End of file]                                                         │
│                                                                       │
│                                                                       │
│ ▓Buffer: LETTER.TXT▓▓▓▓▓▓▓▓▓▓▓▓▓▓▓▓▓Write │ Insert │ Forward▓ │
╰─────────────────────────────────────────────────────────────────────╯
```

Figure 3.4 *The Completed Letter*

delete characters, use the ⟨ × ⟩ key on the VT200 or Delete on the VT100, which deletes the character to the left of the cursor, or the ERASE CHARACTER line command, which deletes the character at the cursor position.

Deleting a word is just as easy. Position the cursor on the word and use the ERASE WORD command (F13 function key on the VT200 or Comma on the VT100 numeric keypad). To delete a line of text, position the cursor at the beginning of the line and use the ERASE LINE line command. Explore the use of these keys and commands by following Experiment 3.5.

Experiment 3.5 *Deleting Text*

1. The first text you need to delete is the misspelling in the word *Deer.* Move the cursor to the end of this word. Press the ⟨ × ⟩ key or Delete twice to delete the last two characters. Then type *ar* to correct the spelling.

2. Move to the beginning of the second line of the first paragraph. Activate the command line by pressing Do. Use the ERASE CHARACTER line command to delete the *t* in *to.*

3. Move to the beginning of the third line and use the ERASE WORD command to delete the first word, *position*.

4. Move to the beginning of the fourth line of text and use the line command ERASE LINE to delete the line. Notice that the lines below the deleted line move up. The deleted text is stored by EVE in a workspace called the *Delete buffer*. This buffer contains the most recently deleted character, word, or line. You can use the contents of the buffer to restore the most recent text that you have deleted.

3.5.4   Undeleting Text

To restore deleted text stored in the Delete buffer, use the RESTORE line command. Use this line command in Experiment 3.6 to restore the text you deleted previously.

Experiment 3.6 *Undeleting Text*

1. The last text deleted was the line previous to the current editing line. Use the RESTORE line command to restore the line.

2. You also deleted the character *t* from the word *to,* and the word *position*. Because EVE can restore only the most recently deleted text, you will need to retype these deletions.

3. If you want to work more with the delete and undelete functions, add several lines to the bottom of the file and work with the keys and commands using that text. When you are finished, delete the extra text from the file.

3.6   Leaving an EVE Editing Session

When you have finished editing a file of text, you need to leave the EVE editing session and save the completed file. You can use either the Ctrl/Z key sequence (VT200 and VT100) or the EXIT line command (F10 on a VT200) to save the results of an editing session. In either case, when you exit the editing session, EVE copies the contents of the Main buffer to a file in your user directory. The file has the same name but a higher version number, as illustrated in Figure 3.5.

During the course of an editing session, you may realize that you are editing the wrong file or that you have accidentally deleted information you need. To avoid saving the contents of the current buffer, you can leave an EVE editing session by using the QUIT line command rather than the EXIT line command. The QUIT line command ends an editing session without saving the

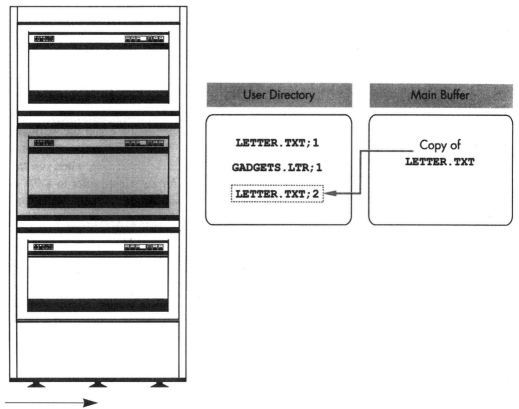

Figure 3.5 *Saved File with Higher Version Number*

buffer's contents. Experiment 3.7 demonstrates various methods of leaving an EVE editing session.

Experiment 3.7 *Leaving an EVE Editing Session*

1. First try leaving the EVE editing session and saving the changes using the Ctrl/Z key sequence.

2. You are at the DCL prompt, $. The changes to the file are now saved in a new version of LETTER.TXT. Verify this by using the DIRECTORY command to get a listing of files:

```
$ directory letter.txt
Directory DUA1: [YOURGROUP.YOU]
LETTER.TXT;2    LETTER.TXT;1
Total of 2 files.
$
```

3. Return to EVE as if you were going to edit LETTER.TXT:

```
$ edit/tpu letter.txt
```

4. This time, leave EVE using the QUIT line command.

5. With QUIT, the contents of the buffer are not saved in a file. Use the DIRECTORY command to check that a new version of LETTER. TXT has not been saved:

```
$ directory letter.txt

Directory DUA1: [YOURGROUP.YOU]

LETTER.TXT;2          LETTER.TXT;1

Total of 2 files.
$
```

3.7   Creating a File with EVE

Earlier in the chapter, you created the LETTER.TXT file using the DCL CREATE command. You also can create a new file from EVE by specifying a new file name when you enter the EDIT/TPU command. Experiment 3.8 demonstrates how to create a new file, which contains a C program that prints Fahrenheit temperatures and the centigrade, or Celsius, equivalents.

Experiment 3.8   *Creating a New File from EVE*

1. Activate EVE using the file name TEMP.C:

```
$ edit temp.c
```

Once EVE finishes painting the screen with text, the cursor appears in the upper left-hand corner, and the symbol [End of file] flags the end of the file.

2. Enter the following text exactly as it appears. Remember to press Return to start a new line. Notice that, as you enter more than 21 lines of text, the text scrolls off the top of the screen:

```
/*   This program will print a table of Fahrenheit
     temperatures and the corresponding temperatures in
     centigrade, or Celsius */
main ()
{
     int lowest, highest, increment;
     float fahrenheit, celsius;
     lowest = 0;/* lowest temperature */
     highest = 300;/* highest temperature */
     increment = 10;/* temperature increment */
     fahrenheit = lowest;
```

```
            while (fahrenheit <= highest) {
                celsius = (5.0/9.0) * (fahrenheit - 32.0);
                printf(''%4.0f %6.1f\n'', fahrenheit, celsius);
                fahrenheit = fahrenheit + increment;
            }
        }
```

3. Return to the beginning of the file using the arrow keys.

3.8   Getting Help with EVE Commands

EVE's on-line Help facility allows you to obtain help on a specific EVE key or command during your editing session. While in the keypad mode, you can use the HELP command (Help on the VT200 or PF2 on the VT100) to get help about keypad commands. A Help screen appears. You then can press any key to obtain help about that key.

To get help from the command line, type HELP at the Command: prompt and press Return. A Help screen appears. You then can type HELP and the name of a command to obtain help about that command. For example, you could type HELP BOTTOM to see information about the BOTTOM command. To view a complete list of commands, type just HELP and press Return. Experiment 3.9 explores the Help facility.

Experiment 3.9   *Getting Help*

1. You should be in the EVE keypad mode to begin. If you have been following the experiments, the file TEMP.C will be on the screen. Issue the HELP command (Help on the VT200 or PF2 on the VT100). The screen should resemble Figure 3.6.

2. Read the instructions on the screen. Press any of the keypad keys to see information about that key's command.

3. Once you have finished reading the Help text, return to the editing session by pressing Return.

4. Use the Do key to activate the command line. The Command: prompt should appear on the screen.

5. Type HELP and press Return. The screen should resemble Figure 3.7.

6. Read the instructions on the screen. You now can obtain information about a particular command or topic. Enter text to explore a topic; for example, DELETE.

7. Once you have finished reading the Help text, return to the keypad mode editing session by pressing Return.

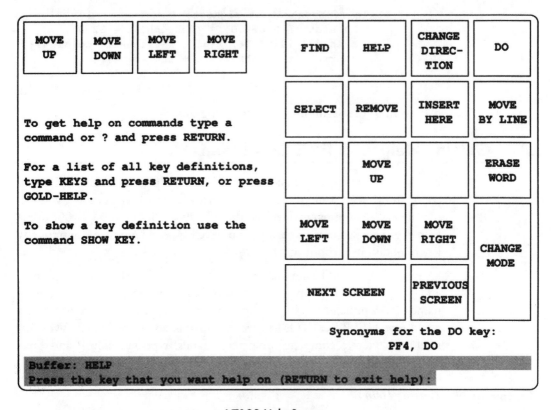

VT100 Help Screen

Figure 3.6 *Keypad Mode Help*

3.9   More EVE Commands and Functions

Many useful keypad functions are provided by EVE for editing a file or text. They include changing the editing direction, searching for text strings, and cutting and pasting portions of text. The following sections introduce many of these functions.

3.9.1   Changing the Editing Direction

When you begin an EVE editing session, the cursor movement through the text in a file is forward, or toward the end of the buffer. This is the default editing direction. For example, when you use the MOVE BY LINE command, the cursor moves to the ends of lines; or when you use the FIND command to search for a text string, the search advances from the cursor toward the end of the file.

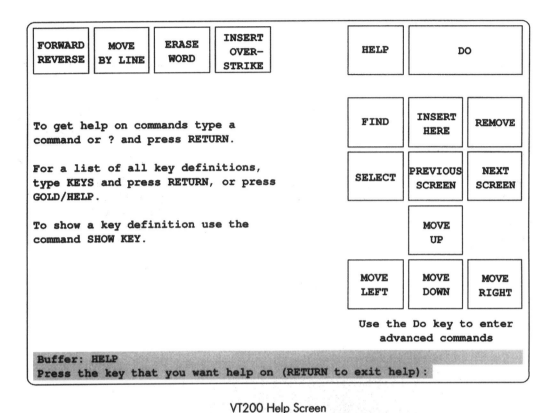

VT200 Help Screen

Figure 3.6 *Keypad Mode Help (Continued)*

By using the FORWARD/REVERSE command (F11 on the VT200 or PF3 on the VT100), you can change the editing direction. After you issue this command, movement through the file will be back toward the beginning of the file. To return to forward movement, you must press the same key again. The status line reflects the current editing direction each time this key is pressed. Being able to control the editing direction is advantageous when working with many EVE functions, as demonstrated in Experiment 3.10.

Experiment 3.10 *Changing the Editing Direction*

1. Change the editing direction to reverse with the FORWARD/ REVERSE command. The status line should display

```
Buffer: TEMP.C                        | Write | Insert | Reverse
```

```
List Of Topics (Commands)

For help on EVE topics, type the name of a topic and press RETURN.

   · For a keypad diagram, press HELP.
   · For help on TPU builtins, type TPU and press RETURN.
   · To exit from help and resume editing, press RETURN.

EDITING TEXT

      Change Mode              Erase Word              Restore Character
      Copy                     Insert Here             Restore Line
      Cut                      Insert Mode             Restore Selection
      Delete                   Overstrike Mode         Restore Sentence
      Erase Character          Paste                   Restore Word
      Erase Line               Quote                   Select
      Erase Previous Word      Remove                  Select All
      Erase Start Of Line      Restore                 Store Text

BOX EDITING
```

```
Buffer: HELP                To see more, use: | Prev Screen | Next Screen
Type the topic you want help on(press RETURN if done):
```

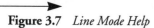

Figure 3.7 *Line Mode Help*

2. Activate the command line by pressing Do. Then type the MOVE BY WORD command and press Return.

3. To move by the line, use the MOVE BY LINE command. Notice that in reverse the MOVE BY LINE command moves the cursor to the beginning of lines. (If you are in the middle of a line, the cursor moves to the beginning of that line; if you are at the beginning of a line, the cursor moves to the beginning of the previous line.)

4. Use the FORWARD/REVERSE command to change the editing direction. Then use the MOVE BY LINE command again. In the forward direction, this command moves the cursor to the end of lines. (If you are in the middle of a line, the cursor moves to the end of that line; if you are at the end of a line, the cursor moves to the end of the next line.)

5. When you are finished experimenting, return the editing direction to forward.

3.9.2   Other Ways of Moving the Cursor

You have been moving the cursor around the screen up to this point by moving a character, word, or line at a time. In addition to these methods, EVE provides ways to move the cursor in larger increments. For example, the TOP and BOTTOM line commands move the cursor to the beginning or the end of the file quickly. These commands are particularly useful when you are working with large files.

You also can move the cursor through the file a screenful of text at a time using the PREV SCREEN (Previous Screen) command (Prev Screen on the VT200 or Period on the VT100 numeric keypad) or the NEXT SCREEN command (Next Screen on the VT200 or KP0 on the VT100). This brings a different section of text into view with a single keystroke. Follow Experiment 3.11 to try out these commands.

Experiment 3.11   *More Cursor Movement Commands*

1. Move to the end of the file with the BOTTOM line command.

2. To move to the top of the file, activate the command line again and enter the TOP line command.

3. Move to the bottom of the file using the BOTTOM line command.

4. Issue the PREV SCREEN command to move from the [End of file] marker up toward the beginning of the file.

5. Use the NEXT SCREEN command to move from the current position toward the end of the file.

3.9.3   A Simple Method of Locating Text

Moving the cursor a character or a word at a time in a small file can be time consuming but acceptable. However, using this method on large files can be tedious. EVE provides a simpler method of locating text with the FIND command (Find on the VT200 or PF1 on the VT100). FIND searches through the current file for a previously specified word, character, or short phrase. It quickly locates an item, minimizing the time required to scan the file.

When the FIND command is activated, it searches for the specified item in the current editing direction. EVE prompts you for the text string to search for, or the search string. You type the search string and press Return, then EVE searches for the string. EVE moves the cursor to the first occurrence of the search string that it encounters.

EVE accepts either lowercase or uppercase letters. If the word is typed in all lowercase letters, EVE finds the word whether it is in lowercase, uppercase, or a combination of the two. If the word is typed in all uppercase letters, EVE finds the word only if it is in all uppercase letters. If the word is typed in a combination of lowercase and uppercase, EVE finds only those occurrences that have the same combination of lowercase and uppercase letters.

If you want to find the next occurrence of the search string, you can press the Find key twice and EVE will search for the previously entered search string.

This method of locating text can save a considerable amount of time when searching for a set of characters within a lengthy document. Keep in mind that, when searching for text, it is important to make the search string unique. You should try to include in the search string as many landmarks surrounding the text as possible, so that EVE can locate the text on the first attempt.

If EVE is unable to locate a search string, it gives a message to that effect. This happens when a search string is mistyped, a string does not exist, or the direction of the search is moving away from the string in the text. In the last case, if the search string is found in the opposite direction, EVE will display a message indicating this and prompt you to continue the search. You can try using the FIND command by following Experiment 3.12.

Experiment 3.12 *Using FIND to Locate Text*

1. Move the cursor to the beginning of the TEMP.C file.

2. Issue the FIND command. EVE prompts you for the search string, as shown in Figure 3.8.

3. Type the character { and press Return. EVE searches toward the end of the file for the first occurrence of {.

4. Search for the next occurrence by pressing the Find key twice. EVE moves to the next occurrence of {.

5. Press the Find key twice again. EVE did not find another occurrence of the search string in the current editing direction and so it displays a message, as shown in Figure 3.9.

6. Type *y*(*es*) and press Return. EVE moves the cursor to the first occurrence of the search string in the reverse direction, or toward the beginning of the buffer.

3.10   Working with a Selected Range of Text

Up to this point, you have experimented with several methods of moving the cursor around the screen and manipulating small sections of text. EVE provides several additional features that enhance its editing abilities further. One

```
/* This program will print a table of
   Fahrenheit temperatures and the
   corresponding temperatures in
   centigrade, or Celsius */

main ()
{
 int lowest, highest, increment;
 float fahrenheit, celsius;

 lowest = 0;        /* lowest temperature */
 highest = 300;     /* highest temperature */
 increment = 10;    /* temperature increment */

fahrenheit = lowest
 while (fahrenheit <= highest){
         celsius = (5.0/9.0) * (fahrenheit - 32.0);
         printf ("%4.0f %6.1f\n", fahrenheit, celsius);
         fahrenheit = fahrenheit + increment;
 }
}


 Buffer: TEMP.C                          Write | Insert | Forward
 Forward Find::
```

Figure 3.8 *The Find Prompt*

particularly useful feature allows you to select a larger portion of text that can be manipulated as a unit.

3.10.1 Selecting a Range of Text

The SELECT command (Select on the VT200 or KP7 on the VT100) allows you to select a section, or range, of text. The section of text can be made up of one or more words or one or more lines of text. On the screen a highlight identifies the selected text.

To select a range of text, move the cursor to the beginning of the text to be manipulated, press SELECT, then use any of the cursor movement keys or line commands to highlight the text. For example, you can use the arrow keys to extend the highlight up or down a line or left or right, or you can use the MOVE BY WORD line command. You can highlight text in either the

```
/* This program will print a table of
   Fahrenheit temperatures and the
   corresponding temperatures in
   centigrade, or Celsius */

main ()
{
 int lowest, highest, increment;
 float fahrenheit, celsius;

 lowest = 0;        /* lowest temperature */
 highest = 300;     /* highest temperature */
 increment = 10;    /* temperature increment */

fahrenheit = lowest
 while (fahrenheit <= highest){
         celsius = (5.0/9.0) * (fahrenheit - 32.0);
         printf ("%4.0f %6.1f\n", fahrenheit, celsius);
         fahrenheit = fahrenheit + increment;
 }
}
```

Buffer: TEMP.C   Write | Insert | Forward
Forward in reverse direction. Go there?

Figure 3.9   *Search Text Not Found*

forward or reverse direction simply by using FORWARD/REVERSE to
change the editing direction.

Portions of text can be excluded from a selected range by moving the cursor back until the unwanted text is no longer highlighted. You can cancel any
selection by pressing SELECT a second time. You can practice selecting
ranges of text by following Experiment 3.13.

Experiment 3.13   *Selecting a Range of Text*

1. In the earlier experiments in this section, you worked with the LET-
   TER.TXT file. Retrieve that file by exiting EVE and then reactivating
   EVE with LETTER.TXT as the file name. When you exit EVE, you
   must enter a file name for the TEMP.C file because you created it in
   EVE and so it exists only in memory.

2. Select the first four lines of text with the SELECT command and highlight the lines. As you move the cursor down, EVE extends the highlight, as shown in Figure 3.10.

3. All the highlighted text is selected. You could now use other keys and commands to manipulate the selected range. Instead, press SELECT to cancel this selection.

3.10.2 Removing and Inserting a Range of Text

Previously, you deleted text by the character, word, or line. In addition to these delete capabilities, EVE provides a REMOVE command (Remove on the VT200 or KP8 on the VT100) that lets you delete the text in a selected range. This method allows you to remove larger portions of text with a single keystroke.

```
Dear Mr. Smith:
Just a brief note to thank you for taking the time
to talk with me today about the computer programming
position you are looking to fill.  I enjoyed our
conversation and found your comments very helpful.

As I told you during the interview, I would like
the chance to show how well I can handle the job.
I would be delighted to discuss the matter further
with you at your convenience.

I look forward to hearing from you.  Thank you again
for your time and encouragement.

Sincerely,
[End of file]




Buffer: LETTER.TXT                    Write | Insert | Forward
Move the text cursor to select text.
```

Figure 3.10 *Selecting Text*

REMOVE erases any selected highlighted text or blank spaces. The removed text is stored in the Insert buffer. The text remains in the Insert buffer until it is replaced by other text or until the editing session is completed. If you select and remove another portion of text while the earlier one is in the Insert buffer, the earlier text will be deleted from the buffer.

It is important to keep in mind when selecting a portion of text for removal that you should move the cursor one space beyond the last character you want to remove. The character or space the cursor is on is not included in the removed text.

Once the text has been removed, the contents of the Insert buffer can be placed anywhere in the current editing buffer. This is accomplished by positioning the cursor at the location where the text is to be placed and using the INSERT HERE command (Insert Here on the VT200 or KP9 on the VT100). All text to the right of the cursor will be moved to the right to accommodate the addition of the new text. You can see how REMOVE and INSERT HERE work by following Experiment 3.14.

Experiment 3.14   *Removing and Inserting Text*

    1. Move the cursor to the beginning of the file.

    2. Use the SELECT command to move the cursor to the beginning of the blank line following the first paragraph.

    3. Use the REMOVE command to remove the selected text from the file. The selected text is now in the Insert buffer, as shown in Figure 3.11.

    4. To restore the removed portion of text, you can insert it back into its previous location. If you wanted to insert it elsewhere, you would move the cursor to the new location. Leave the cursor in its current position and use the INSERT HERE command to insert the contents of the Insert buffer into the file.

3.11   Discovering Some of EVE's Special Features

EVE has additional features that make it unique compared to other full-screen editors like EDT. These features are discussed in the following sections.

3.11.1   Finding and Replacing Text

EVE provides a way to find and replace text. You can use the REPLACE line command to specify which text should be replaced and what should replace it. This method is useful when you have numerous occurrences of text that need to be replaced, because once you find and replace the first occurrence, you can continue replacing other occurrences easily.

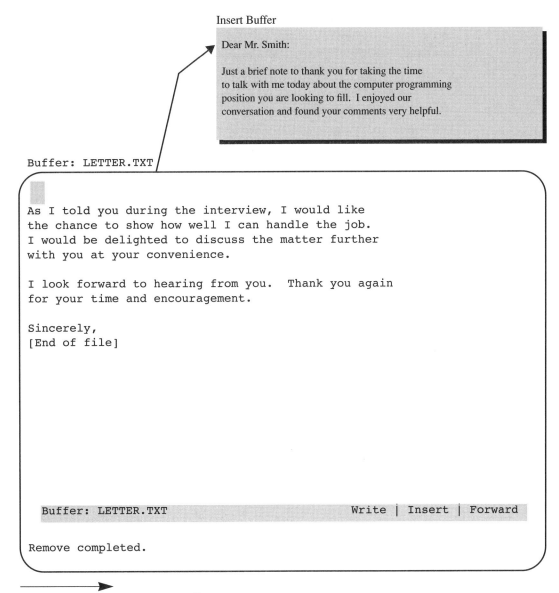

Figure 3.11   *The Insert Buffer*

When you enter the REPLACE line command, EVE prompts you for the string to be replaced, or the old string. When you enter the old string, EVE then prompts for the string that should replace the old string, the new string.

Once you have entered the new string, EVE highlights the first occurrence of the text to be replaced and prompts you for an action with Replace? type yes, no, all, last, or quit:. You may respond by typing *y*(*es*) to replace the occurrence, *n*(*o*) not to replace the occurrence, *a*(*ll*) to replace all occurrences without further prompting, *l*(*ast*) to replace the current occurrence or stop, or *q*(*uit*) to stop the replace process completely.

The REPLACE line command is case sensitive. If the old string is in all lowercase letters, EVE finds all uppercase and lowercase occurrences. If the old string is in uppercase or mixed uppercase and lowercase letters, EVE finds only occurrences that match exactly. If the new string is in lowercase letters, the replacement will match the case of the occurrence being replaced. If the new string is in uppercase or mixed uppercase and lowercase letters, the replacement will be exact regardless of the case of the occurrence being replaced. Follow Experiment 3.15 to see how the REPLACE line command works.

Experiment 3.15   *Finding and Replacing Text*

1. Move the cursor to the beginning of the file, and press the Do key to move to the command line prompt.

2. Use the REPLACE line command to replace the word *you* with *YOU*. Type the string of text to be replaced, *you*, at the old string prompt and press Return. Type the new string, *YOU*, at the new string prompt and press Return.

3. EVE highlights the first occurrence of the old string and prompts you for an action. Type *a*(*ll*) and press Return to change all occurrences of you to *YOU*.

4. A message appears that the old string is found in the reverse direction. Remember that you entered *you* (all lowercase letters) as the old string and that EVE will match it with uppercase or lowercase letters. Because you started the search at the top of the file, the string found in the reverse direction already has been changed. Press Return to accept the default response, *n*(*o*).

3.11.2 Typing over Existing Text

By default, when EVE is first activated, the editing session is in insert mode. As you type, the characters to the right of the cursor are moved to the right to make room for the newly typed characters. However, simple editing such as deleting and typing characters could become tedious. EVE provides the INSERT/OVERSTRIKE command (F14 on the VT200 and Enter on the VT100) as an efficient method for performing these simple edits. Use this key to change to overstrike mode so that you can type over an existing word, easily correcting typographical errors, reversing lowercase and uppercase letters, or replacing a word with another one of equal length.

To change from the insert to the overstrike mode or vice versa, press the INSERT/OVERSTRIKE key. The status line on the bottom of the screen will reflect this change. Try Experiment 3.16 to see how INSERT/OVER-STRIKE works.

Experiment 3.16 *Typing over Existing Text*

1. Move to the first occurrence of *YOU*.

2. Change to overstrike mode with the INSERT/OVERSTRIKE command.

3. Type *you* in place of *YOU*.

4. Press the INSERT/OVERSTRIKE key to return the editing mode to insert mode.

3.11.3 Reformatting a Paragraph

The FILL PARAGRAPH line command fills, or reformats, the current paragraph so that all the lines of text run from the left to the right margin (columns 1 and 80, by default). This command is particularly useful when paragraphs you have edited extensively no longer fit properly between the margins.

EVE recognizes blank lines and Runoff (Digital's standard text-formatting program) command lines as paragraph boundaries. To reformat a paragraph, place the cursor anywhere in the paragraph and enter the FILL PARA-GRAPH line command. The paragraph is reformatted and the cursor moves to the end of the paragraph. Try Experiment 3.17 to see how the FILL PARA-GRAPH command works.

Experiment 3.17 *Reformatting a Paragraph*

1. Move the cursor to middle of the first paragraph and press Return to break the line.

2. Leaving the cursor in its current position, activate the command line, and enter the FILL PARAGRAPH command.

3.11.4 Editing a Different File

Sometimes you may want to view or edit a different file during an editing session. You can use the GET FILE line command to fetch the contents of the specified file, store it in an editing buffer, and display the file on the screen. The status line indicates the name of the new file being edited. This command becomes most useful when working with more than one file, or two editing windows, which is discussed in the next section. You can see how the GET FILE command works by following Experiment 3.18.

Experiment 3.18 *Editing a Different File*

1. Activate the EVE command line by pressing Do, and type the GET FILE command followed by the file name TEMP.C. Then press Return. TEMP.C appears on the screen, replacing LETTER.TXT.

2. Activate the EVE command line again, but this time type GET FILE and the file name LETTER.TXT.

3.11.5 Creating Two Editing Windows

One of EVE's many powerful features is the ability to allow two files to be edited at the same time. This section explains how to split the screen to view two different sections of a long document or two different documents at the same time.

When EVE is first activated, the contents of the file to be edited are placed in a buffer having the same name. The file then is displayed on the screen in an area called a *window*. By using the TWO WINDOWS line command, you can split the screen into two sections, or windows.

When you do so, these two windows will contain the same file, which you can verify by looking at the status lines. Because the same file is displayed in both windows, whatever changes you make to the text in one window occur at the same time in the other. This is true even if you are viewing different portions of the file at the same time. If you want to view two different files on the screen, you can use the GET FILE command to retrieve a different file into one of the windows.

To move the cursor from one window to the other, use the OTHER WINDOW line command. You can use the ONE WINDOW line command to return the screen to its original state. The window the cursor is in becomes the current window. Try splitting the screen into two windows by following the steps in Experiment 3.19.

Experiment 3.19 *Creating Two Windows*

1. Activate the command line by pressing the Do key. Create a second window by entering the TWO WINDOWS command. The cursor is positioned in the second, or lower, window.

2. Use the GET FILE command to retrieve the TEMP.C file. Activate the command line, type GET FILE followed by the file name TEMP.C, and press Return.

3. Now the LETTER.TXT file appears in the top window and the TEMP.C file appears in the lower window. Activate the command line again, but this time type ONE WINDOW. Then press Return. Notice which of the two files is displayed on the screen.

4. Exit from EVE when you are finished. A message appears, asking if the changes to LETTER.TXT should be saved; right now they exist only in the buffer in memory. Type *y*(*es*) and press Return.

3.12   Recovering from Interruptions

Four common circumstances can interrupt or end your editing session without your consent:

1. Noise in a communication channel, which may cause extraneous characters to appear on the screen during an editing session

2. Accidentally pressing Ctrl/Y, which interrupts command processing

3. A system crash without warning

4. Exceeding your disk quota

The methods that allow you to recover from such circumstances are discussed in the sections that follow.

3.12.1   Deleting Extraneous Characters

During an editing session, you may receive broadcast messages or messages indicating that you have received electronic mail. In other instances, garbage characters may appear on the screen while you are using a dial-up modem to access the computer system.

To purge uninvited characters or messages, clear and redraw the screen by pressing Ctrl/W. Using Ctrl/W is especially important when foreign characters appear on the screen, as it will ensure that the cursor is in the correct position.

3.12.2   Resuming an Interrupted Editing Session

You can interrupt an editing session by mistakenly pressing Ctrl/Y. Luckily there is a simple solution. By entering the CONTINUE command at the DCL $ prompt, you can return to the EVE editing session. Follow Experiment 3.20 to see how this works.

Experiment 3.20   *Interrupting an Editing Session with Ctrl/Y*

1. Activate EVE to edit the LETTER.TXT file.

2. Interrupt the editing session by pressing Ctrl/Y.

3. Locate the DCL $ prompt and the cursor. Type CONTINUE, and press Return.

3.12.3 Recovering a Lost Session

On some computers a system crash means that the contents of the file you were editing are lost. But with EVE you can recover text lost because of a system failure.

Like EDT, EVE has a Journal facility that records all your keystrokes during an editing session in a special file called a *journal file*. If your editing session ends abruptly because of a system crash, EVE saves the journal file. Even though the text of your editing work has been lost, the keystrokes you used are saved. Using the journal file, EVE can restore almost all your editing work. (Sometimes, the last few commands you typed or the last few keys you pressed may not have been recorded in the journal file at the time of the interruption.)

The journal file normally is stored in the current directory with the same file name as the file you were working on, but with the file type .TPU$JOURNAL. When you next activate EVE, use the /RECOVER qualifier and specify the name of the file you want to recover. When EVE begins the recovery process, do not touch the keyboard until the file is restored. EVE reproduces the editing session, reading the commands from the journal file and executing them on the screen. EVE re-edits your file in exactly the same fashion and sequence as you did prior to the interruption.

Once EVE has finished processing all the command information and keystrokes stored in the journal file, it will continue to use the same journal file during your editing session. If you are able to end your editing session successfully, using the EXIT command or the QUIT line command, EVE discards the journal file from your directory. However, if you find journal files in your directory that you do not plan to use, simply delete them. To simulate a system crash, try Experiment 3.21.

Experiment 3.21 *Simulating a Crash and Recovering*

1. Add several lines to the LETTER.TXT file, perhaps repeating the last few lines of text.

2. Simulate a system crash by pressing Ctrl/Y and then logging off the system.

3. Log back into the system.

4. Activate EVE to edit LETTER.TXT but include the /RECOVER qualifier before the file name:

```
$ edit/tpu/recover letter.txt
```

Sit back and watch as EVE re-edits the file. Remember two important things when you recover an interrupted EVE session. First, you must use the same type of terminal you used during the original editing session. In fact, the terminal should be identical in all characteristics. Second, never modify the file you were editing before you attempt its recovery.

3.12.4   Exceeding Your Disk Quota

Essentially, you can exceed your disk quota while using EVE in two ways. Your disk quota might be full prior to activating EVE, or there may be enough disk storage in your user account prior to activating EVE but not enough to store the contents of the editing buffer on leaving. These two events occur more often than you might think, especially in environments in which disk storage is limited and many computer programs are compiled.

When you exceed your disk quota prior to activating EVE, a message similar to the following appears:

```
Error opening PACK2:[YOURGROUP.YOU]TOTAL.TXT as output
ACP file extend failed
Disk quota exceeded
```

To solve this problem, purge or delete files to recover space on the disk or request additional disk space.

When you exceed your disk quota while saving a file, a message similar to the following appears:

```
Output file could not be created
Filename: PACK2:[YOURGROUP.YOU]LIST.TXT
ACP file create failed
Disk quota exceeded
Press Return to continue
```

To solve this problem, press Return and then Ctrl/Y to return to the DCL $ prompt. This will not save the contents of the file you are working on, but it does save the journal file for later use. Once out of EVE, you can purge or delete obsolete files. In some instances, you may have to request additional disk space.

To start editing your file again, type the same command line used to begin the original editing session but include the /RECOVER qualifier so that EVE can reconstruct your editing session. For example, to recover a file called EXAMPLE.PAS, you would type

```
$ edit/tpu/recover example.pas
```

Summary

EVE, the extensible versatile editor, is an interactive text editor on the Open-VMS operating system. You can use EVE to edit different types of files such as letters, memos, or complex programs. With EVE, you can create new files, insert text into them, and edit and manipulate that text. You also can edit and manipulate text in existing files. Changes being made to a file can be viewed on the screen as you make them.

To activate EVE, your character-based terminal or windowing device must be either VT200 or VT100 compatible. Each of these keyboards has an editing keypad and some additional keys that EVE uses to perform editing functions. EVE also uses the Ctrl key with some main keyboard keys to perform other editing functions. In addition, EVE uses some of the function keys on the VT200 keyboard.

EVE assigns various commands to the numeric keypad on the VT100 terminal. The VT200 keyboard includes an eight-key auxiliary editing keypad and four arrow keys. The VT200's numeric keypad is used by EVE only for numeric entries.

As an interactive editor, EVE provides two ways to enter editing commands: keypad mode and line mode. You can move from one mode to the other during the same editing session. In addition, you can enter text in two ways: insert mode and overstrike mode. Both modes can be used interchangeably.

You gain access to EVE by typing the EDIT command with the /TPU qualifier at the DCL $ prompt. If a requested file does not exist, EVE displays the [End of file] marker and a message that the file does not exist. If the file exists in your user directory, EVE puts a copy of the file into the main editing buffer and displays a portion of it on the screen.

EVE's on-line Help facility allows you to get help during your editing session without disturbing your work. In the keypad mode, you press HELP or F2 to get information about keypad functions. For help on line commands, you type HELP on the command line.

EVE's Journal facility acts as a safety net for your editing work. It can save you hours of work should your editing session stop unexpectedly because of a system interruption. While you are editing or inserting text, EVE keeps track of every keystroke you enter at your terminal. EVE records this information in a buffer until the buffer is full, and then transfers the information to a journal file. This journal file is deleted as soon as you use the EXIT command or the QUIT line command.

This chapter has only introduced some of the editing capabilities of EVE. However, it describes and demonstrates the most commonly used editing features. You can explore features that are not discussed in this chapter, such as defining keys and extended TPU, on your own. They expand EVE's editing capabilities further.

Tables 3.1–3.4 summarize the functions, commands, special characters, and important terms used in this chapter.

Table 3.1 *Commands on the EVE Editing Keypads*

Command	VT200 Key	VT100 Key	Result
DO	Do	PF4	Activates the EVE command line
ERASE WORD	F13	Comma	Deletes the current word
EXIT	Ctrl/Z or F10	Ctrl/Z	Exits EVE and saves your current editing work in a new file with the same name and a higher version number
FIND	Find	PF1	Locates a search string
FORWARD/ REVERSE	F11	PF3	Switches the editing direction
HELP	Help	PF2	Provides information on the keypad mode editing keys
INSERT HERE	Insert Here	KP9	Inserts the contents of the Insert buffer to the left of the cursor
INSERT/OVERSTRIKE	F14	Enter	Switches the editing mode to Insert or Overstrike
MOVE BY LINE	F12	Minus	Moves the cursor to the end of lines in the forward editing direction; to the beginning of lines in reverse
NEXT SCREEN	Next Screen	KP0	Moves the cursor vertically through a file, a screenful at a time, toward the end of the file
PREV SCREEN	Prev Screen	Period	Moves the cursor vertically through a file, a screenful at a time, toward the beginning of the file
REFRESH	Ctrl/W	Ctrl/W	Clears and redraws the screen
REMOVE	Remove	KP8	Deletes the selected range of text and places it in the Insert buffer
RETURN	Return	Return	Inserts a line terminator in the text and moves the cursor to the beginning of a new line
SELECT	Select	KP7	Marks one end of a selected range

Table 3.2 *DCL and EVE Line Commands*

Command	Result
BOTTOM	Moves the cursor to the end of a file
CREATE	Creates a new file
EDIT	Activates the EVE editor
/RECOVER	Instructs EVE to use the journal file to restore a file editing session after a system interruption
END OF LINE	Moves the cursor to the end of the current line
ERASE CHARACTER	Erases the character the cursor is on
ERASE LINE	Erases the remainder of the line from the current cursor position to the end of the line
FILL PARAGRAPH	Reformats a paragraph within current margins
GET FILE	Gets the contents of a specified file, stores it in an editing buffer, and displays it on the screen
HELP	Provides on-line help for the EVE command line interface
MOVE BY WORD	Moves the cursor to the beginning of the current or next word, depending on the editing direction
ONE WINDOW	Deletes a second editing window
OTHER WINDOW	Switches cursor from one editing window to the other
QUIT	Exits EVE without saving your current editing work in a new file
REPLACE	Replaces the next occurrence of the current search string with a new string
RESTORE	Restores the text last erased
START OF LINE	Moves the cursor to the beginning of the current line
TOP	Moves the cursor to the beginning of the current buffer
TWO WINDOWS	Creates a second editing window

Table 3.3 *Special Characters*

Character	Meaning
Command:	Command line prompt
[End of file]	Designates the end of the file

Table 3.4 *Important Terms*

Term	Definition
Buffer	Temporary work space in EVE specifically for manipulating text
Character	Letter or symbol
Command	Instruction specifying an action for EVE to perform
Cursor	Used by EVE to indicate the current editing position
Editor	Application software package used to create and modify text files
EVE	OpenVMS full-screen editor
Insert buffer	Storage area used in conjunction with the REMOVE command
Journal file	File containing commands from the current editing session
Numeric keypad	Group of keys located on the far right-hand side of the keyboard
Screen editor	Text editor that allows you to view the contents of a file on the screen
Scrolling	Movement of lines of text up or down the screen
Searching	Locating specified text within a text file
Selected range	Portion of text that has been flagged to be manipulated by an EVE command
String	Group of characters
Text file	File containing ASCII characters

Exercises

1. Name the two EVE editing modes.

2. While in EVE, interrupt your editing session using Ctrl/Y. Once out of EVE, type the following DCL commands: DIRECTORY, SHOW PROCESS, PHONE. Now try to reinstate your editing session using the CONTINUE command. Did it work? How can you resume the session?

3. In question 2, you entered DCL commands before reinstating your interrupted EVE session. This time execute a command file, such as LOGIN.COM, and then type the CONTINUE command. What happened?

4. Try pressing the REMOVE key without selecting a range of text first. What happened?

5. Name the various methods of locating text within a buffer.

6. What is the default direction and default editing mode when EVE is first activated?

7. Name the terminals on which you can activate EVE. Why?

8. What is the programming language in which EVE is written?

9. How does EVE indicate the current editing mode and direction?

10. Explore how to redefine the function of a specific key using the DEFINE KEY line command.

11. You can execute DCL commands from EVE's command line. Explain the steps to accomplish this process. Experiment with using various DCL commands such as DIRECTORY and SHOW PROCESS, and see what happens.

12. Explain the process in which EVE searches for text or a search string. How does EVE respond if the search string is not found in the current editing direction?

13. Name all the methods for exiting an EVE editing session.

Review Quiz

Indicate whether the following statements are true or false:

1. The contents of the Main buffer can be saved only to the file specified at the time you activate EVE.

2. The CHANGE command is used in EVE to move from line mode editing to keypad mode editing.

3. The default editing direction when you first enter EVE is forward.

4. Searches using the FIND key can occur only in the reverse direction.

5. Ctrl/A allows you to clear and redraw the screen.

6. EVE can be activated only on VT200 and VT100 character-based terminals.

7. The REPLACE line command exchanges a selected range of text, established using the FIND key, with the contents of the Insert buffer.

8. The INCREMENT FORWARD key moves the cursor in increments of 16 lines at a time.

9. The default editing mode when EVE is first activated is overstrike.

10. When one uses the FIND key, the characters to be searched for must be typed exactly as they appear in the current editing buffer.

Further Reading

Sawey, Ronald M., and Troy T. Stokes. *A Beginner's Guide to VAX/VMS Utilities and Applications,* 2d ed. Newton, Mass.: Digital Press, 1992.

Digital Equipment Corporation, POB CS2008, Nashua, NH 03061:

Printed Documentation	*Extensible Versatile Editor Reference Manual*
	DEC Text Processing Utility Reference Manual
	Guide to the DEC Text Processing Utility
	Guide to the Extensible Versatile Editor
	OpenVMS DCL Dictionary: A–M
	OpenVMS DCL Dictionary: N–Z
	OpenVMS User's Manual
On-Line Documentation	OpenVMS On-Line Help Facility
	OpenVMS Bookreader
	http://www.openvms.digital.com

4

Full-Screen Editing with EDT

*Poetry should surprise by a fine excess, and not by singularity. It should
strike the reader as a wording of his own highest thoughts, and appear
almost as a remembrance.*

—John Keats, Letter to John Taylor, 1818

OpenVMS provides several different text editors, which you can use to create
and edit text files. This chapter explores the text editor EDT. In this chapter,
you will

▶ Learn how to use EDT keypad mode

▶ Learn how EDT stores a text file

▶ Explore commonly used EDT keypad commands

▶ Experiment with various methods of moving the cursor

▶ Explore various ways to locate text

▶ Examine different ways to recover from system interruptions

4.1   About EDT

EDT is one of the full-screen editors offered by OpenVMS. It allows you to
create and modify text files, which are files of characters and include such
things as source programs, command files, and memoranda. EDT is described
as a full-screen editor because text can be edited anywhere on the screen.

EDT has three separate modes (line, nokeypad, and keypad) that can be
used in combination with one another. Line mode allows you to manipulate a

range of one or more lines of text. It is used most frequently on hard-copy, or printing, terminals. In the nokeypad mode, English words and abbreviations are used to manipulate text on the screen. The keypad mode provides easy manipulation of text using simple keystrokes. Using the keys on the numeric keypad, to the right of the main keyboard, you can work with characters as well as with larger portions of text. Cursor position determines how text will be affected by the EDT commands, and you can move the cursor through a file in a variety of ways. In the keypad mode, the keypad commands make it possible to delete, find, insert, substitute, or move text in a file with a single keystroke.

In addition, EDT provides the following features to make your editing easier:

▶ An on-line Help facility, which can be used at any time during an editing session without affecting the work in progress

▶ A fail-safe mechanism, called a *Journal facility*, which allows retrieval of edit changes after a system crash

▶ Several methods of searching for text rapidly

▶ Multiple cursor movement functions

This chapter emphasizes editing in the keypad mode. Occasionally, line mode commands that are essential to the editing process are discussed. A more detailed treatment of line mode commands is given in Appendix C. Before you explore EDT, follow Experiment 4.1, which uses the DCL CREATE command to set up a file. The text in this file is a familiar verse from Augustus De Morgan's *A Budget of Paradoxes* (c. 1850). You will use this file during experiments in this chapter.

Experiment 4.1 *Creating the Initial File*

1. Use the DCL CREATE command to create the file FLEAS.TXT:

```
$ create fleas.txt
```

2. Type the following text, which has a missing line. Use the Tab key to indent the appropriate lines:

```
      upon their backs bite 'em,
And little fleas have lesser fleas,
      and so ad infinitum.
And the great fleas themselves, in turn,
      have greater fleas to go on;
While these again have greater still,
      and greater still, and so on.
```

3. Exit by pressing Ctrl/Z:

```
Ctrl/z
Exit
$
```

4.2   Getting Started with EDT

To activate EDT, use the DCL EDIT command with the /EDT qualifier:

`$ edit/edt` *filename*

On some systems, EDT is the default editor. When this is the case, you do not need to use the /EDT qualifier but simply enter the EDIT command. Because the command to activate EDT varies somewhat from place to place, you will need to find out how to activate EDT on your system.

In addition, you can enter the EDIT command with or without the file name. If you do not enter the file name with the command, DCL prompts you for the file name. For example,

```
$ edit/edt
_File:
```

Then enter the file name and press Return.

Once you have entered the EDIT command and the file name, you have activated EDT. On some systems, EDT will be in the line mode and the first line of the file appears followed by the line mode prompt, an asterisk. For example,

```
$ edit/edt test.txt
     1 First line of file appears
*
```

To move from the line mode to the keypad mode, type CHANGE at the line mode prompt and press Return. Then the first 22 lines of the file appear on the screen.

On other systems, a special file, called an *initialization file,* EDTINI.EDT, has been created. It contains the line mode command SET MODE CHANGE, which shifts EDT automatically into the keypad mode. This file may exist in your user directory or in one of the systemwide directories. If it exists, EDT goes directly into the keypad mode, and the first 22 lines of the file appear on the screen. In this case, you do not need to enter the CHANGE command.

Whether EDT activates in the line mode or the keypad mode, it places a copy of the file in a workspace called the *Main buffer,* where you can manipulate the text. In addition, EDT keeps track of each keystroke you make during an EDT session in a special file, called a *journal file.* When you end an editing session normally, by typing EXIT or QUIT, EDT discards the journal file. If the editing session ends abruptly because of system interruption, how-ever, the journal file is saved, and you can use it to restore almost all your lost editing work. Try activating EDT by following Experiment 4.2.

Experiment 4.2 *Activating EDT*

1. Activate EDT by entering the EDIT command and the file name on one line. Retrieve the file FLEAS.TXT, which you created in Experiment 4.1:

```
$ edit/edt fleas.txt
```

EDT either is in the line mode and displays the first line of the file and the line mode asterisk prompt, as follows, or is in the keypad mode and dis-plays all seven lines of the file and the [EOB] symbol, which signifies end of buffer, as shown in Figure 4.1.

```
$ edit/edt fleas.txt
        1 upon their backs to bite 'em,
*
```

2. If EDT is in the line mode, use the CHANGE command to move to the keypad mode:

```
█ upon their backs to bite 'em,
And little fleas have lesser fleas,
    and so ad infinitum.
And the great fleas themselves, in turn,
    have greater fleas to go on;
While these again have greater still,
    and greater still, and so on.
[EOB]
```

Figure 4.1 *Keypad Mode's Full-Screen Display*

```
$ edit/edt fleas.txt
      1 upon their backs to bite 'em,
* change
```

Once EDT finishes painting the screen with text, the cursor appears in the upper left-hand corner and the [EOB] symbol, or end-of-buffer marker, flags the end of the file, as seen in Figure 4.1. Behind the scenes, a copy of FLEAS.TXT has been put into the Main buffer, as shown in Figure 4.2.

4.3 An Overview of the EDT Keypad

The EDT keypad includes the standard numeric keypad, shown in Figure 4.3, and the cursor movement keys. The keys on the numeric keypad (PF1–PF4, 0–9, Minus, Period, Comma, Enter) are assigned different functions, or commands. With the exception of the Gold key (PF1) and the Help key

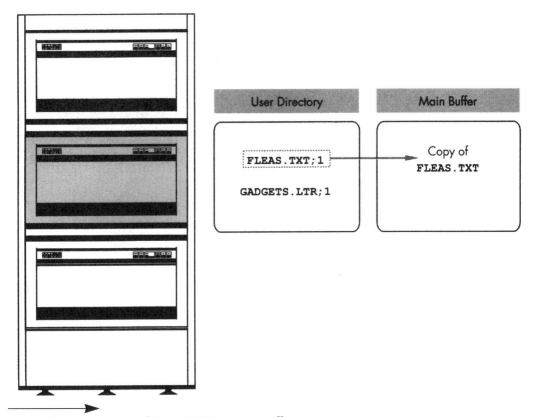

Figure 4.2 *Copy of FLEAS.TXT in Main Buffer*

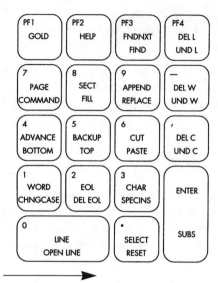

Figure 4.3 *The EDT Keypad*

(PF2), each key is assigned two commands. For instance, key number 4 (or KP4) on the numeric keypad is assigned the ADVANCE and BOTTOM commands (see Figure 4.3). To issue the upper command on a key, press the key. To issue the lower, or alternative, command on a key, press GOLD and press the key. For instance, press 4 to issue the ADVANCE command. Press Gold and KP4 a second time, or Gold 4, to issue the BOTTOM command. In addition, EDT uses the auxiliary keypad on VT200 keyboards and the arrow keys on VT100 keyboards.

4.4   Entering and Editing Text

When you work in EDT, you use keypad commands to modify and manipulate text. Some of the commands move the cursor to particular places in the text, and using the arrow keys will move the cursor as well.

4.4.1   Moving Around the File

The cursor is positioned at the beginning of the file when you enter keypad mode. You can move the cursor through the file using the arrow keys. The Left Arrow and Right Arrow keys move the cursor one character to the left or right, respectively. The Up Arrow and Down Arrow keys move the cursor up or down one line. When using these keys, you cannot move past the beginning of the file or the top of the buffer nor can you move past the end of the file or the end of the buffer.

When you want to move directly to the top or bottom of the buffer, you can use the TOP and BOTTOM commands. Both commands are the lower, or alternative, commands on their respective keys, so you must first press Gold and then press the appropriate key for the command: Gold 5 for the TOP command, or Gold 4 for the BOTTOM command. These keys are particularly useful when you are working with large files.

A quick way to move to the end of the current line of text is through issuing the EOL (end-of-line) command by pressing KP2. Since EOL is the upper command on its key (see Figure 4.3), no Gold key press is needed.

To move to the beginning of the current line, press F12 on the VT200 keyboard or Backspace on the VT100 keyboard. To move to the beginning of the next line, use the LINE command by pressing the KP0 key.

Experiment with these cursor movement keys and commands by following the steps in Experiment 4.3. Consult Figure 4.3 to become familiar with the commands associated with the various numeric keypad keys.

Experiment 4.3 *Exploring Some Cursor Movement Keys and Commands*

1. Try using the arrow keys to move around the file.

2. Issue the TOP command to move to the top of the buffer; and issue the BOTTOM command to move to the bottom of the buffer.

3. Move to the top of the buffer and then press the Up Arrow key. Notice the message that appears. The bell and the message are EDT's way of telling you that the cursor cannot be moved past the beginning of the file. You would get a similar response if you tried to move past the end of the file.

4. Use the EOL, LINE commands VT200 or Backspace on the VT100 to move to the end and beginning of lines of text.

5. When you are finished experimenting, move to the top of the buffer. Several other ways to move around a file are discussed in later sections of this chapter.

4.4.2   Inserting Text

You can add text to a file by moving the cursor to the place where the text should be added and typing the text. As you type each character, EDT pushes the cursor and any text to the right of the cursor further right. You can insert from a single character to many lines of text. The characters always are inserted to the left of the cursor.

When you want to break a line of text, use Return or the OPEN LINE command (Gold 0). To use Return, position the cursor on the character that should be the first character of the new line and press Return. To use the OPEN LINE command, position the cursor *before* the character that should be the first character of the new line and press Gold 0.

The text file that you created in Experiment 4.1 is missing the first line. To practice using the EDT editor to make insertions, insert this line by following the steps in Experiment 4.4.

Experiment 4.4 *Inserting Text*

1. The cursor should be at the top of the buffer. Type the missing line as shown in Figure 4.4. Make sure to misspell the last word as shown.

2. Now break the line by pressing Return. This enters a line terminator and moves the character the cursor is on plus the text to the right of the cursor to the next line, as shown in Figure 4.5.

3. Next try using the OPEN LINE command to break a line. In preparation, you should delete the line terminator, and so move the new sec-

```
Great fleas have little flees▮upon their backs to bite 'em,
And little fleas have lesser fleas,
    and so ad infinitum.
And the great fleas themselves, in turn,
    have greater fleas to go on;
While these again have greater still,
    and greater still, and so on.
[EOB]
```

Figure 4.4 *Entering a Line*

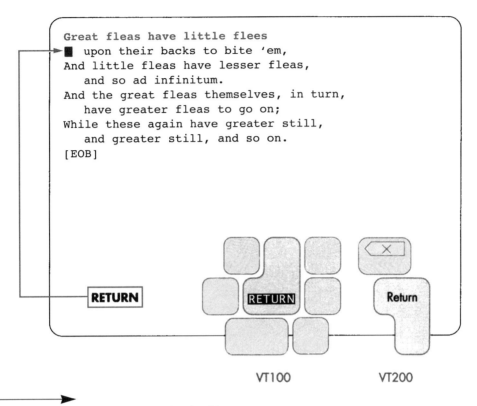

Figure 4.5 *Using Return to Break a Line*

ond line back to the end of the first, by pressing the ⟨ × ⟩ key on the VT200 or Delete on the VT100.

4. Use the OPEN LINE command to break the line. Notice that the text has been moved down a line. This time, however, the cursor remains at the end of the first line, as shown in Figure 4.6.

4.4.3 Deleting Text

With EDT, you can delete text by the character, word, or line. There are two methods of deleting characters. You can use the DELETE command by pressing the ⟨ × ⟩ key on the VT200 or Delete on the VT100, which deletes the character to the left of the cursor; or you can use the DEL C (delete character) command, which deletes the character at the cursor position, by pressing the Comma on the numeric keypad.

To delete a word, position the cursor on the word and issue the DEL W (delete word) command by pressing the Minus on the numeric keypad.

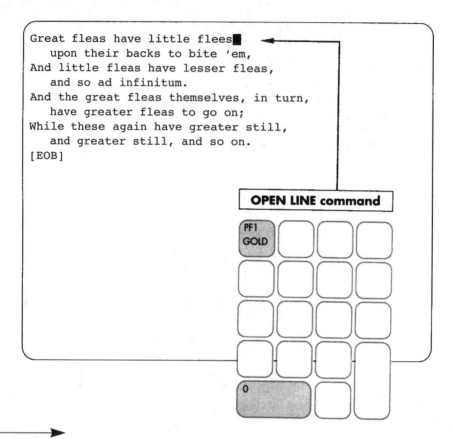

Figure 4.6 *Using OPEN LINE to Break a Line*

To delete a line of text, position the cursor at the beginning of the line and use the DEL L (delete line) command by pressing the PF4 key. Alternatively, you can use the DEL EOL command (Gold 2). It differs from the DEL L command because it does not delete the line terminator and so leaves a blank line on the screen. Both the DEL L and DEL EOL commands delete from the cursor position to the end of the line, so you can use them to delete just part of a line as well. Explore the use of these commands by following Experiment 4.5.

Experiment 4.5 *Deleting Text*

1. The first text you need to delete is the misspelling in the word *fleas*. The cursor is at the end of the line containing this error. Press the ⟨ ✕ ⟩ key or Delete twice to delete the last two characters of the line. Then type *as* to correct the spelling.

2. Move to the beginning of the second line and issue the DEL C command to delete the tab character and the *u* in *upon.*

3. Move to the beginning of the third line and issue the DEL W command to delete the first word, *And.*

4. Move to the beginning of the fourth line and use the DEL L command to delete the line. Notice that the lines below the deleted line move up.

5. The cursor is at the beginning of the fifth line of text, *And the great fleas* . . . Use the DEL EOL command to delete to the end of that line. Notice that, although the text disappears, a blank line remains, as shown in Figure 4.7.

When you delete text with these commands, EDT stores the text in buffers. The Character buffer stores the most recently deleted character, the Word buffer stores the most recently deleted word, and the Line buffer stores the most recently deleted line. You can use the contents of these buffers to restore the most recent character, word, or line that you have deleted.

```
Great fleas have little fleas
pon their backs to bite 'em,
little fleas have lesser fleas,
█
   have greater fleas to go on;
While these again have greater still,
   and greater still, and so on.
[EOB]
```

Figure 4.7 *Results of the Deletions*

4.4.4   Undeleting Text

The undelete commands are used to restore deleted text that was stored in buffers. The UND L (undelete line) command (Gold PF4) restores the most recently deleted line. The UND W (undelete word) command (Gold –) restores the most recently deleted word, and the UND C command (Gold ,) restores the most recently deleted character. Use these functions to restore the text you deleted in Experiment 4.5.

Experiment 4.6   *Undeleting Text*

1. The cursor is at the beginning of the fourth line, which is blank (see Figure 4.7). Use the UND L command to restore the line.

2. You also deleted the line *and so ad infinitum,* but because the line buffer holds only the most recently deleted line, this line cannot be restored using the UND L command. Instead, open a line with the OPEN LINE command and retype the line of text.

3. Next move to the *p* in *pon* and use the UND C command to restore the *u*. Then add a tab character to indent the line, as shown in Figure 4.8.

```
Great fleas have little fleas
   upon their backs to bite 'em,
And little fleas have lesser fleas,
   and so ad infinitum.
And the great fleas themselves, in turn,
   have greater fleas to go on;
While these again have greater still,
   and greater still, and so on.
[EOB]
```

Figure 4.8   *Results of Undeleting Text*

4. If you want to work more with deleting and undeleting text, add several lines to the bottom of the file and work with the commands on the new text. When you are finished, delete the extra text from the file.

4.5   Leaving an EDT Editing Session

You have finished editing this file of text, so you need to leave the EDT editing session and save the completed poem in FLEAS.TXT. To save the results of an editing session, you can use the COMMAND command (Gold 7) to remain in the keypad mode but cause EDT to prompt for a line mode command, as shown in Figure 4.9. You then can enter the line mode command EXIT and press Enter. Alternatively, you can move from the keypad mode to the line mode by pressing Ctrl/Z. The line mode prompt * appears. Then enter the EXIT command and press either Return or Enter.

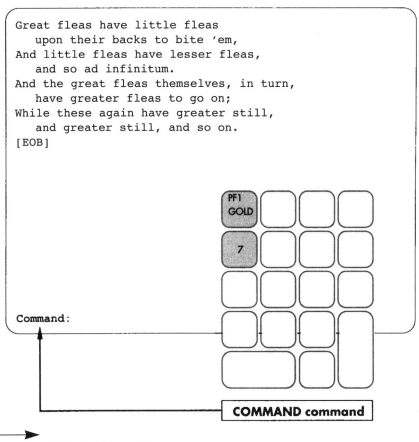

```
Great fleas have little fleas
   upon their backs to bite 'em,
And little fleas have lesser fleas,
   and so ad infinitum.
And the great fleas themselves, in turn,
   have greater fleas to go on;
While these again have greater still,
   and greater still, and so on.
[EOB]
```

Command:

COMMAND command

Figure 4.9   *Using COMMAND*

In either case, the EXIT command copies the contents of the Main buffer to a file in your user directory. The file has the same name but a higher version number, as illustrated in Figure 4.10.

You also can exit an EDT editing session and save the contents of the Main buffer in a file having a different name. To do this, type the new file name after the EXIT command. For example, to save the FLEAS.TXT file under a new name, type

Command: **exit newfleas.txt**

Remember to press Enter (and not Return) when using COMMAND to exit.

There may come a time when you realize that you are editing the wrong file or you have accidentally deleted information that you need. You can leave an EDT editing session without saving the file in the Main buffer by using the QUIT command rather than the EXIT command. Experiment 4.7 demonstrates various methods of leaving an EDT editing session.

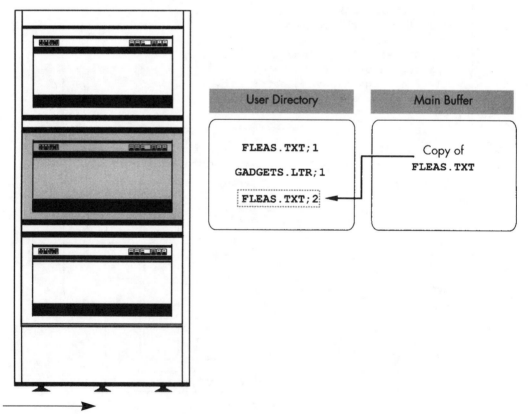

Figure 4.10 *Saved File with Higher Version Number*

Experiment 4.7 *Leaving an EDT Editing Session*

1. First, try leaving the EDT editing session and saving the changes to the file under the same name. Move to the line mode by pressing Ctrl/Z.

2. At the line mode asterisk prompt, type the EXIT command and press Return.

3. You are back at the DCL prompt, $. The changes to the file are saved in a new version of FLEAS.TXT. You can verify this by using the DIRECTORY command to get a listing of files. Notice the higher version number for FLEAS.TXT:

```
$ directory fleas.txt

Directory PACK2:[YOURGROUP.YOU]

FLEAS.TXT;2  FLEAS.TXT;1

Total of 2 files.
$
```

4. Now return to EDT as if you were going to edit FLEAS.TXT.

```
$ edit/edt fleas.txt
```

5. If EDT moves automatically to the keypad mode, press Ctrl/Z to change to the line mode. Otherwise, remain in line mode at the * prompt.

6. Try exiting the EDT session and saving the file with a new name, FLEAS1.TXT.

7. The file now is saved under FLEAS1.TXT. Check this by using the DIRECTORY command to see all files beginning with FLEAS and having the .TXT extension:

```
$ directory fleas*.txt

Directory PACK2:[YOURGROUP.YOU]

FLEAS.TXT;2  FLEAS.TXT;1  FLEAS1.TXT;1

Total of 3 files.
$
```

8. Once again, return to EDT as if you were going to edit FLEAS.TXT (if you need to, move to keypad mode):

```
$ edit/edt fleas.txt
```

9. Try using the COMMAND command to see the line mode * prompt while running in the keypad mode. At the Command: prompt, enter the QUIT command rather than EXIT. Then press Return. Because Return is not the correct key for processing with the COMMAND command, ^*M* appears, as shown in Figure 4.11.

10. Delete the ^*M* and press Enter to enter the QUIT command.

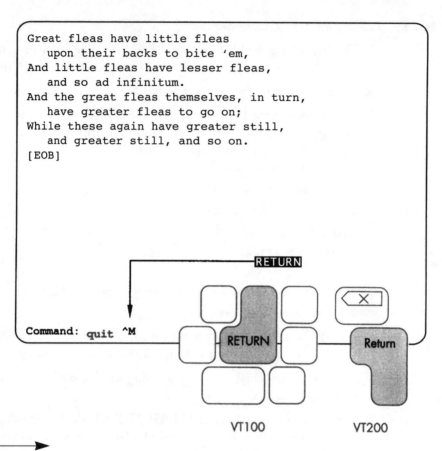

```
Great fleas have little fleas
   upon their backs to bite 'em,
And little fleas have lesser fleas,
   and so ad infinitum.
And the great fleas themselves, in turn,
   have greater fleas to go on;
While these again have greater still,
   and greater still, and so on.
[EOB]
```

Command: quit ^M

RETURN

VT100   VT200

Figure 4.11   *Results from Pressing Return*

11. With QUIT, the contents of the buffer are not saved in a file. Use the
    DIRECTORY command to check that a new version of FLEAS.TXT
    has not been saved.:

    $ directory fleas.txt

    Directory PACK2:[YOURGROUP.YOU]

    FLEAS.TXT;2 FLEAS.TXT;1

    Total of 2 files.
    $

4.6   Creating a File with EDT

You used the DCL CREATE command to create the FLEAS.TXT file and then
moved to EDT to make changes to that file. You also can create a new file from

EDT by specifying a new file name when you enter the EDIT/EDT command. Follow Experiment 4.8 to create a new file, which contains a Pascal procedure to do a bubblesort. (The bubblesort procedure enables a small set of data to be manipulated easily, by comparing pairs of elements in a list. As the sort moves down the list, elements are compared, and the smaller data items eventually *float* to one end, while the larger data items move to the other end.)

Experiment 4.8 *Creating a New File with EDT*

1. Activate EDT using the file name BUBBLE.PAS:

```
$ edit/edt bubble.pas

Input file does not exist
[EOB]
*
```

Because EDT cannot locate the file BUBBLE.PAS in your user account, it displays a message, an end-of-buffer symbol, and possibly, the line mode asterisk prompt.

2. If necessary, use the CHANGE command to change from the line mode to the keypad mode.

3. Enter the following text exactly as it appears. Remember to press Return to start a new line. Notice that, as you enter more than 21 lines of text, the text scrolls off the top of the screen.

```
const
     max = 512;
     ListMax = 10000;
type
     KeyType = integer;
     OtherInfo = packed array[1..max] of char;
     ItemType = record
          bytes: OtherInfo
          key: KeyType
          end; (*ItemType*)
     ListType = array[1..ListMax] of ItemType;

procedure BubbleSort (var list: ListType; ListSize: integer);

var SwapMade: Boolean; (*to detect if swap was made*)
    index: integer; (*array index*)

begin
     SwapMade := true;
     while (Listsize > 1 and SwapMade do begin
          Listsize := ListSize - 1; SwapMade := false;
          for index := 1 to ListSize do
               if list[index].key > list[index + 1].key then
```

```
                              begin
                                  swap(list, index); (*hidden procedure*)
                                  SwapMade := true (*signal swap was made*)
                              end
                      end
              end; (*BubbleSort*)
```

4. Use the TOP command to return to the beginning of the file.

4.7   Getting Help with EDT Commands

At some point, you may forget a specific EDT command or need additional information on it. EDT has a built-in Help facility that allows you to obtain information on the keypad and the line mode commands during an editing session.

To get help while in keypad mode, use the HELP command (Help on the VT200; PF2 on the VT100). A Help screen appears. You then can press any key to obtain help about that command.

To get help while in the line mode, type HELP at the asterisk prompt and press Return. A Help screen appears. Or you can type HELP and the name of a command to obtain help about that command. For example, you could type HELP COPY to see information about the COPY command. Explore the Help facility by following the steps in Experiment 4.9.

Experiment 4.9 *Getting Help*

1. You should be in the EDT keypad mode to begin. If you have been following the experiments, the file BUBBLE.PAS will be on the screen. Press the Help key to move to the Help screen, which should resemble Figure 4. 12.

2. Read the instructions on the screen. Press any of the numeric keypad keys to see information about that key's commands.

3. Once you have finished reading the help text, return to the editing session by pressing the Spacebar.

4. Shift into the line mode by pressing Ctrl/Z. The line mode asterisk prompt should appear on the screen.

5. Type HELP and press Return. The screen should resemble Figure 4.13.

6. Read the instructions on the screen. You can now obtain information about a particular command or topic. Enter text to explore a topic; for example, HELP COPY.

7. Once you have finished reading the Help text, return to the keypad mode editing session by typing CHANGE and Return at the asterisk prompt.

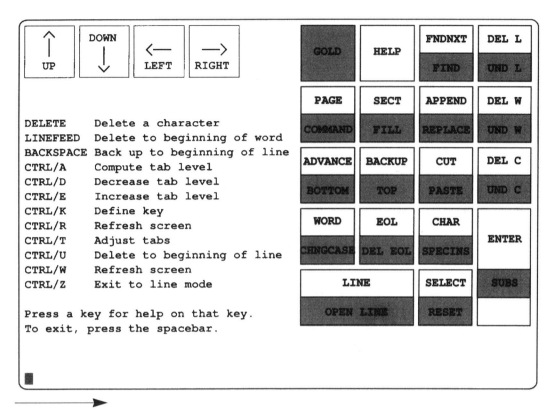

Figure 4.12 *Keypad Mode Help*

4.8 More Editing Commands

EDT provides many useful editing commands in the keypad mode. You can change the editing direction, search for text strings, cut and paste portions of text, and so on. The following sections introduce these commands.

4.8.1 Changing the Editing Direction

By default, movement through the text in a file is forward, or toward the end of the file. For example, when you use DEL W, the word following the cursor is deleted; or when you use FIND to search for a text string, the search advances from the cursor toward the end of the file.

You can change this editing direction using the BACKUP command (KP5) and the ADVANCE command (KP4). After you select BACKUP, movement through the file will be back toward the beginning of the file. To

```
    HELP topic subtopic subsubtopic...

A topic can have one of the following forms:

    1. An alphanumeric string (e.g. a command name, option, etc.)
    2. The match-all or wildcard symbol (*)

Examples: HELP SUBSTITUTE NEXT
          HELP CHANGE SUBCOMMAND
          HELP CH

If a topic is abbreviated, HELP displays the text for all topics that
match the abbreviation.


Additional information available:

CHANGE        CLEAR    COPY      DEFINE    DELETE      EXIT      FILL
FIND          HELP     INCLUDE   INSERT    JOURNAL     KEYPAD    MOVE
PRINT         QUIT     RANGE     REPLACE   RESEQUENCE  SET       SHOW
SUBSTITUTE    TAB      TYPE      WRITE

*█
```

Figure 4.13 *Line Mode Help*

return to forward movement, you must select ADVANCE. Being able to control the editing direction is advantageous when working with many EDT functions, as you will see in the sections that follow.

4.8.2   Other Ways of Moving the Cursor

Up to this point, you have been moving the cursor around the screen by the character or line or by moving to the top or bottom of the file. Exploring EDT further, you will find other cursor movement commands available.

You can use the CHAR (character) command (KP3) to move one character at a time. The CHAR command can be used as an alternative to the Left Arrow and Right Arrow keys. Use the WORD command (KP1) to move one word at a time. A word is any group of characters bounded by a space, horizontal tab, line feed, vertical tab, form feed, or carriage return.

The direction the cursor moves depends on the editing direction. If BACKUP is in effect, the cursor moves to the previous character or word. If

ADVANCE is in effect, the cursor moves to the next character or word. Explore these cursor movement options by following Experiment 4.10.

Experiment 4.10 *More Cursor Movement Options*

1. Move to the beginning of a line of text and use the CHAR command several times. The default editing direction is forward, so the cursor moves forward along the line.

2. Use the BACKUP command to change the editing direction. Then use the CHAR command several times. The cursor moves back toward the beginning of the file.

3. Now use the WORD command several times. Because BACKUP still is in effect, the cursor moves to the previous word.

4. Use the ADVANCE command to change the editing direction. Use the WORD command again. Now the cursor moves forward through the file.

You can move the cursor in increments of 16 lines at a time using the SECT (section) command (KP8). This command brings a different section of text into view with a single keystroke. The direction of movement depends on the editing direction. Follow Experiment 4.11 to try out the SECT command.

Experiment 4.11 *Viewing Sections of Text*

1. First, use the BOTTOM command to move to the end of the file.

2. Reverse the editing direction using the SECT command.

3. Use the SECT command to move 16 lines from the [EOB] marker up toward the beginning of the file.

4. Use the ADVANCE command to set the editing direction forward and then use the SECT command again to move the cursor back to its original position.

4.8.3 Dividing the Text into Pages

When you are working with long files, it sometimes is useful to divide the text into pages. You can then speed up movement through the text by moving page by page. To divide the text into pages, enter a page marker. The default page marker is the form feed character, <FF>, which is accepted by many printers as an end-of-page delimiter. Insert this character by holding down the Ctrl key and pressing the l key.

Once page markers are set, you can use the PAGE command (KP7) to move to the markers. The direction in which the cursor moves depends on the editing direction. If no page markers are set, the PAGE command moves the cursor to the top or bottom of the file. Follow the steps in Experiment 4.12 to see how this command works.

Experiment 4.12 *Defining Page Boundaries*

1. Move the cursor to the blank line that appears after the following line in your BUBBLE.PAS file:

```
ListType = array[1 . . ListMax] of ItemType;
```

2. Enter a page marker by pressing Ctrl/L. The form feed character <FF> appears, as shown in Figure 4.14.

3. Move the cursor to the beginning of the file using the TOP command.

4. Use the PAGE command to move to the first page marker.

```
   KeyType = integer;
   OtherInfo = packed array[1..max] of char;
   ItemType = record
      bytes: OtherInfo
      key: KeyType
      end;   (*ItemType*)
   ListType = array[1..ListMax] of ItemType;
<FF> ▓
procedure BubbleSort (var list: ListType;
                          ListSize: integer);

var SwapMade: Boolean;     (*to detect if swap was made*)
      index: integer;      (*array index*)

begin
   SwapMade := true;

   while (ListSize > 1) and SwapMade do begin
      ListSize := ListSize - 1;
      SwapMade := false;

      for index := 1 to ListSize do
```

Figure 4.14 *The Form Feed Character*

4.8.4   A Simple Method of Locating Text

Up to this point, you have located text by moving the cursor through the file. Using this method on small files is tedious but tolerable. On larger files, however, it would not be tolerable. Using the FIND command (Gold PF3) and the FNDNXT (find next) command (PF3), you can move directly to a specified text string. When you use FIND, EDT prompts for the text string to search for, or search string. You type the search string and press Enter. EDT searches for the string and moves the cursor to the first occurrence of the search string that it encounters. The direction of the search depends on the current editing direction.

If you want to find the next occurrence of the search string, use FND-NXT. EDT moves the cursor to the next occurrence.

This method of locating text can save a considerable amount of time when searching for a sequence of characters within a lengthy document. Keep in mind, when searching for text, it is important to make the search string unique. Try to include in the search string as many landmarks surrounding the text as possible, so that EDT can locate the text on the first attempt.

It is possible for EDT to be unable to locate a search string and to give a message to that effect. This happens when a search string is mistyped, a string does not exist, or the direction of the search is moving away from the string in the text. In the last case, you can switch the editing direction to search in the opposite direction. Try using the FIND and FNDNXT commands by following Experiment 4.13.

Experiment 4.13 *Using FIND and FNDNXT to Locate Text*

1. Move the cursor to the beginning of the BUBBLE.PAS file. The editing direction is set forward.

2. Use the FIND command. EDT prompts you for the search string, as shown in Figure 4.15.

3. Type *begin* and press Enter. EDT searches toward the end of the file for the first occurrence of *begin.*

4. Search for the next occurrence by using the FNDNXT command. EDT moves to the next occurrence of *begin.* Use FNDNXT again, to find the next occurrence.

5. Use FNDNXT again. EDT found no other occurrence of the search string and so displays a message, as shown in Figure 4.16.

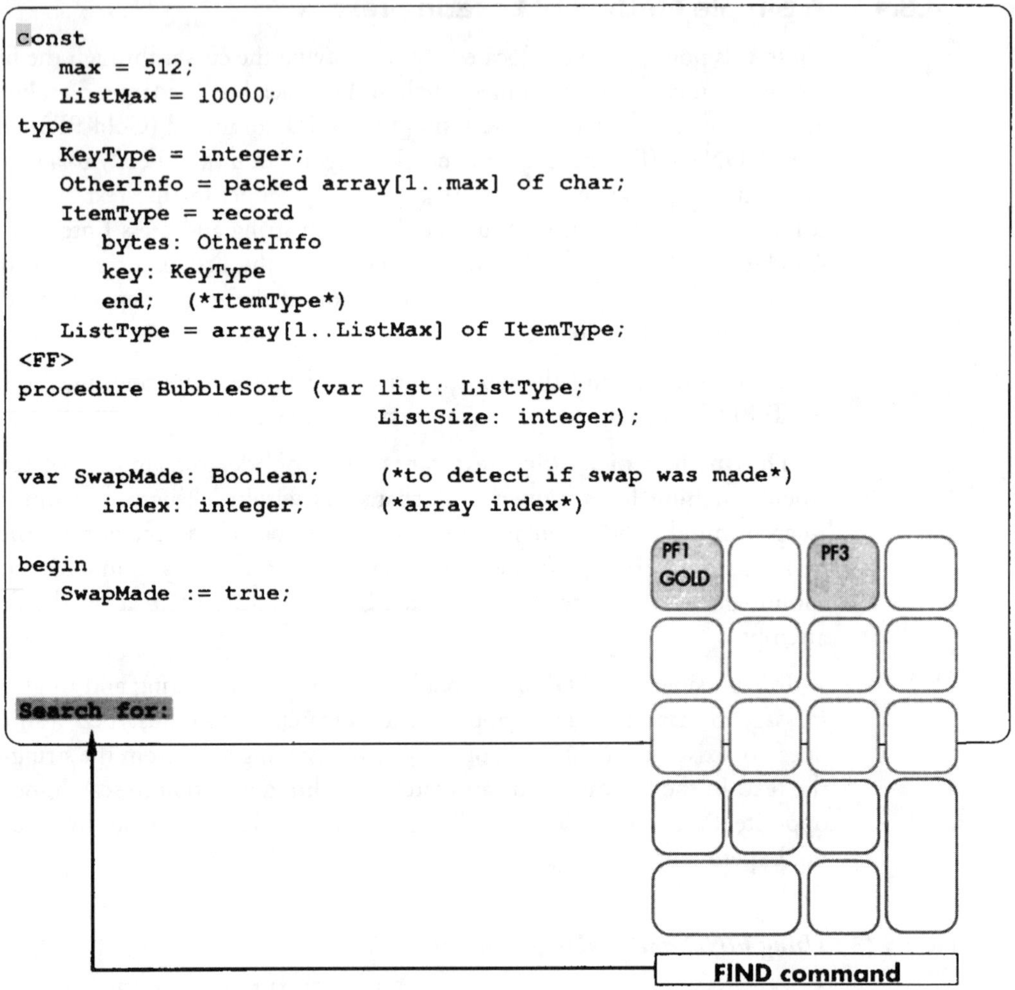

```
const
   max = 512;
   ListMax = 10000;
type
   KeyType = integer;
   OtherInfo = packed array[1..max] of char;
   ItemType = record
       bytes: OtherInfo
       key: KeyType
       end;   (*ItemType*)
   ListType = array[1..ListMax] of ItemType;
<FF>
procedure BubbleSort (var list: ListType;
                          ListSize: integer);

var SwapMade: Boolean;      (*to detect if swap was made*)
       index: integer;       (*array index*)

begin
   SwapMade := true;



Search for:
```

FIND command

Figure 4.15   *The Search Prompt*

6. Use BACKUP to change the editing direction. Then use FNDNXT again. Now EDT searches backward through the file for the search string.

7. Finally, use ADVANCE to reset the editing direction to forward.

4.9   Working with a Selected Range of Text

As you have seen, EDT has a great deal of editing capability. You have explored various methods of moving the cursor around the screen and manip-

```
  Var SwapMade: Boolean;     (*to detect if swap was made*)
      index: integer;        (*array index*)

  begin
    SwapMade := true;

    while  (ListSize > 1) and SwapMade do begin
      ListSize := ListSize - 1;
      SwapMade := false;

      for index := 1 to ListSize do
          if list(index).key > list(index + 1).key then

            begin
              swap(list,index);         (*hidden procedure*)
              SwapMade := true          (*signal swap was made*)
            end

      end
  end;  (*BubbleSort*)
  [EOB]

  Search for:
  String was not found
```

Figure 4.16 *String-Not-Found Message*

ulating small portions of text. However, EDT has several other features that enhance its editing abilities. In particular, EDT allows you to select a larger portion of text, which you can then manipulate as a unit, moving it, reformatting it, replacing it, and so on.

4.9.1   Selecting a Range of Text

You can use the SELECT command (Period) to select a range of text. Move to the beginning of the range, issue SELECT, and then use any of the cursor movement keys to highlight the appropriate text. For example, you can use the arrow keys to extend the highlight up or down a line, or left or right, or you can use the WORD command to highlight the next word. To highlight in the opposite direction, change the editing direction.

If you decide that portions of the selected text should not be included in the selected range, you can move the cursor back until you exclude any unwanted text. EDT also provides a RESET command (Gold .), which allows you to cancel an active selected range at any time. (RESET also resets the editing direction to forward.) A selected range stays active until you either use the RESET command or execute a function or command that uses the selected range. Practice selecting ranges of text by following Experiment 4.14.

Experiment 4.14 *Selecting a Range of Text*

1. In the experiments in this section, work with the FLEAS.TXT file. Retrieve that file by exiting EDT and then reactivating EDT, specifying the FLEAS.TXT file. If necessary, move to the keypad mode.

2. Select the first four lines of text by using SELECT and then use the LINE command to move the cursor down to the beginning of the fifth line. As you move the cursor down, EDT extends the highlight, as shown in Figure 4.17.

3. All the highlighted text is selected. You could now use other commands to manipulate the selected range. If you decide you do not want to work with this range, cancel the selection with RESET.

```
Great fleas have little fleas
   upon their backs to bite 'em,
And little fleas have lesser fleas,
   and so ad infinitum.
And the great fleas themselves, in turn,
   have greater fleas to go on;
While these again have greater still,
   and greater still, and so on.
[EOB]
```

Figure 4.17 *Selecting a Range of Text*

4.9.2   Changing the Case of a Range of Text

A change you can make to a range of text is to its case. The CHNGCASE command (Gold 1) switches lowercase letters to uppercase or uppercase letters to lowercase. You may use CHNGCASE for individual letters or for all text in the selected range. To see how this works, try Experiment 4.15.

Experiment 4.15   *Changing the Case of a Range of Text*

1. Move the cursor to the beginning of the file.

2. Use the SELECT command to mark the beginning of the selected range.

3. Move the cursor to the end of the file with the BOTTOM command.

4. Use the CHNGCASE command to change the case of the selected range. Notice that the uppercase letters become lowercase and vice versa.

5. Repeat steps 1 through 4 to return the text to its previous state.

4.9.3   Cutting and Pasting a Range of Text

In previous experiments, you worked with commands that deleted text by the character, word, or line. EDT also has a command, CUT (KP6), that lets you delete the text in the selected range. Using this method, you can choose large sections of text to be cut with a single keystroke.

Like the delete commands discussed previously, the CUT command saves deleted text in a special storage area, called the Paste buffer. The text stored in the Paste buffer can be pasted back into the file using the PASTE command (Gold 6), a keystroke combination similar to the UND C, UND W, UND L commands. The contents of the Paste buffer remain until you execute another CUT command or end the EDT session. You can see how CUT and PASTE work by following Experiment 4.16.

Experiment 4.16   *Cutting and Pasting Text*

1. Move the cursor to the beginning of the file.

2. Use the SELECT command and move the cursor to the beginning of the fifth line.

3. Use CUT to cut the selected text (the first four lines) from the file. The selected text now is in the Paste buffer, as seen in Figure 4.18.

4. To restore the cut portion of text, you can paste it back into its previous location, or if you want to paste it elsewhere, you can move the cursor to the new location. Move the cursor to the beginning of the third line, *While these . . .*, and use PASTE to paste the contents of the Paste buffer into the file.

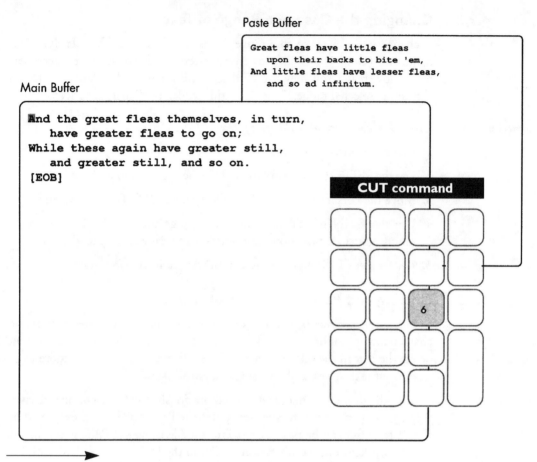

Paste Buffer

```
Great fleas have little fleas
    upon their backs to bite 'em,
And little fleas have lesser fleas,
    and so ad infinitum.
```

Main Buffer

```
And the great fleas themselves, in turn,
    have greater fleas to go on;
While these again have greater still,
    and greater still, and so on.
[EOB]
```

CUT command

6

Figure 4.18 *The Paste Buffer*

4.9.4   Using the Paste Buffer to Replace Text

You can use the Paste buffer to temporarily store text that you want to use to replace other text. The REPLACE command (Gold 9) deletes a selected range of text and replaces it with the contents of the Paste buffer. Follow Experiment 4.17 to replace the first two lines of text with the contents of the Paste buffer.

Experiment 4.17 *Replacing a Selected Range of Text*

1. The Paste buffer still contains the first four lines of the poem. Use SELECT to establish a selected range containing the current third and fourth lines of text in the file, or Main buffer, *Great fleas . . . to bite 'em.*

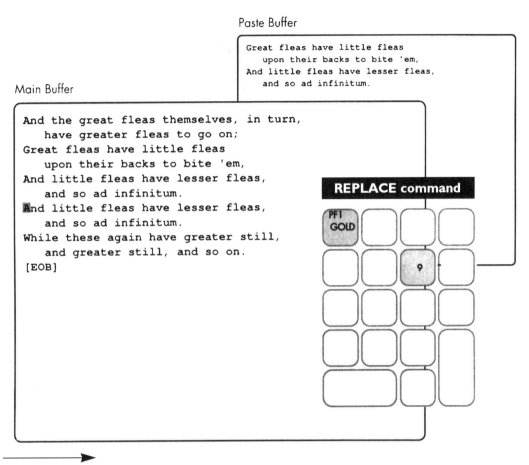

Figure 4.19   *Using REPLACE*

2. Use REPLACE to replace these two lines with the contents of the Paste buffer, as shown in Figure 4.19.

4.9.5   Finding and Replacing Text

There is another way to select and replace text. You can use the FIND command to establish which text should be replaced with the contents of the Paste buffer and then use the SUBS (substitute) command (Gold Enter) to replace that text with the contents of the Paste buffer. This method is useful when you have numerous occurrences of text that need to be replaced, because once you find and replace the first occurrence you can continue finding and replacing other occurrences just by using SUBS. Follow Experiment 4.18 to see how this works.

Experiment 4.18 *Finding and Replacing Text*

1. Move the cursor to the top of the file.

2. You want to replace *fleas* with *FLEAS*. First, type *FLEAS*. Then move to the beginning of the word and use the SELECT command to select *FLEAS*. Use the CUT command to move *FLEAS* to the Paste buffer.

3. Use the FIND command, entering *fleas* as the search string and pressing Enter.

4. Use the SUBS command to replace the first occurrence of *fleas*, and move to the next occurrence. Use SUBS to replace each remaining occurrence.

5. Restore the word *fleas* by following steps 1 through 4 and using *fleas* to replace *FLEAS*.

4.9.6 Adding to the Paste Buffer

The contents of the Paste buffer remain intact until you cut more text or end the EDT session. Sometimes, however, you want to add more text to the Paste buffer without destroying its current contents. You can add selected text to the Paste buffer using the APPEND command (KP9). APPEND removes the selected text from the Main buffer and adds it to the end of the Paste buffer. It is particularly useful for correcting the order of text, as Experiment 4.19 demonstrates.

Experiment 4.19 *Using APPEND to Add to the Paste Buffer*

1. The lines of the poem are out of sequence. Using CUT and APPEND, you can reassemble them in the paste buffer in the proper order. First, move to the beginning of the current third line of the file, *Great fleas . . .*

2. Use the SELECT command to select the third through the sixth lines.

3. Use the CUT command to remove those lines and place them in the Paste buffer.

4. Move to the current first line of the file, *And the great fleas . . .*, and use the SELECT command to select the first and second lines.

5. Now use the APPEND command to append these lines to the contents of the Paste buffer.

6. Move to the fifth line, *While these . . .*, and use the SELECT command to select the fifth and sixth lines.

7. Use the APPEND command to append these two lines to the contents of the Paste buffer.

8. Move to the beginning of the first line, and use the SELECT command to select the remaining lines on the screen. Then use the REPLACE command to replace this selected text with the contents of the Paste buffer.

4.9.7 Reformatting a Paragraph

When EDT is first activated, it establishes the margin boundaries at columns 1 and 80. Though these default values are set, they do not affect the length of text that can be typed on each line. To readjust text (within a paragraph) that extends beyond 80 columns, use the FILL command (Gold 8).

The FILL command allows you to reformat a selected range of text neatly between the pre-established margins. This is particularly useful when you have added and deleted text in an existing document paragraph, creating short lines within the paragraph. Follow the steps in Experiment 4.20 to see how the FILL command works.

Experiment 4.20 *Readjusting Document Paragraphs*

1. Exit EDT and then reactivate it using the file name LETTER.TXT (if necessary, change from the line mode to the keypad mode):

```
$ edit/edt letter.txt
Input file does not exist
[EOB]
```

2. Enter the following text exactly as it appears. Remember to press Return to start each new line as shown:

```
                              Today's Date


Gentlemen:

We are in the process of contacting firms or individuals
who have sent information for which we have no interest.
Attached is the label from such a mailing list sent by
you.

We request that you please remove us from your mailing list.
Should you have any question regarding
this, please feel free to contact me.

Sincerely!

Your Signature
```

3. Position the cursor at the beginning of the first *We.*

4. Use the SELECT command to mark the beginning of the selected range.

5. Move the cursor to the end of the paragraph using any of the cursor movement functions.

6. Use the FILL command to reformat the paragraph.

4.10   Discovering Some of EDT's Special Features

EDT has special features that are not apparent until you begin to explore further. Two of these are introduced in the following sections.

4.10.1   Repeating a Keystroke Automatically

When you know you want to repeat a keypad editing command a certain number of times, you can use the REPEAT function. As its name suggests, this function repeats a keystroke the number of times that you specify.

To use this function, first press the Gold key and then press a keyboard number key or keys to indicate the number of times you want the next keystroke repeated. Note that this is the number key on the regular keyboard, not the numeric keypad. EDT displays the number in the lower portion of the screen, and the next keystroke you make will be repeated as many times as you have specified. To try this, follow the steps in Experiment 4.21.

Experiment 4.21   *Repeating Keystrokes*

1. Suppose you want to move the cursor two words to the right. Press Gold and then the number 2 on the regular keyboard. The number 2 appears in the lower left-hand corner of the screen. Now use the WORD command. The cursor moves right past the next two words.

2. You can use this function to repeat characters as well. Move the cursor to the end of the file. Press Gold and then type 6. Now type the keyboard period character. The last line of LETTER.TXT now contains six periods.

4.10.2   Inserting Special Characters

Another EDT feature is the SPECINS command (Gold 3). This command allows you to insert into text any character from the DEC multinational character set, ranging from ASCII control characters to letters with accent marks. To enter a character, press Gold, type the decimal value of the ASCII character, and then use the SPECINS command. Table F.1 in Appendix F lists these decimal values.

4.11   Recovering from Interruptions

The four most common circumstances that can interrupt or end your editing session without your consent are

1. Noise in a communication channel, which may cause extraneous characters to appear on the screen during an editing session

2. Accidentally pressing Ctrl/Y, which interrupts command processing

3. A system crash without warning

4. Exceeding your disk quota

The methods that allow you to recover from such misfortunes are discussed in the sections that follow.

4.11.1   Deleting Extraneous Characters

During an editing session, you may receive broadcast messages or messages indicating that you have received electronic mail. In other instances, garbage characters may mysteriously float across the screen while you are using a dial-up modem to access the computer system.

To purge uninvited characters or messages, press Ctrl/W. This clears and redraws the screen. Using Ctrl/W is especially important when foreign characters appear on the screen, because it will ensure that the cursor is in the correct position. If the garbage characters actually get inserted into a file, you can delete them using any of the delete commands.

4.11.2   Resuming an Interrupted Editing Session

Imagine that you have just spent the last two hours typing a computer program or important document into an EDT file. As you are typing, you accidentally press Ctrl/Y. Panic sets in when you realize you do not have a backup copy of your work.

This has happened to most of us at one time or another. Luckily there is a simple solution. By typing CONTINUE at the DCL $ prompt, you can return to the EDT session. Follow Experiment 4.22 to see how this works.

Experiment 4.22   *Interrupting an Editing Session with CTRL/Y*

1. Exit EDT and reactivate it using the FLEAS.TXT file. Change into the keypad mode if necessary.

2. Interrupt the editing session by pressing Ctrl/Y.

3. Locate the DCL $ prompt and the cursor. Enter the CONTINUE command and press Return.

4. You are back in EDT. Now press Ctrl/W to restore the screen to its state before the interruption.

4.11.3   Recovering a Lost Session

Suppose your system has just crashed. On some computers, this would mean that the contents of the file you were editing would be lost forever. Not so with EDT; you can recover text lost because of a system failure.

EDT has a Journal facility that keeps track of each keystroke you make during your editing session in a special file, called a *journal file*. If your editing session should end abruptly because of a system crash, EDT saves the journal file. Even though the text of your editing work has been lost, the keystrokes you used are saved; so, using the journal file, EDT can restore almost all your editing work. However, sometimes the last few commands you typed or the last few keystrokes you made may not have been recorded in the journal file at the time of the interruption.

The journal file normally is stored in the current directory with the same file name as the file you were working on and .JOU as the file type. When you next activate EDT, you use the /RECOVER qualifier and specify the name of the file you want to recover.

When EDT begins the recovery process, do not touch the keyboard until the file is restored. EDT reproduces the editing session, reading the commands from the journal file and executing them on the screen. EDT will re-edit your file in exactly the same fashion and sequence as you did prior to the interruption.

Once EDT has finished processing all the command information and key-strokes stored in the journal file, it will continue to use that journal file during your editing session. If you are able to end your editing session successfully, using the EXIT or QUIT commands, EDT discards the journal file from your directory. (However, if you find journal files in your directory that you do not plan to use, simply delete them.) To simulate a system crash, try Experiment 4.23.

Experiment 4.23   *Simulating a Crash and Recovering*

1. Enter several new lines to the FLEAS.TXT file. For instance, you can add a copy of the last three lines of the poem.

2. Simulate a system crash by pressing Ctrl/Y and then logging out of the system.

3. Log back into the system.

4. Activate EDT to edit FLEAS.TXT but include the /RECOVER qualifier before the file name:

```
$ edit/edt/recover fleas.txt
```

Sit back and watch as EDT re-edits the file. Remember two important things
when you recover an interrupted EDT session. First, you must use the same
type of terminal you used during the original editing session. In fact, the terminal should be identical in all characteristics. Do not start a recovery operation on a hard-copy terminal when you were working on a VT200 or VT100
terminal. Second, you should never modify the file you were editing before
you attempt its recovery.

4.11.4   Exceeding Your Disk Quota

Essentially, while using EDT, you can exceed your disk quota in two ways.
Your disk storage might be full prior to activating EDT or the disk storage
available in your user account may not be enough to store the contents of the
Main buffer. These two events occur more often than you would think, especially in environments in which disk storage is limited and the revision of files
is frequent.

When you exceed your disk quota prior to activating EDT, a message similar to the following appears:

```
Error opening PACK2:[YOURGROUP.YOU]TOTAL.TXT as output
ACP file extend failed
Disk quota exceeded
```

To solve this problem, you can purge or delete files to recover space on the
disk or request additional disk space.

When you exceed your disk quota while exiting EDT and saving a file, a
message similar to the following appears:

```
Output file could not be created
Filename: PACK2:[YOURGROUP.YOU]LIST.TXT
ACP file create failed
Disk quota exceeded
Press Return to continue
```

To solve this problem, press Return and then Ctrl/Z to return to the line
mode. Then enter the QUIT/SAVE command. The QUIT/SAVE command
does not save the contents of the file you were working on, but it does save
the journal file for later use.

Once out of EDT, you can purge or delete obsolete files to free a minimum number of blocks of disk storage equal to the size of the file you are working on plus a little extra to allow for growth. In some instances, you may have to request additional disk space.

To start editing your file again, type the same command line used to begin the original editing session, but include the /RECOVER qualifier so that EDT can reconstruct your editing session. For example, to recover a file called BUBBLE.PAS, you would type

```
$ edit/edt/recover bubble.pas
```

Summary

EDT is an interactive text editor with three distinct editing modes: keypad, line, and nokeypad. Both the keypad and nokeypad modes are screen editors. The line mode can be used on any type of terminal—hard-copy or screen.

With the EDT editor, you can create and edit text files. When you are editing a file, you can add or delete text, move or copy text from one place to another, and save or discard your editing work. To activate the EDT editor, enter the DCL EDIT command and the name of the file.

If the file does not exist, EDT displays the [EOB] marker and a message that the file does not exist. If the file exists in your user directory, EDT puts a copy of the file into the Main buffer and displays a portion of it on the screen. The next step, in either case, is to insert and edit text using one of the three editing modes.

In some systems, EDT will start in the line mode and you can change to the keypad mode. In other systems, EDT begins in the keypad mode.

You can use EDT's on-line Help facility any time during your editing session. The line mode HELP command supplies general information on EDT as well as details on line mode and nokeypad mode commands. The HELP command by itself provides information on using the Help facility and a list of topics on which you can get help. For help on a specific topic, type the HELP command followed by the name of the topic.

When you are in the keypad mode, press Help on the VT200 or PF2 on the VT100. EDT displays a diagram of the keypad and a list of other keypad commands and tells you to press the key for which you want help.

EDT's Journal facility keeps track of each keystroke you make during an EDT session in a special file, called the *journal file*. When you finish your editing session using the EXIT or QUIT commands, EDT normally discards the journal file. If your editing session ends abruptly because of a system interruption, the journal file is saved even though your editing work has been lost. Using the journal file, EDT can restore almost all your editing work.

This chapter has only scratched the surface when it comes to the editing capabilities of EDT. However, it describes and demonstrates the most commonly used editing features. Features not discussed in this chapter, such as defining keys and creating macros and initialization files, can be explored on your own and used to expand EDT's editing capabilities further.

Tables 4.1–4.5 summarize the functions, commands, special characters, and important terms discussed in this chapter.

Table 4.1   *EDT Keypad Commands and Functions*

Command/Function	Key	Result
ADVANCE	KP4	Sets the editing direction to forward
APPEND	KP9	Deletes the selected range from the current buffer and appends it to the end of the Paste buffer
BACKUP	KP5	Sets the editing direction to backward
BOTTOM	Gold 4	Moves the cursor to the end of the current buffer
CHAR	KP3	Moves the cursor one character in the current editing direction
CHNGCASE	Gold 1	Changes the case of all letters in the selected range or at the current cursor position
COMMAND	Gold 7	Accesses line mode commands while in the keypad mode
CUT	KP6	Deletes the selected range of text and places it in the Paste buffer
DEL C	Comma	Deletes the character that the cursor is on
DEL EOL	Gold 2	Deletes the text from the cursor to the end of the line
DEL L	PF4	Deletes the text from the cursor to the beginning of the next line, deleting the line terminator
DEL W	Minus	Deletes characters from the cursor to the beginning of the next word

Table 4.1   *EDT Keypad Commands and Functions (Continued)*

Command/Function	Key	Result
ENTER	Enter	Sends a command or search to EDT for processing
EOL	KP2	Moves the cursor to the next line terminator in the current editing direction
FILL	Gold 8	Reformats the text in the selected range so that as many whole words as possible are included in the lines, within the current margins
FIND	Gold PF3	Locates the search string that you specified when EDT displayed the Search for: prompt
FNDNXT	PF3	Locates the next occurrence of the current search string in the current editing direction
GOLD	PF1	Accesses the alternative keypad commands
HELP	PF2	Provides information on keypad mode editing keys
LINE	KP0	Moves the cursor to the beginning of the next line in the current editing direction
OPEN LINE	Gold 0	Adds a line terminator to the right of the cursor, which does not move
PAGE	KP7	Moves the cursor to the next EDT page boundary in the current editing direction or, if no page boundary is present, moves the cursor to the top or bottom of the buffer
PASTE	Gold 6	Inserts the contents of the Paste buffer to the left of the cursor
REPLACE	Gold 9	Deletes the selected range of text and replaces it with the contents of the Paste buffer
RESET	Gold .	Cancels the selected range and sets the editing direction to forward
SECT	KP8	Moves the cursor 16 lines in the current editing direction
SELECT	Period	Marks one end of a selected range
SPECINS	Gold 3	Allows you to insert any character from the DEC multinational character set into your text by entering the decimal value for that character

Table 4.1 *EDT Keypad Commands and Functions (Continued)*

Command/Function	Key	Result
SUBS	Gold Enter	Replaces the next occurrence of the current search string with the contents of the Paste buffer
TOP	GOLD 5	Moves the cursor to the beginning of the current buffer
UND C	Gold ,	Inserts the contents of the delete character buffer to the left of the cursor
UND L	Gold 4	Inserts the contents of the Delete Line buffer to the left of the cursor
UND W	Gold –	Inserts the contents of the Delete Word buffer to the left of the cursor
WORD	KP1	Moves the cursor to the beginning of the next word in the current editing direction

Table 4.2 *Keyboard Key Functions*

Key	Result
Backspace or F12	Moves the cursor to the beginning of the current line or to the previous line
Ctrl/L	Inserts a form feed character in text
Ctrl/W	Clears and redraws the screen
Ctrl/Z	Shifts from the keypad mode to the line mode
Delete or ⟨ X ⟩	Deletes the character to the left of the cursor
Down Arrow	Moves the cursor down to the next line
Left Arrow	Moves the cursor one character to the left
Return	Inserts a line terminator in the text and moves the cursor to the beginning of the new line
Right Arrow	Moves the cursor one character to the right
Up Arrow	Moves the cursor up to the previous line

Table 4.3 *DCL and Line Mode Commands*

Command	Short Form[a]	Result
CHANGE	C	Shifts EDT to the keypad mode
CREATE	CR	Establishes a new file
EDIT		Activates the EDT editor
/RECOVER		Instructs EDT to use the journal file to restore a file after a system interruption
EXIT	EX	Ends the EDT session, saving a copy of the Main buffer text to an external file
HELP	H	Activates the line mode Help facility
QUIT	QU	Ends the EDT session without saving a copy of your editing work
QUIT/SAVE		Ends the EDT session without saving a copy of your editing work but does save the journal file

[a] Short forms of commands can be used only in the line mode. Using the short form while in the keypad mode (with the COMMAND command) causes an error.

Table 4.4 *Special Characters*

Character	Meaning
Command:	COMMAND function prompt
[EOB]	Designates the end of a buffer (or file)
<FF>	EDT symbol designating a form feed
_File:	EDT input file prompt
.JOU	Identifies an EDT journal file
Search for:	FIND command prompt
^M	A control character for a carriage return
*	Line mode editing prompt
$	DCL prompt

Table 4.5 *Important Terms*

Term	Definition
Alternative command	Secondary command sequence executed by a key on the numeric keypad
Buffer	Temporary work space in EDT specifically for manipulating text
Character	Letter or symbol
Command	Instruction specifying an action for EDT to perform
Cursor	Used by EDT to indicate the current editing position
Editor	Application software package used to create and modify text files
EDT	OpenVMS full-screen editor
Journal file	File containing commands from the current editing session
Main buffer	Space containing an input file while changes and additions take place during an EDT editing session
Numeric keypad	Group of keys located on the far right-hand side of the keyboard
Paste buffer	Storage area used in conjunction with the CUT command
Primary command	Principal command sequence executed by a key on the numeric keypad
Screen editor	Text editor that allows you to view the contents of a file on the screen
Scrolling	Movement of lines of text up or down the screen
Searching	Looking for specified text within a text file
Selected range	Portion of text that has been flagged to be manipulated by an EDT command
String	Group of characters
Text file	File containing ASCII characters
Word	Group of characters bounded by a space, horizontal tab, line feed, vertical tab, form feed, or carriage return

Exercises

1. Name the three EDT editing modes.

2. What is the difference between the CUT and APPEND commands?

3. Make a list of all the EDT keypad commands that only work with a selected range of text.

4. Which of the commands in Exercise 3 use the Paste buffer to manipulate text within the Main buffer?

5. Use the SPECINS command to create an ASCII character chart.

6. Find out how to redefine or relocate preset keypad editing keys.

7. What is the maximum number of characters that can be typed on one line during an EDT editing session?

8. Determine the minimum amount of disk storage required to create the journal file when you activate EDT.

9. Define the key sequence Gold E to locate a semicolon (;) and delete to end of line.

10. Describe all the ways you can change the case of two letters preceding the cursor.

11. What are two ways of inserting a form feed into a text file?

12. Create a directory of terms (acronyms, DCL commands, special symbols, and so on) that you have encountered so far. Use the following format when creating your table:

    Term   Meaning   Example

13. While in EDT, interrupt your editing session using Ctrl/Y. Once out of EDT, type the following DCL commands: DIRECTORY, SHOW PROCESS, MAIL. Now try to reinstate your editing session using the CONTINUE command. Did it work? How can you resume the session?

14. In Exercise 13, you entered DCL commands before reinstating your interrupted EDT session. This time, execute a command file such as LOGIN.COM, and then enter the CONTINUE command.

15. Name all the possible methods of searching for text within a file.

16. Exit from an EDT session saving the contents of the Main buffer to a subdirectory in your user account.

17. Try saving a file to another user directory. Explain what happens.

18. Explain the result of the following experiment:
   a. Activate EDT using any text file stored in your user directory.
   b. Move the cursor to the end of the third line.
   c. Use the EOL command and watch what happens.
   d. Set the editing direction to backward.
   e. Repeat step c.

19. Modify Exercise 18 using the Backspace key instead of the EOL command.

20. Try the following experiment:
   a. Activate EDT using any text file stored in your user directory.
   b. Set the line width to 132 columns.
   c. Use the SELECT command.
   d. Move the cursor to the end of the file.
   e. Use the FILL command.

21. Try using the CUT command without selecting a range of text first. What happened?

22. Try the following experiment:
   a. Activate EDT using any text file stored in your user directory.
   b. Move the cursor to the beginning of the third line.
   c. Set the editing direction to backward.
   d. Use the LINE command.
   What happened?

Review Quiz

Indicate whether the following statements are true or false:

1. The contents of the Main buffer can be saved only to the file specified at the time you activated EDT.

2. The SHIFT command is used to move from the line mode to the keypad mode.

3. There are two ways of specifying an input file name when you activate EDT.

4. The default editing direction when you first enter EDT is backward.

5. The file stored in the Main buffer is only a copy of the original file.

6. The Delete key deletes one character to the right of the cursor.

7. To process a line mode command using the COMMAND command, you need to press Return.

8. Searches using the FIND command can occur only in the forward direction.

9. The CHARACTER command can be used as an alternative to the Left Arrow and Right Arrow keys.

10. The PAGE command moves the cursor in increments of 16 lines at a time.

11. The REPLACE command exchanges a selected range of text, established using the FIND command, with the contents of the Paste buffer.

12. The GOLD/REPEAT function allows you to repeat a keypad editing function a specific number of times.

13. Ctrl/X allows you to clear and redraw the screen.

14. You can start a recovery operation after a system crash on a hard-copy terminal when you were working on a VT200 or VT100 terminal.

15. EDT will not activate successfully if there is not enough disk storage to create the journal file.

16. The QUIT/SAVE command sequence saves the contents of the Main buffer even though there is not enough disk storage.

Further Reading

Digital Equipment Corporation, POB CS2008, Nashua, NH 03061:

Printed Documentation	*OpenVMS DCL Dictionary: A-M*
	OpenVMS DCL Dictionary: N-Z
	OpenVMS EDT Reference Manual
	OpenVMS User's Manual.
On-Line Documentation	OpenVMS On-Line Help Facility
	OpenVMS Bookreader
	http://www.openvms.digital.com

5

The Phone and Mail Utilities

At the instant I first became aware of the cosmos we all infest I was sitting in my mother's lap and blinking at a great burst of lights, some of them red and others green, but most of them only the bright yellow of flaring gas.

—H. L. Mencken, *Happy Days*, 1940

VMS provides two utilities that help you communicate with other system users: the Phone utility and the Mail utility. This chapter explores these two utilities. In this chapter, you will

▶ Learn to place a call using the Phone utility

▶ Learn to answer a phone call from someone else

▶ Explore different methods of sending mail messages

▶ Understand the use of mail folders

▶ Create a file from a mail message

5.1   Using the Phone Utility

The Phone utility is an interactive utility that enables you to talk to other users on your system via your terminal screen. You can place a call, answer an incoming call, and get a list of users that you can call, and even place conference calls.

To enter the Phone utility, type

```
$ phone
```

The Phone utility screen appears, as shown in Figure 5.1. The % is the Phone prompt. You can type Phone commands after this prompt, such as DIRECTORY to see a list of available users or HELP to get information about the various Phone features.

The two sections of the split screen are used to carry on a conversation. The upper section, or window, will display your comments, and the lower window will display the other person's comments. You generally do not invoke the Phone utility unless you are placing or answering a call.

5.1.1   Placing a Call

To place a call to another person, type

```
$ phone username
```

The screen changes to the Phone utility screen, and a message appears indicating that the utility is ringing the other person. When the person answers, another message appears—the user name of the person you are calling appears in the lower window— and you can begin your conversation.

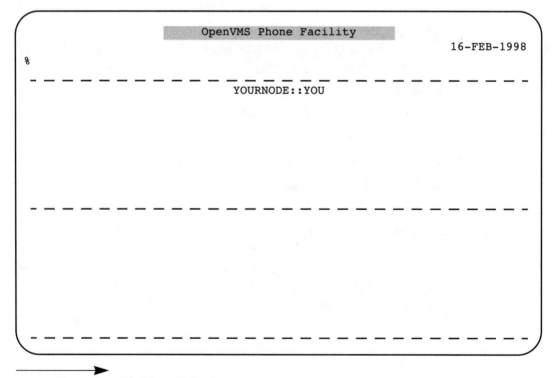

Figure 5.1   *The Phone Utility Screen*

As you type your comments, they appear in the upper window. The other person's responses appear in the lower window. For example, the conversation might start something like that shown in Figure 5.2.

If you need to issue a Phone command during a conversation, you can move back to the Phone prompt by typing %. When the conversation is over, press Ctrl/Z to hang up and move back to the Phone prompt. Exit the Phone utility by typing

```
% exit
```

5.1.2 Answering a Call

If someone calls you, you will receive a message to that effect. You can answer the call by moving to the Phone utility and then, at the Phone prompt, entering the ANSWER command. The ANSWER command completes the connection when someone is calling you.

You can experiment with the Phone utility by calling yourself. By doing this, you avoid bothering others on the system while you learn to use Phone. Follow the steps in Experiment 5.1.

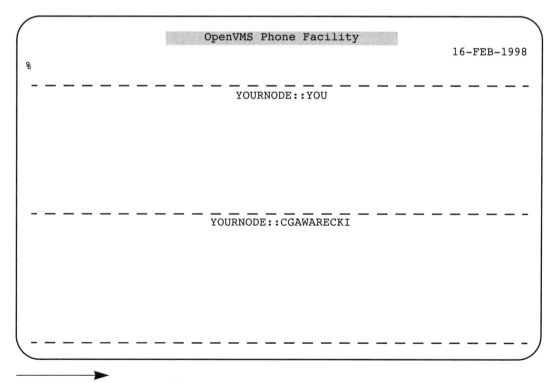

Figure 5.2 *A Sample Phone Conversation*

Experiment 5.1 *Phoning Yourself*

> **1.** Phone yourself by entering the PHONE command and your user name:
>
> ```
> $ phone your-username
> ```
>
> **2.** When the phone rings, the call is answered automatically because you are calling yourself. (If the call were from another user, you would enter the PHONE command at the $ prompt and then the ANSWER command at the % prompt.)
>
> **3.** Your user name appears in both the upper and lower windows because you are calling yourself. Enter some text as a conversation. Both windows will reflect your comments. To finish the conversation and to hang up, press Ctrl/Z.
>
> **4.** Use the EXIT command to exit the Phone utility:
>
> ```
> % exit
> ```

Once you understand how the Phone utility works, try calling someone else. Use the SHOW USERS command at the DCL $ prompt to get a list of people currently logged on and then select a person to phone. Or you can activate the Phone utility and use the DIRECTORY command to see a list of users available for phoning. The directory listing indicates whether a user is accepting broadcast messages and so can be phoned.

5.1.3 Phone Courtesies

Keep in mind that this phone dialogue is carried on in silence. The other person can only guess when you are finished saying something. Thus, it helps to have some sort of symbols that simulate CB talk. For example, try using (o) for over and (oo) for over and out at the end of your comments. There may be times when you do not want to be interrupted by phone messages. You can use the SET BROADCAST command to disable incoming phone calls. For example, you might type

```
$ set broadcast=nophone
```

To enable incoming phone messages, you would type

```
$ set broadcast=phone
```

5.2 Using the Mail Utility

Using the Mail utility, you can exchange messages with other users on your system or on any other computer that is connected to your system by way of a network. You can send a file using the MAIL command at the $ or you can move to the Mail utility, where you can create and send messages, read messages, and perform other mail management tasks.

If mail messages have been sent to you since the last time you logged in, you will see a message like the following when you log in:

```
You have 2 new Mail messages.
```

You will also receive a message if someone sends you mail while you are logged on.

5.2.1   Sending and Reading Mail

To send a message you will need to know if the recipient is located on your computer system or on a computer that is part of a network (on a different node or the Internet).

To invoke the Mail utility, enter the DCL command MAIL, as follows

```
$ mail
MAIL>
```

Once you are in Mail, you can enter Mail commands by entering a command at the MAIL> prompt and pressing either the Return or Enter key.

To send a mail message from within the Mail utility, enter the SEND command. The Mail utility then prompts you for the recipient's user name, a subject line and the text of the message. Enter the message, pressing Ctrl/Z when you are finished to send the message. To send a message to jmuggli on your computer system, you would type

```
$ mail
MAIL> send
To:     jmuggli
Subj:   schedule
Enter your message. Press CTRL/z when complete, or CTRL/c to quit:
John,
The new schedule will be out next week.
Joe
Ctrl/z
Exit
```

To send mail to someone on a different node precede the recipient's user name with the appropriate node name at the To: prompt. If the user name contains special characters or spaces, you must enclose the user name in quotation marks (""). In the following example, a message is sent to user SSIMONETT on node TRUMPET.

```
$ mail
MAIL> send
To:      trumpet::ssimonett
```

Mail will display a message if the network connection to the remote node is not available.

If you are sending mail via the Internet, supply the recipient's e-mail address, consisting of a user name and domain name, at the To: prompt. To send a message by way of the Internet you might type

```
$ mail
MAIL> send
To:      cgarwecki@pooh.computing.analysts.com
```

In an Internet e-mail address, the domain name follows the @ sign and is read from left to right. The domain name in this example is *pooh.computing. analysts.com*. The components *pooh* and *computing* describe the host name and subdomain respectively. The term *analysts* is the location name (or second-level domain) and *.com* describes the classification type (or first-level domain). Table 5.1 lists the more common classifications.

Table 5.1 *Common Classification Types (First-Level Domain Names)*

Type	Description
.com	Commercial
.org	Nonprofit organization
.net	Network operations
.gov	U.S. government
.edu	Educational organization
.mil	U.S. military
.au	Australia
.ca	Canada
.fr	France
.jp	Japan
.uk	United Kingdom
.us	United States

Alternatively, you can send a preexisting message or file from the DCL level by typing

```
$ mail files-specification username
```

The file specification is that of the file you want to mail. The recipient name is the user name of the person to whom you are sending the file. For example, to mail a copy of the OPENVMS.DAT file to jmuggli, you would type

```
$ mail openvmsbks.dat jmuggli
```

To send a mail message to more than one user, simply enter a list of user names at the To: prompt, separating the names with commas.

To read your mail, activate the Mail utility. A message tells you how many new mail messages you have. Press the Return key to see the first new message. If you have more than one message, press Return after reading each message to see the next message.

You can begin exploring the Mail utility's capabilities by sending mail to yourself, following the steps in Experiment 5.2.

Experiment 5.2 *Sending Mail to Yourself*

1. Begin by creating a short file using the CREATE command:

```
$ create mail.txt
This file can be sent as a mail message
 Ctrl/z 
 Exit 
$
```

2. Now use the MAIL command in a single command line to send a copy of the existing file to yourself (in the following command line, enter your *user name* in place of *YOU*):

```
$ mail mail.txt you
New mail on node YOURNODE from YOURNODE::YOU
$
```

3. Now move to the Mail utility, where you can create and send messages as well as read your mail:

```
$ mail

You have 1 new message.

MAIL>
```

4. You can read the new message by pressing Return:

```
MAIL>
#1                8-DEC-1997 20:34:52.39              NEWMAIL
From:    YOURNODE::YOU
To:      YOU
CC:
Subj:

This file can be sent as a mail message

MAIL>
```

5. Now create and send a message using your computer node name from within the Mail utility. Use the SEND command, which prompts you for the name of the user or users to whom you want to send the message, the subject, and then the message. When you are finished entering the message, press Ctrl/Z:

```
MAIL> send
To:      YOUR_NODENAME::YOU
Subj:    experience with send
Enter your message below.  Press CTRL/z when complete, or
CTRL/c to quit:
...message from me
 Ctrl/z
 Exit
New mail on node YOURNODE from YOURNODE::YOU

MAIL>
```

6. Repeat step 5, entering your Internet e-mail address at the To: prompt:

```
MAIL> send
To:      YOUR_USERNAME::YOUR_DOMAINNAME
Subj:    experience with send
Enter your message below.  Press CTRL/z when complete, or
CTRL/c to quit:
...message from me
 Ctrl/z
 Exit
New mail on node YOURNODE from SMTP%"YOUR_USERNAME@your_domainname"

MAIL>
```

7. You have sent yourself two messages. Now exit the Mail utility:

```
mail> exit
$
```

5.2.2   Using Folders

The Mail utility stores messages in *folders*. By default, it stores unread messages in a folder called *NEWMAIL* and read messages in a folder called *MAIL*. Mail also uses a WASTEBASKET folder to temporarily store messages you have deleted. When you exit the Mail utility, the WASTEBASKET folder is discarded. You can create as many additional folders as you like, and you can move messages between folders.

Use the MOVE command to move a message to a different folder. For example, if you have just read a new message and you want it stored in a folder called SCHEDULES, you would type

```
MAIL> move schedules
```

You create a folder by moving a message to it and responding to the prompts so that the new folder is created. For example, if the folder called SCHEDULES did not exist, the Mail utility would respond as follows:

```
MAIL> move schedules
Folder SCHEDULES does not exist.
Do you want to create it (Y/N, default is N)? y
%MAIL-I-NEWFOLDER, folder SCHEDULES created

MAIL>
```

By default, the Mail utility begins in the NEWMAIL folder or, if no new messages exist, the MAIL folder. To access a different folder, use the SELECT command and specify the folder's name. For example, to access the SCHEDULES folder, you would type

```
MAIL> select schedules
%MAIL-I-SELECTED, 1 message selected

MAIL>
```

5.2.3   Listing Messages

When you are in the Mail utility, you can perform other mail management tasks. For example, you can ask for a directory listing of your messages, using the DIRECTORY command. This command lists the messages by author, date, subject, and message number. You can use the message number to refer to that message during mail management tasks.

Unless you specify a folder name or have selected a different folder, the DIRECTORY command lists the messages in the NEWMAIL folder or, if that is empty, in the MAIL folder. Here is a sample directory listing:

```
MAIL> directory
```

```
                                                                        NEWMAIL
      # From                    Date          Subject

      1 YOURNODE::YOU           8-DEC-1997    experience with send
      2 SMITH                  22-AUG-1997    test
      3 OSOKO                  24-AUG-1997

MAIL>
```

Try Experiment 5.3 to see how to use the DIRECTORY command to read mail messages.

Experiment 5.3   *Using the DIRECTORY Command*

1. First move to the Mail utility:

```
$ mail

You have 1 new message.

MAIL>
```

2. Because you have not read the last message you received, you have one message in the NEWMAIL folder. Ask for a directory listing of your mail messages in this folder:

```
MAIL> directory
                                                             NEWMAIL
  # From                    Date          Subject

  1 YOURNODE::YOU           8-DEC-1997    experience with send

MAIL>
```

3. Press Return to read this message:

```
#1              8-DEC-1997 20:34:52.39            NEWMAIL
From:    YOURNODE::YOU
To:      YOU
CC:
Subj:    experience with send

. . . message from me

MAIL>
```

4. Now that the message has been read, it is copied to the MAIL folder. Get a listing of messages in the MAIL folder:

```
MAIL> directory mail                                    MAIL

# From                    Date            Subject

1 YOURNODE::YOU           8-DEC-1997
2 YOURNODE::YOU           8-DEC-1997      experience with send

MAIL>
```

5. To read a message, select the message by specifying the message's number. Try reading message 2:

```
MAIL> 2

#2              12-DEC-1997 22:01:59.32              NEWMAIL
From:   YOURNODE::YOU
To:     YOU
Subj:   experience with send

...message from me

MAIL>
```

6. Now exit the Mail utility:

```
MAIL> exit

$
```

5.2.4   Two Useful SEND Qualifiers

The Mail utility's SEND command has two qualifiers that often are useful. The /SELF qualifier lets you send a copy of a message you send to someone else back to yourself. The syntax for this form of the SEND command is

send/self

You also can specify the subject of the message with the /SUBJECT qualifier. If you specify a subject in the command, the Mail utility does not prompt you for that information, and the information appears in the mail message directory. The syntax for this form of the SEND command is

send/subject="*subject text*"

Notice that you must enter the subject text enclosed in quotation marks if it is longer than a single word. Try using these two qualifiers in Experiment 5.4.

Experiment 5.4   *Sending a Message to Another User and Yourself*

1. Move to the Mail utility:

   ```
   $ mail

   MAIL>
   ```

2. Now use the SEND command with both the /SELF and /SUBJECT qualifiers to create and send a new message:

   ```
   MAIL> send/self/subject="Secret life"
   To:      another user
   Enter your message below. Press CTRL/z when complete, or
   CTRL/c to quit:
   Marcel Vogel found plants reading persons' thoughts. Peter
   Thompkins, Christopher Bird. The Secret Life of Plants.
   Avon, 1974, p. 43.
   Ctrl/z
   Exit

   New mail on node YOURNODE from YOURNODE::YOU

   MAIL>
   ```

3. The message has been sent to another user and to yourself. Use the DIRECTORY command to check this. Because there is a new message, the DIRECTORY command lists the contents of the NEWMAIL folder. Notice that this last message has a subject listed.

   ```
                                                            NEWMAIL
   # From                  Date         Subject

   1 YOURNODE::YOU          8-DEC-1997   Secret life

   MAIL>
   ```

4. Press Return to read the new message:

   ```
   #1             14-JAN-1998 10:36:25.51              NEWMAIL
   From:   YOU
   To:     ANOTHER USER
   CC:     YOURNODE::YOU
   Subj:   Secret life

   Marcel Vogel found plants reading persons' thoughts. Peter
   Thompkins, Christopher Bird. The Secret Life of Plants. Avon,
   1974. p. 43.

   MAIL>
   ```

5. Now exit from the Mail utility:

```
MAIL> exit

$
```

5.2.5 Extracting Mail Messages

A mail message created and sent through the Mail utility is not an OpenVMS file. However, you may find that you want a message's information to be in a file. The Mail utility has an EXTRACT command that makes it possible to write a mail message to a file. The Mail EXTRACT command has the following syntax:

extract *filespec*

The file specification is the name of the file you want to create.

To extract a mail message, first read the message and then extract it to a new file. To see how the EXTRACT command works, try Experiment 5.5.

Experiment 5.5 *Extracting a Mail Message*

1. First, activate Mail and check your mail directory. Because there are no new messages, the DIRECTORY command lists the messages in the MAIL folder:

```
$ mail
MAIL> directory
                                              NEWMAIL
# From              Date           Subject

1 YOURNODE::YOU     14-JAN-1998
2 YOURNODE::YOU     14-JAN-1998    experience with send
3 YOURNODE::YOU     14-JAN-1998    Secret life

MAIL>
```

2. Read the "secret life" message:

```
MAIL> 3
     #3          14-JAN-1998 10:53:08.94           NEWMAIL
From:    YOURNODE::YOU
To:      ANOTHER_USER
CC:      YOURNODE::YOU
Subj:    Secret life

Marcel Vogel found plants reading persons' thoughts. Peter
Thompkins, Christopher Bird. The Secret Life of Plants.
Avon, 1974, p. 43.

MAIL>
```

3. Now use the EXTRACT command to copy the message to a new file:

```
MAIL> extract plantlife.dat
%MAIL-I-CREATED, PACK2:[YOURGROUP.YOU]PLANTLIFE.DAT;1
created
```

4. Exit from Mail and verify that you now have a new file named PLANTLIFE.DAT in your current directory:

```
MAIL> exit
$ directory plantlike.dat
Directory PACK2:[YOURGROUP.YOU]

PLANTLIFE.DAT;1

Total of 1 file.
$
```

When the message is extracted to the file, it includes the To, From, and Subject headings from Mail. If you use the TYPE command to inspect the new file, these headings will appear. You can prevent the headings from being copied when you extract a message by using the /NOHEADER qualifier for the Mail EXTRACT command. For example, after reading the message, you could type

```
MAIL> extract/noheader secretlife.dat
```

The copy of the message in this new file would not have the Mail headers.

Summary

The OpenVMS Phone and Mail utilities make it possible for system users to communicate with each other. With these utilities, you have a choice of either interactive exchanges via the Phone utility or sending messages to other users via the Mail utility.

Both utilities provide a HELP command. When you begin using either utility, you can get help on a topic by typing

```
help topic
```

For example, while you are in Mail, you can obtain information on all the Mail commands by typing

```
MAIL> help *
```

To display a list of available topics, type

```
MAIL> help
```

Experiment with the HELP command to see what commands are available for each utility.

The Phone utility works only if the user you wish to talk to is logged in when you make the call by entering

```
$ phone username
```

When you enter this command line, the phoned user will see the *Ringing You...* message flash on the screen. You will want to use this utility with care to avoid distracting another user unnecessarily.

You can print a list of users you may call on your system by entering the DIRECTORY command while you are in Phone. The Mail utility also has a DIRECTORY command that you can use to see a listing of your mail messages. In both cases, you need to be *inside* the utility to use the commands provided by that utility. You can tell if you are inside either utility by observing the special prompt that is displayed. The Phone utility prompt is %, and the Mail utility prompt is MAIL>.

Exercises

1. Give the command lines to do the following things:
   a. Mail a file named EXPRESS.DAT to a user named Susan.
   b. Mail EXPRESS.DAT;14 to Susan.

2. Using the HELP command provided by the Phone utility, list and give a brief explanation of each of the Phone commands available on your local system.

3. Using the HELP command provided by Mail, list and give a brief explanation of each of the Mail commands available on your local system.

4. Give the command line to mail a file named T.DAT;5 to yourself.

5. Which Phone command allows you to respond to another user phoning you while you are using Phone?

6. Give the command used by both Phone and Mail to terminate a utility session.

7. What happens when you type the following while you are in the Mail utility?

```
MAIL> mail
```

8. Give two ways to terminate a Phone session.

9. What technique is used to block incoming phone messages? Give the command line to do this.

10. If you have blocked incoming phone messages, how do you remove the block? Give the command line to do this.

11. Assume you have 12 mail messages. Give the Mail command lines to do the following:
  a. List your mail messages.
  b. Delete messages 5 and 9.
  c. Copy message 6 to a file named MSG.6.

Review Quiz

Indicate whether the following statements are true or false:

1. The SET command can be used to block incoming phone messages.

2. You can use the WRITE command to copy a mail message to a file while you are in Mail.

3. Extracting a mail message means writing the message to a designated file.

4. The Mail SEND command has a /SUBJECT qualifier that must be used when you send a mail message.

5. You can use the Mail SEND command to mail a file to yourself.

6. If you type the following, then the Mail utility next prompts you for the message to send:

`MAIL> send`

7. The Mail utility allows you to keep a copy of messages you send.

8. The Phone utility allows you to reject calls from designated users.

9. The Phone FACSIMILE command makes it possible to send the contents of a file as part of a Phone conversation.

10. You must type the following to respond to an incoming Phone message:

`$respond`

Further Reading

McBride, R. A., K. W. Wong, J. F. Peters, and E. A. Unger. *Rule-Based Active Message Systems.* Proceedings of the Association for Computing Machinery Workshop on Applied Computing, March 30–31, 1989.

Sawey, Ronald M. and Troy T. Stokes. *A Beginner's Guide to VAX/VMS Utilities and Applications,* 2d ed. Newton, Mass.: Digital Press, 1992.

Digital Equipment Corporation, POB CS2008, Nashua, NH 03061:

Printed Documentation	*OpenVMS DCL Dictionary: A-M*
	OpenVMS DCL Dictionary: N-Z
	OpenVMS Software Overview
	OpenVMS User's Manual
On-Line Documentation	OpenVMS On-Line Help Facility
	OpenVMS Bookreader
	http://www.openvms.digital.com

6

More Work with Files

The brain is, in fact, an associating machine. To recall a name, date, or fact, what the brain needs is a cue, a clue.

—Robert L. Montgomery, *Memory Made Easy,* 1979

Yea, from the table of my memory I'll wipe away all trivial fond records.

—Shakespeare, *Hamlet,* Act I, Scene 5

Chapter 2, "A Beginner's Guide to OpenVMS File Management," introduced you to some basics of file handling with OpenVMS. This chapter extends your understanding of working with files. In this chapter, you will

▶ Learn how to search files

▶ Explore uses of the Sort and Merge utilities

▶ Explore another way to create files

▶ Begin using logical names

▶ Learn how to print files

▶ Learn how to set up local help libraries

6.1   Searching Files

The SEARCH command scans one or more files for a specified string or strings and lists all occurrences of the lines containing the string or strings. This command is useful in constructing special-purpose glossaries, for example. Even though a text may have a mixture of ideas, you can cull from it all lines pertaining to a selected set of keywords.

The SEARCH command has the following syntax:

```
search filespec[,...] search-string[,...]
```

The file specification is the name of at least one file that should be searched. If more than one file should be searched, list the names, separating them with commas. You may include wildcard characters in the file specification.

The search string is the string of characters to be searched for. If it includes any spaces, lowercase letters, or nonalphanumeric characters, the search string must be enclosed in double quotation marks (" ").

For example, to search the OPENVMSDEF.TXT file (created in Experiment 2.1) for occurrences of the string *one file*, you would type

```
$ search openvmsdef.txt "one file"
A wildcard char. can specify more than one file.
$
```

To list all lines in OPENVMSDEF.TXT with the string *information*, you would type

```
$ search openvmsdef.txt "information"
A file is a named piece of information.
$
```

You can practice using the SEARCH command by following the steps in Experiment 6.1.

Experiment 6.1   *Searching Files*

1. Use the CREATE command to create the following sample file:

```
$ create authors.dat
Cather, Willa Five Stories
Cather, Willa A Lost Lady
Cather, Willa My Mortal Enemy
Cather, Willa Obscure Destinies
Cather, Willa One of Ours
Cather, Willa The Professor's House
Camus, Albert The Stranger
Bolt, Robert A Man for All Seasons
 Ctrl/z 
 Exit 
$
```

2. Now search the file for the string *One:*

```
$ search authors.dat "One"
Cather, Willa One of Ours
$
```

3. The SEARCH command also has a /LOG qualifier, which displays the file name, number of records, and number of matches for each file searched. For example, to search all your files of type .TXT for the string *file*, you would type

```
$ search/log *.txt "file"
%SEARCH-S-NOMATCH, PACK2:[YOURGROUP.YOU]A.TXT;1 -1 record
%SEARCH-S-NOMATCH, PACK2:[YOURGROUP.YOU]AI.TXT;1 -13 records
.
.
.
*****************************
PACK2:[YOURGROUP.YOU]MAIL.TXT;1
This file can be sent as a mail message
%SEARCH-S-MATCHED, PACK2:[YOURGROUP.YOU]MAIL.TXT;1 -1 record, 1

match

*****************************
.
.
.
PACK2:[YOURGROUP.YOU]OPENVMSDEF.TXT;1
A wildcard char. can specify more than one file.
A file is a named piece of information.
%SEARCH-S-MATCHED, PACK2:[YOURGROUP.YOU]OPENVMSDEF.TXT;1 -4 records, 2 matches
$
```

6.2   Another Method of Creating Files

Up to this point, you have used the CREATE, EDIT, COPY, and Mail EXTRACT commands to establish new files. OpenVMS also offers a variety of other ways to create new files. For example, many DCL commands have an /OUTPUT qualifier that makes it possible to create a new file. By default, OpenVMS sends a command's response or output to the terminal or, in a batch job, to a batch job log file. (This default output stream or file is specified by SYS$OUTPUT, a system logical name.) The /OUTPUT qualifier directs the output from a command to a specified file instead. Table 6.1 lists a selection of DCL commands that have this qualifier.

6.2.1   Redirecting the DIRECTORY Command Output

You can use the /OUTPUT qualifier with the DIRECTORY command to redirect the listing of files from the terminal to a specific file. You might do this to save a copy of the listing from an old directory when you anticipate making many changes to it and want to have a record of the old directory structure.

Table 6.1 *Commands with the /OUTPUT Qualifier*

Command	Example	Result
DIRECTORY	`directory/output=d.dat`	Writes the output from a DIRECTORY command to a new file; in this case, D.DAT
RUN	`run/output=r.dat pgm`	Writes the output from the execution of PGM, an executable program, to a file; in this case, R.DAT
SEARCH	`search/output=se.dat pgm begin`	Writes the output from a SEARCH command; in this case, the search scans the PGM file for occurrences of *begin* and the output file is SE.DAT
SHOW	`show/output=sh.dat users`	Writes the output from a SHOW command that lists current users to a file; in this case, SH.DAT
TYPE	`type/output=t.dat`	Writes the output from a TYPE command to a file; in this case; T.DAT

The DIRECTORY command with the /OUTPUT qualifier has the following syntax:

`directory/output`[`=filespec`]

Although the file specification is optional for the /OUTPUT qualifier, if you do not enter it, the output is sent to the default output device (generally, the terminal) rather than to a file. Try redirecting the output of the DIRECTORY command by following Experiment 6.2.

Experiment 6.2 *Redirecting the Output from a DIRECTORY Command*

1. Send the output from a DIRECTORY operation to a file named DIR.OUT:

```
$ directory/output=dir.out
$
```

2. The directory history is now in a new file called *DIR.OUT.* Verify this by entering a DIRECTORY command for DIR.OUT files:

```
$ directory dir.out
Directory PACK2:[YOURGROUP.YOU]

DIR.OUT;1

Total of 1 file.
$
```

3. You can see the contents of the DIR.OUT file by entering a TYPE command:

```
$ type dir.out

Directory PACK2:[YOURGROUP.YOU]

A.TXT;1   AI.TXT      AUTHORS.DAT;1     BUBBLE.PAS;1
    .
    .
    .

Total of 35 files.
$
```

When you create a file of the directory results, everything that normally would appear on the screen is placed in the file. You can suppress the directory heading, which contains the device and directory names, by using the /NOHEADING qualifier. For example, you could type

```
$ directory/noheading/output=dirnh.out
```

The /NOHEADING qualifier tells the DIRECTORY command to use single-column format in its output. As a result, the pathname of each file appears with each file name. To see this, type

```
$ type dirnh.out
PACK2:[YOURGROUP.YOU]A.TXT;1
PACK2:[YOURGROUP.YOU]AI.TXT;1
        .
        .
        .

PACK2:[YOURGROUP.YOU]VAXMAN.DAT;1
PACK2:[YOURGROUP.YOU]OPENVMS.DIR;1

Total of 35 files.
$
```

If you want to direct the output to a different directory, be sure to include the pathname for that directory or subdirectory when you enter the file specification. Remember, pathnames are enclosed in brackets. For example, to direct the output to a file in a subdirectory called DIRLISTS, you would type

```
$ directory/output=[.dirlists]dir.out
```

6.2.2   Redirecting the SEARCH Command Output

You can redirect the output from the SEARCH command to a specified file using the /OUTPUT qualifier. By redirecting the output from the

SEARCH command, you can establish special-purpose files that provide a permanent record of the output. The syntax for this form of this command is

```
search/output[=filespec] filespec[,...] string[,...]
```

For example, to create a file that contains the lines in OPENVMSDEF.TXT with the string information, you would type

```
$ search/output=info.dat openvmsdef.txt "information"
$
```

6.3   Sorting File Contents

Sorting the contents of a file is a useful procedure that can help you organize information in a specific way. A sorted list arranges the items in ascending or descending order. Each item is considered a record. A record can consist of one or more fields. For example, the list in Table 6.2 shows the most common English words, taken from Gaines (1956). The list has two fields, Word and Frequency, and each word and its frequency number constitute one record.

A sort key is the field of the records that is used to order the list. For example, in the Gaines word list, the frequency field has been used as the sort key. These most common English words appear in descending order relative to frequency counts. The DCL Sort utility makes it possible to sort file records in terms of one or more sort keys.

Table 6.2 *Most Common English Words*

Word	Frequency
the	15,568
of	9,767
and	7,638
to	5,739
a	5,074
in	4,312
that	3,017
is	2,509

6.3.1   Sorting Files with the Sort Utility

You use the DCL Sort utility to sort the records of a file or files by one or more sort keys. The SORT command, which invokes the Sort utility, has the following syntax:

sort *input-filespec*[,...] *output-filespec*

The input file specification is the name of at least one file to be sorted. Up to ten files can be sorted to create one output file. If more than one file should be sorted, list the file names, separating them with commas. The output file specification is the file that will be created and that will contain the sorted records.

In its simplest form, without any qualifiers, the SORT command sorts the file using the entire record as the sort key and produces an output file with the records in ascending order. Follow the steps in Experiment 6.3 to explore how a simple sort works.

Experiment 6.3   *Using the SORT Command without Qualifiers*

1. First create a file, GAINES.DAT, to be sorted:

   ```
   $ create gaines.dat
   the      15568
   of       9767
   and      7638
   to       5739
   a        5074
   in       4312
   that     3017
   is       2509
   Ctrl/z
   Exit
   $
   ```

2. Now enter a SORT command without qualifiers. This sorts the records of the file by the entire record. The input file is GAINES.DAT and the output file can be WORDS.DAT:

   ```
   $ sort gaines.dat words.dat
   $
   ```

3. Use the TYPE command to see the contents of WORDS.DAT:

   ```
   $ type words.dat
   a        5074
   and      7638
   in       4312
   ```

```
is      2509
of      9767
that    3017
the     15568
to      5739
$
```

If you want the output from a sort to be written directly to the screen, specify SYS$OUTPUT as the output file. Then the SORT command displays the results of the sort rather than creating a file containing the results. For example, to see the results of a sort of GAINES.DAT directly on the screen, you would type

```
$ sort gaines.dat sys$output
a       5074
and     7638
in      4312
is      2509
of      9767
that    3017
the     15568
to      5739
$
```

6.3.2   Using the SORT Command with the /STATISTICS Qualifier

At times it is helpful to use the /STATISTICS qualifier with the SORT command. This qualifier gives you a way of checking what the Sort utility has done because it lists information about the sort procedure—the number of records read and sorted, the elapsed time, and much more. For example, to produce statistics for a sort of the GAINES.DAT file, you would type

```
$ sort/statistics gaines.dat words.dat
                OpenVMS Sort/Merge Statistics
Records read:             8      Input record length:     10
Records sorted:           8      Internal length:         12
Records output:           8      Output record length:    10
Working set extent:  163840      Sort tree size:         102
Virtual memory:         400      Number of initial runs:   0
Direct I/O:               7      Maximum merge order:      0
Buffered I/O:            11      Number of merge passes:   0
Page faults:             31      Work file allocation:     0
Elapsed time:  00:00:00.09       Elapsed CPU:     00:00:00.01
$
```

6.3.3   Sorting with Sort Keys

By default, the Sort utility uses the entire record as the sort key and sorts the records in ascending order. If you want to sort by a specific field in the records, you must specify that field by using the /KEY qualifier. The syntax for the /KEY qualifier is

```
sort/key=(position:column-number,size:key-length,
[data_type],[sort-order]) input-filespec output-filespec
```

The position and size arguments of the /KEY qualifier are mandatory, and the type and order arguments are optional. The position argument specifies the position of the leading column of the field that will be used as the sort key.

The size argument specifies the size, or the exact number of columns, of this key field. Acceptable values for this argument depend on the data type of the entries in the key field, or sort key, as follows:

▶ 1 to 32,767 characters for char (character) data

▶ 1, 2, 4, 8, or 16 bytes for binary data

▶ 1 to 31 digits for decimal data

▶ No value for floating-point data (f_floating, d_floating, g_floating, or h_floating)

The optional type argument specifies the data type of the sort key. Type *char* is the default type used by the Sort utility if no type is specified.

The optional order argument specifies the order of the sort operation and can be either ascending or descending. By default, the sort will be in ascending order. For example, to sort the lines in the GAINES.DAT file in descending order using the first field as the sort key, you would type

```
$ sort/key=(pos:1,siz:4,descending) gaines.dat sys$output
to      5739
the     15568
that    3017
of      9767
is      2509
in      4312
and     7638
a       5074
$
```

Before you can specify a field of a record to be used as a sort key, you must first determine the position and size of a key in a file record. (The illustrations in this section will be in terms of stream files, or files of characters, and single sort keys.)

An easy way to pinpoint the position and size of a sort key is to use an editor such as EVE or EDT to add a line to the file that will be sorted. This line could contain alternating groups of five *x*s and five *y*s, or numbers, to serve as a counting mechanism, so that you could count over to the sort key field to determine the column in which the field starts and the size of the field. For example, to determine the position and size of the Frequency field in GAINES.DAT, you could add a line, as follows:

```
a       5074
and     7638
xxxxxyyyyyxxxxxyyyyy
in      4312
is      2509
of      9767
that 3017
the     15568
to      5739
```

Alternatively, the line might contain numbers, as follows:

```
a       5074
and     7638
12345678901234567890
in      4312
is      2509
of      9767
that 3017
the     15568
to      5739
```

In either case, you can then determine that the Frequency field starts at position 10 and has a size of 5.

You can explore using a different sort key by following the steps in Experiment 6.4. This experiment creates a file of records with multiple fields by using the /DATE, /SIZE, and /OUTPUT qualifiers with the DIRECTORY command.

Experiment 6.4 *Sorting with Sort Keys*

1. Use the DIRECTORY command with the /DATE, /SIZE, and /OUTPUT qualifiers to create the file GOODPLACE.DAT. The directory listing can include only files of type .DAT:

   ```
   $ directory/date/size/output=goodplace.dat *.dat
   $
   ```

2. Examine the contents of GOODPLACE.DAT by entering a TYPE command:

   ```
   $ type goodplace.dat
   ```

   ```
   Directory PACK2:[YOURGROUP.YOU]
   ```

```
AUTHORS.DAT;1 1 13-JAN-1998 12:49:41.52
.
.
.
WORDS.DAT;1 1 25-SEP-1997 15:00:32.42

Total of 9 files, 8 blocks.
$
```

The /DATE qualifier in the DIRECTORY command included the creation date of the file in the listing, and the /SIZE qualifier included the number of blocks used by the file.

3. Use EVE or EDT to edit GOODPLACE.DAT so that you can pinpoint the position and size of the field you will use as the sort key. Move to the second line and press Return to insert a blank line. Then enter alternating groups of five *x*s and five *y*s as follows:

```
Directory PACK2:[YOURGROUP.YOU]

AUTHORS.DAT;1 1 13-JAN-1998 12:49:41.52
xxxxxyyyyyxxxxxyyyyyxxxxxyyyyy
CSBKS.DAT;1 10 25-SEP-1997 11:38:30.53
.
.
.
WORDS.DAT;1 1 25-SEP-1997 15:00:32.42

Total of 9 files, 8 blocks.
$
```

4. Count the groups of *x*s and *y*s to determine the first column used by the key field. In this example, the Blocks field starts in column 24 (this is the position), and this key uses two columns (this is the size). Your results might be slightly different. Exit the editor without saving a new version of the file.

5. Next, you need to determine the key data type. The /OUTPUT qualifier on the DIRECTORY command creates a stream file, or a file of characters; so each sort key chosen for such a file will have a type of char. Also, for easy reading, you will want the sort to be in descending order so that the largest files appear at the top.

6. Sort the GOODPLACE.DAT file and write the output from the sort to a NEWLIST.DAT file. Use the values for the position and size arguments that you determined in step 4:

```
$ sort/key=(pos:24,siz:2,char,descending) goodplace.dat
newlist.dat
$
```

7. Now display the contents of the NEWLIST.DAT file by using the TYPE command (your results might be slightly different):

```
$ type newlist.dat
Total of 9 files, 8 blocks.
Directory PACK2:[YOURGROUP.YOU]
CSBKS.DAT;1      10 25-SEP-1997 11:38:30.53
LIST.DAT;1        9 25-SEP-1997 11:42:32.43
GAINES.DAT;1      1 25-SEP-1997 11:46:28.34
  .
  .
  .
$
```

You may have found the NEWLIST.DAT file produced by the SORT command in Experiment 6.4 surprising. It puts the Directory header line and Total files line at the top of the sorted file. Keep in mind that, by default, the SORT command uses the ASCII table to determine the order of a character. (The block number symbols are evaluated as characters, not as integers.) The lowercase letters *ck* (in the word *blocks*) occupy columns 24 and 25 in the Total files line, as do the uppercase letters *UP* in the word *YOURGROUP*. Because you specified that the sort keys were to be put in descending order, and uppercase letters and lowercase letters come after any of the numerals in the ASCII table (see Table F.1, Appendix F), the SORT command puts the Total files line and the Directory header line at the top of the sorted file. The keys with the highest ASCII character values move to the top of the sorted file.

6.4   Merging Sorted Files

If you have sorted several files and then decide you want the results of these sorts in one file, you can use the MERGE command to merge together the sorted files into a single sorted file. The syntax for the MERGE command is the same as the syntax for the SORT command (with the exception of several qualifiers):

merge *input-filespec,input-filespec[,...] output-filespec*

The input file specifications are the names of the files to be merged. The same key must be used when you sort the files, or they cannot be merged. Up to ten files may be merged to create one output file. Separate the input file specifications with commas. The output file specification is the file that will be created and that will contain the merged list of sorted records.

In its default form, the MERGE command is simple to use, as you can see by following Experiment 6.5. In this experiment, you set up a second list of the most common English words, sort this new file and the GAINES.DAT file, and then merge these two files together.

Experiment 6.5 *Merging Sorted Files*

1. Begin by creating a second file to sort, GAINES2.DAT:

```
$ create gaines2.dat
it      2255
for     1869
with    1849
you     1336
Ctrl/z
Exit
$
```

2. Sort the GAINES.DAT file and the GAINES2.DAT file just created. The output files for these sorts can be FIRST.DAT and SECOND.DAT:

```
$ sort gaines.dat first.dat
$ sort gaines2.dat second.dat
```

3. The same key (in this case, the entire record) sorted both files, so the sorted files can be merged. Merge the two files created by the sort. Instead of sending the results to an output file, you can have them displayed on the screen by entering SYS$OUTPUT:

```
$ merge second.dat,first.dat sys$output
a       5074
and     7638
for     1869
in      4312
is      2509
it      2255
of      9767
that    3017
the     15568
to      5739
with    1849
you     1336
$
```

6.5   Logical Names

A logical name is one you can use in place of a file specification, part of a file specification, or another logical name. You can use logical names to assign a short, easy-to-remember name to a file or directory whose full file name specification is long and complex. For instance, a file may be nested within subdirectories or on a device other than your default. Typing a logical name is quicker and easier than typing full specifications. Because logical names can represent devices, such as disks or tape, they are useful for ensuring device independence.

6.5.1   Defining Logical Names

Use the DEFINE command to create logical names. This command has the following syntax:

define *logical-name equivalence-string[,...]*

The equivalence string is the file specification or the part of a file specification that you are equating to the logical name. It is a sequence of from 1 to 255 characters and can be any string such as [.OPENVMS] or PACK2: or [YOURGROUP.YOU].

For example, to create the logical name AGENDA for the file specification PACK2:[YOURGROUP.YOU.MTGS] AG3.DAT, you would type

```
$ define agenda pack2:[yourgroup.you.mtgs]ag3.dat
```

You then could use the logical name AGENDA anywhere you need to enter the file specification. For example,

```
$ copy agenda report.dat
```

To define a logical name for a device, for example, PACK2, you would type

```
$ define disk PACK2:
```

When defining a logical name for a device, be sure to end the equivalence string with a colon to indicate that it is a device.

If you define only a part of a file specification with a logical name, the logical name must be the leftmost component of the file specification. Then, when you use the logical name, you must separate it from the rest of the specification with a colon. For example, you could define a subdirectory by typing

```
$ define mtgs pack2:[yourgroup.you.mtgs]
```

To create a file in that subdirectory, you would type

```
$ create mtgs:newfile.dat
```

Finally, you can check the equivalence of a logical name by using the SHOW LOGICAL command. For example, to check the meaning of the logical name AGENDA, you would type

```
$ show logical agenda
"AGENDA" = "PACK2[YOURGROUP.YOU.MTGS]AG3.DAT" (LNM$PROCESS_TABLE)
$
```

To explore logical names, follow the steps in Experiment 6.6.

Experiment 6.6 *Defining and Using Logical Names*

1. Begin by creating a subdirectory of your current directory. If you already have a OPENVMS subdirectory, go on to step 2:

   ```
   $ create/directory [.openvms]
   $
   ```

2. Define OPENVMS as a logical name for the OPENVMS subdirectory:

   ```
   $ define openvms [.openvms]
   $
   ```

3. Use the SHOW LOGICAL command to display the value of the logical name OPENVMS:

   ```
   $ show logical openvms
   "OPENVMS" = "[.OPENVMS]" (LNM$PROCESS_TABLE)
   $
   ```

4. Try using the logical name to copy files to the OPENVMS subdirectory. Then get a directory listing of the files just copied:

   ```
   $ copy *.txt openvms
   $ directory openvms:*.txt

   Directory PACK2[YOURGROUP.YOU.OPENVMS]

   A.TXT;1  AI.TXt;1  FLEAS.TXT;4  FLEAS1.TXT;1
   .
   .
   .
   Total of 11 files.
   $
   ```

6.5.2   System Logical Names

OpenVMS defines a number of logical names whenever the system comes up. It uses these logical names when it processes the DCL commands that you issue. These logical names identify devices and files, and all have the *SYS$* prefix. Some of these system logical names are specifically associated with your process, while others are systemwide. Table 6.3 lists some of the most common system logical names associated with a process.

Table 6.3 *Common System Logical Names*

Logical Name	Equivalence Name
SYS$COMMAND	Name of the file or input stream from which DCL reads commands (usually, the name of your terminal)
SYS$DISK	Name of the default disk
SYS$ERROR	Name of the device that displays all error messages (usually, the name of your terminal)
SYS$INPUT	Name of the file or input stream from which data and commands are read (usually, the name of your terminal)
SYS$OUTPUT	This is the default file or output stream to which DCL sends its output (usually, the name of your terminal)

When you log in, the files named by the process logical names identify the default files that DCL uses for its input and output streams. When you execute a file of commands like your LOGIN.COM file, DCL uses SYS$COMMAND to keep track of the original input stream. It then redefines SYS$INPUT to identify a file of commands it is executing as the file from which to read its input.

6.5.3   Logical Name Tables

OpenVMS stores logical names in logical name tables. There are different types of logical name tables; each type contains the logical names available for specific groups of users. For example, the system logical name table lists the logical names available to all users of the system, and the group logical name table lists the logical names available to all users in your user identification code (UIC) group. The job logical name table contains the logical names available to your process and any of its subprocesses, and the process logical name table contains the logical names available only to your process.

When you define your own logical names, they are stored in the process logical name table. To see the list of logical names you defined as well as the process logical names defined by the system, you can use the SHOW LOGICAL command with the /PROCESS qualifier. Follow Experiment 6.7 to see how this works.

Experiment 6.7 *Viewing Your Process Logical Name Table*
Use the SHOW LOGICAL command to see your process logical name table:

```
$ show logical/process

(LNM$PROCESS_TABLE)
  "SYS$COMMAND" = "_TINY$NTY496:"
  "SYS$DISK" = "PACK2:"
  "SYS$ERROR" = "_TINY$NTY496:"
  "SYS$INPUT" = "_TINY$NTY496:"
  "SYS$OUTPUT" [super] = "_TINY$NTY496:"
  "SYS$OUTPUT" [exec] = "_TINY$NTY496:"
  "TT" = "_NTY496:"
$
```

You will probably see other logical names in your process logical name (LNM) table in addition to those shown in this sample output.

6.6   Printing Files

When you want to print a file, use the PRINT command. This command sends the file to the specified (or default) print queue. The print queue is the list of jobs waiting to be printed on a device. Only one job is printed at a time, and jobs are printed in turn, with the actual order of printing dependent on the priority, size, or submission time of each job.

The syntax for the PRINT command is

print *filespec*[,...]

The file specification can be replaced with a logical name. It also can specify more than one file, with each file specification separated from the others by a comma. For example, to print two files, GAINES.DAT and GAINES2.DAT, in one print job, you would type

```
$ print gaines.dat,gaines2.dat
Job GAINES (queue SYS$PRINT, entry 231) started on SYS$PRINT
```

This command sends the print job to the default print queue, SYS$PRINT. The message that appears shows the job's name, which is taken from the first file specified; the queue name; the job number; and whether the job has started or is pending. Once a job is submitted to a queue, use the job number to refer to it.

To see a list of your jobs in the print queue, use the SHOW ENTRY command. This command displays each job's status in the queue. For example,

```
$ show entry
 Entry     Jobname    Username     Blocks     Status

 231       GAINES     YOU             10      Printing
           On printer queue SYS$PRINT
```

If you want to delete an entry that you have entered in the queue, use the DELETE command with the /ENTRY qualifier and specify the entry number, as follows:

```
$ delete/entry=231
```

The PRINT command has many useful qualifiers. If you want the system to notify you when your print job is done, you can use the /NOTIFY qualifier. To send the print job to a print queue other than the default print queue, use the /QUEUE qualifier and specify the queue name. (SHOW QUEUE displays a list of all queues initialized for the system and their job lists.)

You can use the /COPIES qualifier to specify the number of copies that should be printed. The default number of copies is 1. For example, to print three copies of GAINES.DAT, you would type

```
$ print/copies=3 gaines.dat
```

If you are printing more than one file in a print job, the position of the /COPIES qualifier is important. If you place /COPIES immediately after the PRINT command, all the listed files will be printed that number of times. If you place the /COPIES qualifier after one of the file specifications, only that file will be printed that number of times.

6.7   Creating Library Files

The OpenVMS Librarian utility allows you to create specially formatted files called *library files*. A library file can store groups of files as modules. Library files make it possible to maintain a single file of related modules rather than having a group of individual files. For example, you could have different files, each of which describes a procedure; or you could have a library file whose modules each describe a procedure. Manipulating the single library file is easier than working with many different files.

You can use library files in various ways. You might create a library of program source code or technical references. One particularly good application is to create your own help library. This discussion of library files focuses on creating a help library.

To create a library file, use the LIBRARY command with a qualifier that indicates the type of library and the /CREATE qualifier. Possible library types are /TEXT, /HELP, /SHARE, /OBJECT, and /MACRO.

The specified type controls the default file type specification for the library file and the input files that make up the modules. For example, the syntax to create a help library file is

```
library/help/create library-filespec [input-filespec[,...]]
```

The /HELP qualifier specifies that a help library is being created and that the library file specification will be type .HLB and the input file specification will be type .HLP. The *input-filespec* is optional; you can create the library file and then later add input files containing a module or modules, or you can create the library file and at the same time enter input files to it.

6.7.1   Creating a Help Library File

Before creating the help library, you can create an input file that contains the modules for the library. Input files are created with a program or a text editor. Each input file can contain one or more modules.

The input files for help libraries must have a particular format. Each module in the input file is made up of the lines of text that relate to a single topic, or key. The topic can have up to eight levels of subtopics. The topic, or module name, is key 1; the subtopics are keys 2 through 9. As in an outline, each key level is subordinate to the next higher key level. The lines containing the topic and subtopics begin with the key number indicating their level.

Here is the sample format for a help input file:

```
1 topic/module name        (this identifies a help topic)
first-level text           (any number of lines)
2 subtopic name            (each subtopic name begins with a 2)
second-level text          (any number of lines)
3 sub-subtopic name        (optional topic related to subtopic)
third-level text           (any number of lines)
```

(Other subtopics on levels below 3 go here. The presence of subtopics is optional.)

```
2 next subtopic name
second-level text
3 sub-subtopic name
third-level text
1 next topic/module name   (identifies next help topic)
first-level text
2 subtopic name
second-level text
```

(Other modules will have similar structures.)

By default, each module name can be up to 15 characters long in a help library. If you want to increase the acceptable length, you can use the KEYSIZE option with the /CREATE qualifier when you create the help library file. For example, to create a help library file with module names that can be 30 characters, you would type

$ **library/help/create=(keysize:30)** *library-filespec input-filespec*

Similarly, there is an initial number of modules the library can contain; this default size is 128 modules. Another option for the /CREATE qualifier, MODULES, however, allows you to change the default. Therefore, if your input file has more than 128 modules (more than 128 level-1 topics), you can increase the number allowed. For example,

```
$ library/help/create=(modules:350) library-filespec input-filespec
```

Once you have set up the input file or files, use the LIBRARY command with the /HELP and /CREATE qualifiers, specifying the name of the library file you are creating and the name of the input file or files that contain the modules for the library file. You can explore this procedure by following the steps in Experiment 6.8.

Experiment 6.8 *Creating a Help Library File*

1. Use the DCL CREATE command or a text editor (EVE or EDT) to create a file named IO.HLP that contains the following lines (remember that each key 1 topic and its subtopics will become a separate module):

```
1 module_format
Starts with level-1 text with possible subtopics.
2 level-2
Always starts with a 2 followed by a level-2 name. The
level-2 heading is followed by level-2 text. There may be
more than one level-2 topic.
3 level-3
Always starts with a 3 followed by a level-3 name. There
may be more than one level-3 topic. (Level-3 topics give
ideas related to the nearest level-2 topic.)
3 other-notes
Keep module names short.
2 limitations
defaults: module names have 15 characters, libraries have
an upper limit of 128 modules.
2 structure
A help library has a tree structure.
1 gethelp
Type help/library=PACK2[YOURGROUP.YOU]io.hlb
1 startlib
Type library/help/create libraryfile inputfile
```

2. Now use the LIBRARY command and the /HELP and /CREATE qualifiers to create the help library file. You can use IO as its name; because of the /HELP qualifier, the file type will be .HLB. Change the default keysize to 32 so that the module names can be up to 32 characters long.

Also, add a /LOG qualifier, which simply causes OpenVMS to verify each operation.

```
$ library/help/create=(keysize:32)/log io io
%LIBRAR-S-INSERTED, module module_format inserted in
PACK2:[YOURGROUP.YOU]IO.HLB;1
%LIBRAR-S-INSERTED, module gethelp inserted in PACK2:
[YOURGROUP.YOU]IO.HLB;1
%LIBRAR-S-INSERTED, module startlib inserted in
PACK2:[YOURGROUP.YOU]IO.HLB;1
$
```

6.7.2 Accessing a Local Help Library

You can list the contents of a help library by using the /LIST qualifier and specifying the file name. In addition to a list of module names, this qualifier displays the creation and last revision dates, the number of modules, the maximum key length, and so on. For example,

```
$ library/help/list io
Directory of HELP library PACK2:[YOURGROUP.YOU]IO.HLB;1 on
14-JAN-1998 23:54:16
Creation date:14-JAN-1998 23:48:11 Creator:    Librarian A09-19
Revision date:14-JAN-1998 23:48:11 Library format:        3.0
Number of modules:            3 Max. key length:        32
Other entries:                0 Preallocated index blocks: 9
Recoverable deleted blocks:   0 Total index blocks used:   1
Max. Number history records: 20 Library history records:   0

gethelp
module_format
startlib
$
```

The Librarian utility has an /EXTRACT qualifier that makes it possible to display a selected module in a library. When used alone, /EXTRACT writes the module to a file in the current directory. When used with the /OUTPUT qualifier set to SYS$OUTPUT, /EXTRACT displays the module on the screen. For example, to display the GETHELP module, you would type

```
$ library/help/extract=gethelp/output=sys$output io
1 gethelp
Type help/library=PACK2:[YOURGROUP.YOU]io.hlb
$
```

Generally, however, you want to access the entire help library. Your system probably has a systemwide help library that you can access by typing

```
$ help
```

To get information from your local help library, you use the HELP command with the /LIBRARY qualifier and the file specification. For example, to tell DCL you want to get help from the IO.HLB library, you would type

```
$ help/library=pack2:[yourgroup.you]io.hlb
Sorry, no documentation on HELP

  Additional information available:

  gethelp module_format startlib

Topic?
```

After you get the Topic? prompt, you can enter any of the topics listed (including the names of other local libraries your system might have) to get help on that topic. To exit from a help library, simply press Return.

The first line of the previous example points to another feature of help libraries. If you include in your help library a module named HELP, this module will be displayed first. You can use this HELP module to give instructions on how to use your local help library.

6.7.3   Adding Modules to the Help Library

Once you have created a help library file, you can add more modules to it at any time. Use the /INSERT qualifier to add modules from one or more new input help files. This qualifier has the following syntax:

```
library/help/insert library-filespec input file-spec[,...]
```

The library file specification is the help library file to which you are adding. The input file specification(s) are of type .HLP, and if more than one file is listed, commas separate the file specifications. Following the steps in Experiment 6.9, you can add modules to the IO.HLB library file.

Experiment 6.9   *Adding Modules to a Help Library*

1. Begin by creating three new input files. Because each file is short, use the DCL CREATE command to do so:

```
$ create t1.hlp
1 ideas
See OpenVMS Command Definition, Librarian, and Message
Utilities Manual
 Ctrl/z
 Exit
$ cr t2.hlp
1 insert
```

```
See LIB-27.
Ctrl/z
Exit
$ create help.hlp
1 help
This library gives details on various ways to create a
local help library. Enter ideas to see information on the
librarian utility.
Ctrl/z
Exit
$
```

2. Now insert these new modules into IO.HLB by using the /INSERT qualifier and listing the input files. Use the /LOG qualifier as well so that you can see the operations being performed:

```
$ library/help/insert/log io t1,t2,help
%LIBRAR-S-INSERTED, module ideas inserted in PACK2:
[YOURGROUP.YOU]IO.HLB;1
%LIBRAR-S-INSERTED, module insert inserted in PACK2:
[YOURGROUP.YOU]IO.HLB;1
%LIBRAR-S-INSERTED, module help inserted in PACK2:
[YOURGROUP.YOU]IO.HLB;1
$
```

3. Use the HELP command with the /LIBRARY qualifier to access the help library. Notice that the contents of the newly added help module appear before the Topic? prompt:

```
$ help/library=PACK2:[yourgroup.you]io.hlb

HELP

This library gives details on various ways to create a
local help library. Enter ideas to see information on the
librarian utility.

  Additional information available:

  gethelp  help  ideas  insert  module_format
  startlib

Topic?
```

6.7.4   Replacing Library Modules

You can replace an old module with a revised version by employing the /REPLACE qualifier. Before you use the /REPLACE qualifier, either edit the original version of an input help file or create an entirely new one with the same module name as the module you will be replacing. The /REPLACE qualifier deletes any existing modules in the library that have the same name as modules in the input files and inserts the modules of the input files into the library. Practice replacing a module by following the steps in Experiment 6.10.

Experiment 6.10 *Replacing a Library Module*

1. Use the CREATE command to create CHANGE.HLP:

```
$ create change.hlp
1 change
See LIB-38.
 Ctrl/z 
 Exit 
$
```

2. Insert this module into IO.HLB:

```
$ library/help/log/insert io change
$LIBRAR-S-INSERTED, module change inserted in PACK2:
[YOURGROUP.YOU]IO.HLB;1
$
```

3. Use either EVE or EDT to edit CHANGE.HLP so that the file contains the following text:

```
1 change
See LIB-38 and Openvms Software Overview Manual
```

4. Use the /REPLACE qualifier to replace the old CHANGE module with the edited module. Use the /LOG qualifier to verify the operation:

```
$ library/help/replace/log io change
%LIBRAR-S-REPLACED, module change replaced in
PACK2:[YOURGROUP.YOU]IO.HLB;1
$
```

5. Finally, use the /EXTRACT qualifier to see the CHANGE module:

```
$ library/help/extract=change/output=sys$output io
1 change
See LIB-38 and Openvms Software Overview Manual
$
```

6.7.5   Deleting Library Modules

At times, you will want to delete a module altogether from a help library. The /DELETE qualifier makes it possible to do this. This form of the LIBRARY command has the following syntax:

```
library/help/delete=(module-name[,...]) library-filespec
```

For example, to delete the IDEAS module from IO.HLB, you would type

```
$ library/help/delete=ideas/log io
%LIBRAR-S-DELETED, module IDEAS deleted from PACK2:
[YOURGROUP.YOU]IO.HLB;1
$
```

If you want to delete more than one module, enclose the list in parentheses and separate the module names with commas. For example, to delete the HELP and GETHELP modules, type

```
$ library/help/log/delete=(help,gethelp) io
%LIBRAR-S-DELETED, module HELP deleted from PACK2:
[YOURGROUP.YOU]IO.HLB;1
%LIBRAR-S-DELETED, module GETHELP deleted from PACK2:
[YOURGROUP.YOU]IO.HLB;1
$
```

When you delete modules, the space they occupied remains in the library. To recover the space generated by deleting modules, use the /COMPRESS qualifier with the LIBRARY command. When you use /COMPRESS, the LIBRARY command creates a new library. By default, this new library is in your current directory and has the same file name and type as the original library. The syntax for this form of the LIBRARY command is

```
library/compress[=(option)[,...])]
```

Summary

There are many ways to work with files using DCL. You can search for occurrences of specific strings, and you can sort the contents of files by any specified field. By merging sorted files, you can create a new file of all the information. You can redirect the output from a DCL command using the /OUTPUT qualifier to create a file containing that output so that you have a permanent record. By printing a file, you obtain hard copies of the file's contents.

Logical names provide you a shortcut when referring to file specifications, thus facilitating your work with files. OpenVMS also automatically defines a number of logical names, which it uses when it processes DCL commands. OpenVMS stores logical names in logical name tables, which you can examine.

DCL provides a Librarian utility, which has a variety of uses. One helpful application of this utility is creation and management of help libraries. The Librarian utility makes it possible to organize and retrieve information you might otherwise forget.

Tables 6.4–6.6 give an overview of the commands, special characters, and important terms used in this chapter.

Table 6.4 *DCL Commands*

Command	Result
DEFINE	Defines a logical name
DELETE	
/ENTRY	Deletes the specified entry from the print queue
LOG	Displays what the DELETE command has done
DIRECTORY	
/NOHEADING	Removes the directory heading from the directory listing
/OUTPUT	Redirects the directory listing to an output file
HELP/LIBRARY	Accesses a help library
LIBRARY	Runs the Library utility
/COMPRESS	Restores free space after a deletion
/CREATE	Creates a library
/DELETE	Deletes a library module
/EXTRACT	Extracts a selected module from a library
/HELP	Specifies a help library
/INSERT	Inserts a module into a library
/LIST	Lists the contents of a library
/LOG	Displays what the LIBRARY command has done
/REPLACE	Replaces a library module
MERGE	Merges up to ten sorted files
PRINT	Prints the specified file(s)
/COPIES	Prints the specified number of copies
SEARCH	Searches a file or files for a specified string or strings
/LOG	Displays a record of the search procedure
/OUTPUT	Redirects the results of the search to an output file
SHOW ENTRY	Lists your jobs in the print queue
SHOW LOGICAL/PROCESS	Displays the process logical name table
SORT	Sorts the records of a file or files
/KEY	Sorts by the specified key
/STATISTICS	Lists information about the sort procedure

Table 6.5   *Special Characters*

Character	Meaning
LNM	Logical name
LNM$PROCESS_TABLE	Name of the process logical name table
SYS$COMMAND	Default process permanent file used to identify initial file from which DCL takes its input
SYS$ERROR	Default process permanent file to which DCL writes its error messages
SYS$INPUT	Default process permanent file from which DCL reads its input
SYS$OUTPUT	Default process permanent file to which DCL writes its output
-	The command line continuation operator
_$	Printed by DCL after the continuation operator is entered to continue entering a command on the next line
( )-LIBRARY DELETE	Encloses specification deletion of a library module
( )-MERGE KEY	Encloses specifications for a merge key
( )-SORT KEY	Encloses specifications for a sort key

Table 6.6   *Important Terms*

Term	Definition
Help library	Library of specially formatted modules; each module begins with a line of the form 1 *module-name*
Library	File used to store library modules that have been established by the Librarian utility
Logical name	Name associated with an equivalence string that is all or part of one or more file specifications and possibly other logical names; established with the DEFINE command
Process logical name table	Table that holds definitions of logical names; named LNM$PROCESS_TABLE
Sort key	The field of a record used by SORT and MERGE to order file records

Exercises

Before you do the exercises in this section, create the following file:

```
$ create ada.dat
mesg-based systems: a task can send a mesg to or receive a
mesg from another task.
tasks: components of an Ada program that can execute in
parallel.
task spec: task id is <entry decls> <rep clauses> end id;
rendezvous: communication between two tasks.
 Ctrl/z 
 Exit 
$
```

1. Use the SEARCH command to display the following:
   a. Lines in ADA.DAT containing the word *entry*
   b. Lines in ADA.DAT containing a colon (:)

2. Give the command line to write the output from 1(a) and 1(b) to a file named ENTRY.DAT.

3. Give the SEARCH command line that will display all lines in ADA.DAT following the first occurrence of the word *task*. (Hint: Use the /REMAINING qualifier with SEARCH.)

4. Give the command line to sort the ENTRY.DAT file that was created in Exercise 2.

5. What would be the effect of executing the SORT command in terms of ADA.DAT? Try it to see what happens. Explain the output you get.

6. What is the default output file used by the SEARCH command?

7. List and explain each of the logical names in your process logical name table.

8. Give the SEARCH command line that would search all your files of type .DAT for the string *OpenVMS* and write the lines found to a file named OPENVMSLINES.DAT in your current directory.

9. Use the SORT command with a file (constructed like the GAINES.DAT file) of the command words most used in this chapter.
   a. Create this file, calling it *FILEWORDS.DAT.*
   b. Sort the FILEWORDS.DAT file in ascending order using the default sort key (each entire record). Use SYS$OUTPUT as the output file.
   c. Sort the FILEWORDS.DAT file in descending order using the default sort key. Use SYS$OUTPUT as the output file.

      d. Sort the FILEWORDS.DAT file in descending order with the Frequency (or second) field as the sort key. Use FIRST.DAT as the output file name.

      e. Sort the GAINES.DAT file in descending order with the Frequency field as the sort key. Use SECOND.DAT as the output file name.

10. Show how to merge together the FIRST.DAT and SECOND.DAT files from 9(d) and 9(e).

11. Show how to set up a local help library that gives help on each of the OpenVMS topics covered in this chapter. Call the library file OPENVMS.HLB. In doing this, you should include the following:

      a. Give an example of a module named FILES-11 with at least two levels of subtopics. Construct this module in a file named FILES11.HLP. Give the command line to add this module to your OPENVMS.HLB library.

      b. Give an example of a module named CREATE (constructed in a file named CR.HLP) with three second-level topics and at least two third-level topics for each second-level topic. Give the command line to replace a module named CREATE in your OPENVMS.HLB file with the new module in your CR.HLP file.

Review Quiz

Indicate whether the following statements are true or false:

1. By default, the output from the SORT command is written to SYS$OUTPUT.

2. SYS$OUTPUT is the logical name for a process permanent file.

3. Every help library module begins with a 1.

4. By default, the HELP command opens the most recently created local help library.

5. Unlike the TYPE command, the DIRECTORY command does not have an /OUTPUT qualifier.

6. The Librarian utility creates files of type .HLP.

Further Reading

Gaines, H. F. *Crytanalysis: A Study of Ciphers and Their Solutions.* New York: Dover Publications, 1956.

Sawey, Ronald M., and Troy T. Stokes. *A Beginner's Guide to VAX/VMS Utilities and Applications,* 2d ed. Newton, Mass.: Digital Press, 1992.

Digital Equipment Corporation, POB CS2008, Nashua, NH 03061:

Printed Documentation   *OpenVMS Command Definition, Librarian, and Message Utilities Manual*
                               OpenVMS DCL Dictionary: A–M
                               OpenVMS DCL Dictionary: N–Z
                               OpenVMS Software Overview
                               OpenVMS User's Manual
On-Line Documentation   OpenVMS On-Line Help Facility
                               OpenVMS Bookreader
                               http://www.openvms.digital.com

7

Command Procedures

The guiding principle for making the choice [whether to add a new action or write a new program] should be that each program does one thing.

—Richard Pike and B. W. Kernighan,
Program Design in the UNIX Environment, 1984

Command procedures and the various features you can use in them provide you a way of simplifying and streamlining your use of OpenVMS. In this chapter, you will

► Explore the main features of command procedures

► Form command procedures with familiar groups of command lines

► Experiment with new ways to use logical names

► Begin using global and local symbols to simplify the entry of command lines

► Customize your working environment with enhanced versions of your LOGIN.COM file

► Explore file-handling commands used in command procedures

► Experiment with uses of parameters for command procedures

► Explore uses of literal and quoted strings

► Employ commenting techniques to specify key features of command procedures

7.1   Introduction to Command Procedures

A command procedure is a file containing DCL commands and perhaps some data used by the commands. These procedures can help you to simplify and clarify your use of OpenVMS because you can use them to execute many commands with one statement. Command procedures can be short yet powerful, or they can be more complex, performing program like functions. Using command procedures for repetitive or complex tasks will save you time.

7.1.1   Rules and Guidelines for Writing Command Procedures

You can use an editor such as EVE or EDT to write command procedures, or if it is a short procedure, you can use the DCL CREATE command. When writing a command procedure keep the following in mind:

► The file type of a command procedure is .EXIT.

► A dollar sign ($) must begin each line containing a command, comment, or label.

► If you want to include a line containing data to be used in response to DCL command prompt, omit the dollar sign on that line.

► An exclamation point (!) must be used to indicate the beginning of a comment. Any text on the line following the exclamation point will be ignored.

► Lines containing data used by the commands (responses to DCL prompts) do not begin with a dollar sign.

► Enclose a literal exclamation point in quotation marks (" ") in a command line.

► A command procedure can terminate with an EXIT command.

The basic structure for a command procedure is as follows:

```
$ ! introductory comments
$ !
$ ! comment about next command
$ !
$ command
data used as response to command prompt
$ !
$ ! comment
$ !
$ command
$ command
$ exit
```

Spaces, tabs, and blank lines should be used liberally to improve readability. Comments themselves are an essential part of command procedures. They identify and explain the actions of the procedure and are useful when you need to debug or modify a procedure. A variety of techniques from software engineering can be used to decide what kind of comments to insert into a procedure. A selection of these commenting techniques is given in this chapter.

To execute a command procedure, type the procedure file specification preceded by an at sign (@). For example, to execute a command procedure named CDUP.COM, you would type

```
$ @cdup
```

7.1.2   Sample Command Procedures

Command procedures often are quite short, simple, and designed for a single purpose. For example, you could create the following command procedure to change to the directory one level up from your current directory and execute the SHOW DEFAULT command:

```
$ ! cdup.com
$ !
$ ! action: change directories one level up from the current
$ ! directory and execute show default command.
$ !
$ set default [-] ! move up one directory level
$ show default
$ exit
```

Your LOGIN.COM file also is a command procedure file. Because it is executed each time you log into your system, you can use it to customize the login procedure. For example, your LOGIN.COM file might look like this:

```
$ ! commands executed each time you log in
$ write sys$output "Hello, Pat!"
$ show users
$ show quota
$ exit
```

With this LOGIN.COM file, when you log in, the message *Hello, Pat!* will appear, followed by a list of users and your disk quota.

As with other command procedure files, you can execute your LOGIN.COM file by entering @ and the file name. For example,

```
$ @login
```

When you are customizing LOGIN.COM or another command file, it is helpful to execute the file each time you change it.

7.1.3   Creating a Simple Command Procedure

One guideline for when to write a command procedure is that whenever you find it necessary to type two or more command lines together repeatedly, they can be placed in a command procedure. Suppose you often change from your login directory up to the next directory and then change back to your login directory. Following the steps in Experiment 7.1, you can write command procedures to automate these changes of directories.

Experiment 7.1   *Creating a Command Procedure to Automate Directory Changing*

1. Use the SHOW DEFAULT command immediately after you log in to determine the name of your login directory:

```
$ show default
PACK2:[YOURGROUP.YOU]
```

2. Use EVE, EDT, or the DCL CREATE command to write the following command procedure. Name the command procedure file CDUP.COM and use the SET DEFAULT[-] command to move up one directory level:

```
$ ! cdup.com
$ !
$ ! action: change directories one level up from the current
$ ! directory and execute show default command.
$ !
$ set default [-]
$ show default
$ exit
```

3. Use EVE, EDT, or the DCL CREATE command to write the following command procedure, GOHOME.COM, which changes back to the login directory. Be sure to enter your disk and login directory in place of PACK2:[YOURGROUP.YOU]:

```
$ ! gohome.com
$ !
$ ! action: change back to login directory and display name
$ !
$ set default PACK2:[YOURGROUP.YOU]
$ show default
$ exit
```

4. Starting in your login directory, move up one directory level by executing CDUP.COM:

```
$ @cdup
PACK2:[YOURGROUP]
```

5. Now change back to your login directory by executing GOHOME.COM. Because GOHOME.COM resides in your login directory, which no longer is the current directory, you must give the file specification for GOHOME.COM when you execute it. Otherwise, OpenVMS will not be able to find and execute the command procedure.

```
$ @pack2:[yourgroup.you]gohome
PACK2:[YOURGROUP.YOU]
```

7.2   Using Logical Names in Command Procedures

Using logical names instead of complete file specifications with command procedures can save you time and keystrokes. For example, in Experiment 7.1, you had to specify the complete file specification for the GOHOME.COM procedure because the file did not reside in the current directory. If you define a logical name for that file specification, you can invoke that command procedure from any directory by entering @ and the logical name. For instance, you could define the logical name GOHOME for the file GOHOME.COM by typing

```
$ define gohome pack2:[yourgroup.you]gohome
```

Then, to execute the GOHOME.COM procedure, you use the logical name, which by your definition includes the entire file specification. You would type

```
$ @gohome
```

The choice of a logical name that is the same as the file name for the command procedure is optional. You can choose any logical name for a command procedure. Try using logical names for both the CDUP.COM and GOHOME.COM files. Follow the steps in Experiment 7.2.

Experiment 7.2 *Using Logical Names with Command Procedures*

1. Your login directory should be the current directory. Define logical names for CDUP.COM and GOHOME.COM, giving their full file specifications:

```
$ define cdup pack2:[yourgroup.you]cdup.com
$ define gohome pack2:[yourgroup.you]gohome.com
```

2. Move up one directory level using the logical name to execute CDUP.COM:

```
$ @cdup
PACK2:[YOURGROUP]
```

3. Change back to your login directory using the logical name to execute GOHOME.COM:

```
$ @gohome
PACK2:[YOURGROUP.YOU]
```

The use of logical names simplifies the use of command procedures. However, the lifespan of a logical name is limited to the time when you are logged into your system. When you log in the next time, you will have to redefine the logical names you want to use. Solve this problem by adding the definition of a logical name to your LOGIN.COM file. This automates the creation of the logical names you need. It is good practice to develop a logical names section of your LOGIN.COM file. Follow Experiment 7.3 to see how to do this.

Experiment 7.3 *Defining Logical Names in LOGIN.COM*

1. Use EVE or EDT to edit your LOGIN.COM file so that it looks like the following. Remember to enter your disk and login directory in place of PACK2:[YOURGROUP.YOU]:

```
$ ! login.com
$ !
$ ! action: commands executed each time you log in
$ !
$ ! logical names section:
$ !
$ define cdup PACK2:[YOURGROUP.YOU]cdup.com
$ define gohome PACK2:[YOURGROUP.YOU]gohome.com
$ !
$ ! welcoming actions:
$ !
$ write sys$output "         Hello, Pat!"
$ show users
$ show quota
$ exit
```

2. Because you have changed your LOGIN.COM file, execute it to test the changes:

```
$ @login
```

3. Now use the logical names to move up a directory level and then back to the login director:

```
$ @cdup
PACK2:[YOURGROUP]
$ @gohome
PACK2:[YOURGROUP.YOU]
```

7.3   Introduction to Symbols

A symbol is a name used to represent a character string, integer value, or logical value. When you use a symbol, DCL substitutes the symbol for its value before executing the command line.

You can equate a symbol to a command string and then use the symbol as a synonym for the command. Symbols can represent data in commands and command procedures or as shortcuts for commands themselves. You should be careful, however, not to create a symbol using a name that already is a DCL command.

You can create two types of symbols, local and global. A local symbol is available to the current command level that defined it and command procedures executed from the current command level. A global symbol is accessible at all command levels. Both local and global symbols remain defined until you exit the command level at which they were defined.

Local symbols typically appear inside command procedures for a variety of reasons shown later in this chapter. Global symbols often are used to represent command lines, too.

A symbol name can be from 1 to 255 characters long and it must begin with a letter, an underscore (_), or a dollar sign ($). In a symbol name, lowercase and uppercase letters are treated as uppercase letters, so it does not matter what case you use when defining or using them. Symbol values that are character strings should be enclosed in quotation marks (" "). Numeric values need not be enclosed in quotation marks.

To create a symbol, use the assignment statement (= or ==) or the string assignment (:= or :==). To continue a character string over two lines in a string assignment, use a hyphen (-). Local symbols are created using a single equal sign, and global symbols using two equal signs. Table 7.1 provides examples of creating a local and a global symbol.

Table 7.1 *Local and Global Symbols*

Symbol Type	Meaning	Operator	Example
Global	Accessible at all command levels	==	`dirs=="directory/since"`
Local	Accessible only at the command level at which it is defined and lower levels	=	`history="recall/all"`

7.3.1   Working with Symbols

In addition to creating symbols, you can use the SHOW SYMBOL command to see symbols' values. To see the value of a specific symbol, specify the symbol name. For example, to see the value of the symbol HISTORY, type

```
$ show symbol history
HISTORY = "recall/all"
```

To see the values of all local symbols, you can use the /ALL qualifier. For example,

```
$ show symbol/all
HISTORY = "recall/all"
ADDRESS = "type PACK2:[YOURGROUP.YOU]address.dat"
```

To see all global symbols, use the /GLOBAL qualifier and the /ALL qualifier. For example,

```
$ show symbol/global/all
DIRS == "directory/since"
USERS == "show users"
$RESTART == "False"
$SEVERITY == "1"
$STATUS == "%X0000001"
```

$RESTART, $SEVERITY, and $STATUS are reserved global symbols that DCL maintains.

   If you want to delete a symbol, use the DELETE command with the /SYMBOL qualifier and specify the symbol name. (If the symbol is a global symbol, you also must use the /GLOBAL qualifier.) For example, to delete the local symbol ADDRESS, you would type

```
$ delete/symbol address
```

If ADDRESS were a global symbol, you would delete it by typing

```
$ delete/global/symbol address
```

You can try creating a symbol by following Experiment 7.4, which creates a symbol to represent a command line. The DIRECTORY/SINCE/DATE command line produces a directory of all files created on the current day (/SINCE) and includes each file's creation date in the listing (/DATE).

Experiment 7.4 *Working with Symbols*

1. Create a global symbol for the DIRECTORY/SINCE/DATE command line.

```
$ dirnow=="directory/since/date"
$
```

2. Use the SHOW SYMBOL command to see the value of DIRNOW. Because it is a global symbol, you should use the /GLOBAL qualifier; otherwise, DCL would look for a local symbol:

```
$ show symbol/global dirnow
DIRNOW == "directory/since/date"
```

3. Use the symbol to get a directory listing of the files created today:

```
$ dirnow
Directory PACK2:[YOURGROUP.YOU]
$CDUP.COM;1              25-SEP-1997 10:00:30.10
GOHOME.COM;1            25-SEP-1997 10:20:22.34
LOGIN.COM;1             25-JAN-1997 11:14:48.12
Total of 3 files.
$
```

7.3.2 Abbreviating Symbols

You can include an asterisk (*) abbreviation marker when you define a symbol so that you can abbreviate the symbol name when you use it. Any characters to the right of the asterisk appearing in the symbol may be omitted when you enter the symbol. For example, you can create the following useful global symbol:

```
$ h*istory=="recall/all"
```

Then you can execute the command by entering any of the following for the symbol name:

```
h
hi
his
hist
histo
histor
history
```

7.3.3 Using Symbols with Command Procedures

Symbols can play a role in simplifying the entry of command lines. For example, you can create a global symbol whose value is the command line @CDUP, which executes the CDUP.COM procedure, by typing

```
$ cd=="@cdup"
```

Try creating symbols for the execution of both CDUP.COM and GOHOME.COM by following the steps of Experiment 7.5. Remember that you have already defined logical names for these files and so can use them in the command lines.

Experiment 7.5 *Using Symbols to Execute Command Procedures*

1. Create global symbols for the command lines that execute
CDUP.COM and GOHOME.COM (created in Section 7.1.2). Use
the logical names defined for each file:

```
$ cd=="@cdup"
$ go=="@gohome"
```

2. Now execute the procedures by simply entering the appropriate global
symbol. First execute CDUP.COM to move up one directory and then
execute GOHOME.COM to return to your login directory:

```
$ cd
PACK2:[YOURGROUP]
$ go
PACK2:[YOURGROUP.YOU]
```

Like logical names, global symbols remain defined until you log out. However, you can add the creation of symbols to your LOGIN.COM file, so that
every time you log in, the symbols will be available. Follow Experiment 7.6 to
add a symbol section to your LOGIN.COM file.

Experiment 7.6 *Defining Symbols in LOGIN.COM*

1. Use EVE or EDT to edit your LOGIN.COM file so that it looks like
the following (remember to enter your disk and login directory in place
of PACK2: [YOURGROUP.YOU]):

```
$ ! login.com
$ !
$ ! action: commands executed each time you log in
$ !
$ ! logical names section:
$ !
$ define cdup PACK2:[YOURGROUP.YOU]]cdup.com
$ define gohome PACK2:[YOURGROUP.YOU]gohome.com
$ !
$ ! global symbols section:
$ !
$ cd=="@cdup"
$ go=="@gohome"
$ h*istory=="recall/all"
$ !
$ ! welcoming actions:
$ !
$ write sys$output "        Hello, Pat!"
$ show users
$ show quota
$ exit
```

2. Because you have changed your LOGIN.COM file, execute it to test the changes:

```
$ @login
```

3. Try using the symbol HISTORY to execute the RECALL/ALL command, which recalls the previous command lines you entered:

```
$ h
  1 @login
  2 edit/edit login.com
  .
  .
  .
$
```

7.4   Using Lexical Functions

Lexical functions are built-in OpenVMS routines that return information about character strings and attributes of the current process. For example, the lexical function F$TIME() returns the current date and time.

The results of a lexical function are returned to the point at which the lexical function is used. This allows you to assign the results of the lexical function to a symbol, which you then can use in a command or command procedure. Assign a lexical function to a symbol as you would assign any symbol: Enter the symbol, the equals operator (=), and the lexical function name. For example,

```
$ now=f$time()
```

Lexical functions have the following syntax:

f$lexical-function-name(argument[,...])

The name of a lexical function always begins with F$. After the lexical function name, specify arguments enclosed in parentheses and separated by commas. Some arguments are required and others are optional; the number and type of arguments varies from lexical function to lexical function. For instance, F$LENGTH, which returns the length of a character string, requires one argument:

f$length(*string*)

F$TIME() has no required or optional arguments. If no arguments are required, you must enter an empty set of parentheses after the lexical function name.

You can view a complete list of lexical functions using the Help utility by typing HELP LEXICALS. Experiment 7.7 explores the use of F$LENGTH.

Experiment 7.7   *Using the F$LENGTH Lexical Function*

1. First set up a string variable by typing the following:

```
$ greeting="Hello, world!"
```

2. Store the length of this string in the symbol LEN, which gets its value from the F$LENGTH function:

```
$ len=f$length(greeting)
```

3. Now you can inspect the value of the symbol using the SHOW SYMBOL command.

```
$ show symbol len
LEN = 13    HEX = 0000000D  OCTAL = 00000000015
```

7.5   File-Handling Commands for Command Procedures

Within command procedures, it often is necessary to read and write data from and to files. To do this, use the OPEN, READ, WRITE, and CLOSE commands. Although these DCL commands normally are used only within command procedures, you can explore how they function by working with them at the DCL prompt, outside of a command procedure.

7.5.1   Opening and Closing a File

The OPEN or OPEN/READ command opens a file for reading or writing. You can use the OPEN command to open either an existing file or a new file. Because /READ is the default qualifier for the OPEN command, OPEN and OPEN/READ yield the same results.

When this command opens a file, it assigns a logical name to the opened file and places the name in the process logical name table. The syntax for the OPEN command is

```
open[/read] logical-name filespec
```

For example, each of the following command lines opens OPENVMSBKS. DAT and prepares it for reading:

```
$ open ourfile openvmsbks
```

or

$ **open/read ourfile openvmsbks**

In each case, the OPEN command sets up a pointer to the first line of the file.

If you do not specify a file type in the file specification, the system will use type .DAT as the default type. For example, to open the file OPENVMS-BKS.DAT, using the logical name OURFILE, you would type

$ **open ourfile openvmsbks**

To open a file that is not type .DAT, you must include the type. For example, to open the file AI.TXT, you would type

$ **open aifile ai.txt**

Once opened, the file is referred to by its logical name.

When you finish working with an opened file, use the CLOSE command to close the file. The CLOSE command deassigns the logical name assigned to the opened file. The syntax for the CLOSE command is

close *logical-name*

7.5.2   Reading an Open File

The READ command is used to read from an opened file. To open a file for reading with OPEN or OPEN/READ, you must specify an existing file.

The READ command assigns the contents of a file record to a symbol. A file record is a collection of related items, such as the characters in a line of text. The READ command has the following syntax:

read *logical-name symbol-name*

The logical name is the logical name given the file by the OPEN command. The symbol name is the symbol assigned to the first file record.

Once you have used READ to assign a file record to a symbol, you can use either the WRITE command or the SHOW SYMBOL command to display the value of the symbol. The syntax for these two commands are

write sys$output *symbol-name*
show symbol *symbol-name*

In both cases, OpenVMS will display the file record that the READ command has equated to the symbol.

For example, if you open OPENVMSBKS.DAT with the logical name OURFILE, you can use READ to assign the first record to the symbol THIS-LINE and use WRITE to see the symbol's value:

```
$ read ourfile thisline
$ write sys$output thisline
Goldenberg, R.E. Kenah, L.J. VAX/VMS
```

Alternatively, you can use SHOW SYMBOL to see the symbol's value.

```
$ show symbol thisline
THISLINE = "Goldenberg, R.E. Kenah, L.J. VAX/VMS"
```

After each READ operation, the file pointer set up by the OPEN command moves to the beginning of the next file record. Thus, you can issue the READ command again, assigning the second file record to the symbol, and then view the symbol's new value. In this way, you can read all the records in the file. If you try to read past the end of the file, you get an end-of-file error message. To explore using the OPEN, READ, and CLOSE commands, follow the steps in Experiment 7.8.

Experiment 7.8   *Opening and Reading a File*

1. Use EVE, EDT, or the DCL CREATE command to create a file containing the following text. Name the file QUOTE1.TXT:

```
concurrency control is the activity of coordinating accesses to a
database in a multi-user database management. Concurrency control
permits users to access a database in a multiprogrammed fashion
while preserving the illusion that each user is executing alone on
a dedicated system (Bernstein, P.A., Goodman, N.,
"Concurrency Control in Distributed Database Systems,"
ACM Computing Surveys 13 (1981):185-221.)
```

2. Open QUOTE1.TXT for reading, specifying the logical name MYFILE:

```
$ open myfile quote1.txt
```

3. Use the READ command to assign the file's first record to the symbol THISLINE:

```
$ read myfile thisline
```

4. Use the WRITE command to display the value of the THISLINE symbol:

```
$ write sys$output thisline
concurrency control is the activity of coordinating accesses to a
$
```

5. Read the next two records of the file, assigning them to the THISLINE symbol and displaying the symbol's value:

```
$ read myfile thisline
$ write sys$output thisline
database in a multi-user database management. Concurrency
control
$ read myfile thisline
$ write sys$output thisline
permits users to access a database in a multiprogrammed
fashion
$
```

6. You are finished reading from the open file, so close it:

```
$ close myfile
```

The CLOSE command closes the file and deassigns the logical name.

7.5.3   Opening a File for Writing

In addition to opening a file for reading, you can open a file for writing. To do this, use the OPEN command with the /WRITE qualifier, which prepares a file for writing. This form of the OPEN command has the following syntax:

```
open/write logical-name filespec
```

If the file specification is for a new file, the OPEN/WRITE command creates and opens a new file. If the file specification is for an existing file, then the command creates and opens a new file with a version number greater than the highest version of the existing file. This new version of the file will not contain the contents of the old version of the file.

For example, to open and create a new file, QUOTES.TXT, you would type

```
$ open/write newfile quotes.txt
```

To open and create a new version of an existing file, QUOTE1.TXT, you would type

```
$ open/write newfile quote1.txt
```

If QUOTE1.TXT;2 is the highest version of QUOTE1.TXT, the new file will be QUOTE1.TXT;3.

The OPEN/WRITE command positions the file pointer at the beginning of the opened file. You can then use the WRITE command to add records to the file. The syntax for the WRITE command is

```
write logical-name expression[,...]
```

The logical name is the logical name of the file given by the OPEN command. The expression can be a character string, a value returned by a lexical function, or the value of a symbol; or it can be an expression such as $a + b$. You may enter a list of expressions separated by commas. If the expression is a character string, you must enclose it in quotation marks. For example, to write a character string as the first line of an opened file, you could type

```
$ write newfile "Collected Quotes:"
```

To enter a blank line, enter " " as the expression. Explore opening a file for writing by following Experiment 7.9.

Experiment 7.9   *Opening and Writing to a New File*

1. Open a new file named QUOTES.TXT for writing. Use the logical name PEARLS:

```
$ open/write pearls quotes.txt
```

2. Add some lines of text to the QUOTES.TXT file:

```
$ write pearls "Collected Quotes:"
$ write pearls " "
$ write pearls "The requirements for mastering the art"
$ write pearls "of memory are visualizing, a desire to"
$ write pearls "remember, and a love of people. —R. L."
$ write pearls "Montgomery, Memory Made Easy, NY:"
$ write pearls "AMACOM(Amer. Management Assoc.), 1979."
```

3. Close the file:

```
$ close pearls
```

4. Examine the contents of QUOTES.TXT by using the TYPE command:

```
$ type quotes.txt
```

```
The requirements for mastering the art
of memory are visualizing, a desire to
remember, and a love of people. —R.L.
Montgomery, Memory Made Easy, NY:
AMACOM(Amer. Management Assoc.), 1979.
```

7.5.4   Opening and Appending to a File

If you want to add to an existing version of a file, you can use the OPEN command with the /APPEND qualifier. The OPEN/APPEND command opens an existing file for writing and positions the file pointer at the end of the file. Any records you add using the WRITE command are appended to the end of the file. The /APPEND and /WRITE qualifiers for the OPEN command are mutually exclusive.

This form of the OPEN command has the following syntax:

open/append *logical-name filespec*

Try using the /APPEND qualifier to add to the QUOTES.TXT file. Follow the steps in Experiment 7.10.

Experiment 7.10 *Appending to an Existing File*

1. Open the QUOTES.TXT file using the /APPEND qualifier:

   ```
   $ open/append pearls quotes.txt
   ```

2. The file pointer is at the end of the file. Append three records to the file:

   ```
   $ write pearls " "
   $ write pearls "Time flies like an arrow."
   $ write pearls "—Anonymous"
   ```

3. Close the file and then examine its contents by using the TYPE command:

   ```
   $ close pearls
   $ type quotes.txt

   The requirements for mastering the art
   of memory are visualizing, a desire to
   remember, and a love of people. —R.L.
   Montgomery, Memory Made Easy, NY:
   AMACOM(Amer. Management Assoc.), 1979.

   Time flies like an arrow.
   —Anonymous
   ```

7.5.5 Using File-Handling Commands in a Command Procedure

Now that you are familiar with the file-handling commands OPEN, READ, WRITE, and CLOSE, you can try using them in a command procedure. In Experiment 7.11, you create a command procedure, DTODAY.COM, that creates a file containing the current date and a list of the files created today.

Experiment 7.11 *Using File-Handling Commands in a Command Procedure*

1. Use EVE, EDT, or the DCL CREATE command to write the following command procedure. Call the command procedure file DTODAY. COM. Remember to begin each line with a dollar sign, $:

   ```
   $ ! dtoday.com
   $ !
   ```

```
$ ! assign f$time() to a symbol
$ !
$ now = f$time()
$ !
$ ! open a new file for writing
$ ! and write current time and a heading
$ !
$ open/write infile dir.dat
$ write infile now
$ write infile " "
$ write infile "Files created today:"
$ close infile
$ !
$ ! open dir.dat and append the list
$ ! of new files created today
$ !
$ open/append infile dir.dat
$ directory/since/output = infile
$ close infile
$ exit
```

2. Execute DTODAY.COM. Then examine the file it created, DIR.DAT, using the TYPE command:

```
$ @dtoday
$ type dir.dat
25-SEP-1997 17:05:57.81

Files created today:
Directory PACK2:[YOURGROUP.YOU]
CDUP.COM;1  DIR.DAT;1  DTODAY.COM;1  GOHOME.COM;1
 .
 .
 .
Total of 8 files.
$
```

3. Each time you execute DTODAY.COM a new version of DIR.DAT is created with a new time stamp and a new list of files. Execute DTODAY.COM again:

```
$ @dtoday
```

7.6 Passing Data with Parameters

Command procedures often require that the user provide data to be processed by the procedure. If the data are the same each time the procedure executes, you can include the data in the command procedure in a data line that follows the command requiring the data. A data line does not begin with $. If the data are different each time the procedure executes, you can use one of several mechanisms to specify them. One such mechanism lets you pass the data as one or more parameter values.

Eight local symbols, P1 through P8, called *parameters,* are reserved and available for use with command procedures. When you invoke a command procedure, you can pass it up to eight parameters, which automatically will be equated to the symbols P1 through P8.

Specify parameters on the command line that invokes the command procedure, separating the parameters with one or more spaces or tabs. A parameter can be a character string, integer, or symbol. For example, you might have a command procedure that adds the parameter values and returns the sum. To execute the procedure, you would type

```
$ @add 13 10 37 8
```

You could add up to eight parameters in this example.

If the parameter is a character string that contains spaces, you must enclose the string in quotation marks. Otherwise, each word will be treated as a separate parameter. For example, to execute a command procedure that requires a name as a parameter, you could type

```
$ @name "Fred Bennett"
```

The entire string would be assigned to P1. If you entered

```
$ @name Fred Bennett
```

Fred would be assigned to P1, and Bennett would be assigned to P2. Open-VMS assigns the parameters to the parameter symbols sequentially. If you want to skip a parameter symbol, you must enter a null string, (" "), for that parameter. For example,

```
$ @data "Fred Bennett"   ""    "East St"
          (P1)          (P2)   (P3)
```

Experiment 7.12 explores features of using parameters and shows you a method for displaying parameter values.

Experiment 7.12 *Displaying Parameter Values*

1. Use EDT, EVE, or the DCL CREATE command to create the following command procedure. Call the command procedure file SHOWME.COM:

```
$ !  showme.com
$ !
$ !  action: display values of local symbols P1–P8
```

```
$ !
$ show symbol/local/all
$ exit
```

2. Execute the SHOWME.COM procedure using two parameters:

```
$ @showme Wolfgang Mozart
P1 = "WOLFGANG"
P2 = "MOZART"
P3 = " "
P4 = " "
P5 = " "
P6 = " "
P7 = " "
P8 = " "
```

In this sample run of SHOWME.COM, local parameters P3 through P8 have null values, which are indicated by the empty pairs of quotation marks.

3. Execute SHOWME.COM again, but this time specify that the name be treated as a single parameter by enclosing it in quotation marks:

```
$ @showme "Wolfgang Mozart"
P1 = "Wolfgang Mozart"
P2 = " "
P3 = " "
P4 = " "
P5 = " "
P6 = " "
P7 = " "
P8 = " "
```

Now the local parameter P1 has been assigned the string *Wolfgang Mozart*.

4. Now try running SHOWME.COM without any parameters:

```
$ @showme
P1 = " "
P2 = " "
P3 = " "
P4 = " "
P5 = " "
P6 = " "
P7 = " "
P8 = " "
```

This time each of the local symbols P1 through P8 has a null value.

If you attempt to enter more than eight parameters, OpenVMS will give you the following error message:

```
$ @showme a b c d e f g h i
%DCL-W-DEFOVE too many command procedure parameters-limit to
eight.
$
```

You can pass the value of a symbol by enclosing the symbol in apostrophes ('). For example,

```
$ dowjones = "1936"
$ @showme 'dowjones'
P1 = "1936"
P2 = ""
P3 = ""
P4 = ""
P5 = ""
P6 = ""
P7 = ""
P8 = ""
```

The apostrophes request symbol substitution. In other words, *dowjones* requests that the value of *1936* be substituted when this parameter is passed to SHOWME.COM. You could verify this by leaving out the apostrophes:

```
$ dowjones = "1936"
$ @showme dowjones
P1 = "dowjones"
P2 = ""
P3 = ""
P4 = ""
P5 = ""
P6 = ""
P7 = ""
P8 = ""
```

To request symbol substitution for a symbol within a character string, put two apostrophes before it and one apostrophe after it. For example,

```
$ samplesymbol= "The requirements for mastering the art"
$ write sys$output "Memory: ''samplesymbol'"
Memory: The requirements for mastering the art
```

7.7   Passing Data with the INQUIRE Command

When you use parameters to pass data to a command procedure, you must know what parameters the procedure requires. The procedure does not prompt you for them.

The INQUIRE command can be used in a command procedure to prompt for an input value during the execution of a procedure. This command has the following syntax:

inquire *symbol-name[prompt-string]*

The symbol name is the symbol that will be equated to the data you enter. The prompt string is the prompt that displays on the screen, telling you what data are required. For example, to prompt for the count value, you would type

```
$ inquire count "count"
count: 2010
```

To see the value of the count symbol, you could then type

```
$ show symbol count
COUNT = "2010"
```

Notice that DCL automatically appends a colon and a space to the prompt string. You can prevent this by using the INQUIRE command with the /NOPUNCTUATION qualifier. For example,

```
$ inquire/nopunctuation count "count?"
count? 2011
```

7.8   Concatenating Strings

The + operator makes it possible to concatenate, or glue together, strings. You might concatenate strings when you assign a symbol value. Concatenation of two strings has the following syntax:

symbol=firststring+secondstring

For example,

```
$ here="Wobegon, Minnesota"
$ write sys$output "Lake "+here
Lake Wobegon, Minnesota
```

One practical application of string concatenation can be seen in Experiment 7.13. The command procedure in this experiment simplifies specifying files for the PURGE and DELETE commands. It copies the specified files and deletes the original files. You can use it to move files to another directory.

Experiment 7.13   *Concatenating Strings in a Command Procedure*

1. Use EDT, EVE, or the DCL CREATE command to create the following command procedure. Call the command procedure file *MV.COM:*

```
$ ! mv.com
$ !
$ ! action: copy specified files and delete originals
```

```
$ ! (perform equivalent of UNIX mv command)
$ !
$ wildcard = p1 + ";*"
$ copy/log 'p1' 'p2'
$ delete/confirm 'wildcard'
$ exit
```

This procedure requires two parameters. The first parameter, P1, is the file specification for the file or files you want copied. The second parameter, P2, is the directory to which the files should be copied. The wildcard symbol is assigned to the value of the first parameter, the file specification, concatenated with the specification for all versions of the file. Therefore, the DELETE command will delete all versions of the specified files.

2. Before trying out the command procedure, create a subdirectory called QUOTES:

```
$ create/directory [.quotes]
```

3. Use the GOHOME command procedure to move back to your login directory:

```
$ @gohome
```

4. Now use the MV.COM procedure to move QUOTE1.TXT and QUOTES.TXT to the new subdirectory:

```
$ @mv quote*.txt [.quotes]
%COPY-S-COPIED, PACK2:[YOURGROUP.YOU]QUOTE1.TXT;1 copied to
PACK2:[YOURGROUP.YOU.QUOTES]QUOTE1.TXT;1 (1 block)
%COPY-S-COPIED, PACK2:[YOURGROUP.YOU]QUOTES.TXT;1 copied to
PACK2:[YOURGROUP.YOU.QUOTES]QUOTES.TXT;1 (1 block)
%COPY-S-NEWFILES, 2 files created
DELETE PACK2:[YOURGROUP.YOU]QUOTE1.TXT;1? [N]
```

5. Because of the /CONFIRM qualifier used with the DELETE command, you must confirm whether the files should be deleted from their original location. Confirm the deletions:

```
DELETE PACK2:[YOURGROUP.YOU]QUOTE1.TXT;1? [N] yes
DELETE PACK2:[YOURGROUP.YOU]QUOTES.TXT;1? [N] yes
$
```

6. Get a directory listing of the files in the QUOTES directory:

```
$ directory [.quotes]

Directory PACK2:[YOURGROUP.YOU.QUOTES]

QUOTE1.TXT;1    QUOTES.TXT;1

Total of 2 files.
$
```

7.9   Conditional Execution of Command Procedures

The IF command makes possible conditional execution inside a command procedure. The IF command tests the value of a condition and causes a DCL command to be executed when the condition is true. This command has the following syntax:

if *condition* **then** *command*

The condition used in an IF command line can be one or more numeric constants, string literal, symbols, or lexical functions separated by logical, arithmetic, or string operators. DCL has a rich selection of logical operators that can be used to form expressions. These operators are given in Table 7.2.

The IF command has many applications. For example, Experiment 7.14 creates one command procedure that combines the operations of CDUP.COM and GOHOME.COM.

Experiment 7.14   *Using the IF Command in a Command Procedure*

1. Use EDT, EVE, or the DCL CREATE command to create the following command procedure. Call the command procedure file CD.COM:

```
$ ! cd.com
$ !
$ ! action: change to directory one level below or
$ ! one level up from the current directory
$ !
$ if p1 .eqs. "" then set default [-]
$ if p1 .nes. "" then set default [.'p1']
$ show default
$ exit
```

This procedure references one parameter, the specification for your login directory. If you do not specify a directory, P1 will be null and the procedure will move up one directory level. If you specify a directory one level down, P1 will not equal null, and the procedure will move down to that directory.

2. Before trying the command procedure, simplify the use of CD.COM by creating a global symbol in your LOGIN.COM file. Add the following line to the global symbols section of LOGIN.COM. If LOGIN.COM already has this symbol defined, edit the line as follows:

```
$ cd=="@cd"
```

3. Re-execute LOGIN.COM:

```
$ @login
```

Table 7.2 *String and Numeric Operators*

Operator	Description	Example
.EQS.	Tests if two character strings are equal	`if p1 .eqs. "y" then` `recall/all`
.GES.	Tests if the first string is greater than or equal to the second string	`if p1 .ges. " " then` `recall/all`
.GTS.	Tests if the first string is greater than the second	`if p1 .gts. " " then gohome`
.LES.	Tests if the first string is less than or equal to the second string	`if p1 .les. "aha" then` `directory`
.LTS.	Tests if the first string is less than the second string	`if p1 .lts. "yes" then` `recall 1`
.NES.	Tests if two strings are not equal	`if p1 .nes. "no" then` `directory`
.EQ.	Tests if two integer expressions are equal	`if n .eq. 1 then recall/all`
.GE.	Tests if the first integer expression is greater than or equal to the second integer expression	`if n .ge. 0 then exit`
.GT.	Tests if the first integer expression is greater than the second integer expression	`if n .gt. 50 then exit`
.LE.	Tests if the first integer expression is less than or equal to the second integer expression	`if n .le. 9 then directory`
.LT.	Tests if the first integer expression is less than the second integer expression	`if n .lt. 1 then exit`
.NE.	Tests if two integer expressions are not equal	`if n .ne. 0 then recall/all`
.AND.	Combines two expressions with a logical AND	`if (p1 .eqs. "y") .and. (p2` `.nes. "n") then directory`
.OR.	Combines two expressions with a logical OR	`if (p1 .ges. "n") .or. (p2` `.nes. "y") then recall/all`
.NOT.	Logically negates an expression	`x = 1 if .not. ´ then` `recall/all`

4. Now use the procedure to move up one directory level:

```
$ cd
PACK2:[YOURGROUP]
```

5. Use the procedure to move down one directory level. Enter *cd* and a subdirectory name without the brackets or period:

```
$ cd you
PACK2:[YOURGROUP.YOU]
```

7.10   Branching with the GOTO Command

The GOTO command causes a branch to a labeled location, transferring execution of the command procedure to the commands in that location. You can use GOTO to go around a segment of commands based on a condition tested with the IF command. The syntax for the GOTO command is

goto *label*

A label is a name assigned to a command or group of commands in the procedure. The label appears before the command or commands and always has a colon (:) suffix. The GOTO command transfers execution to those commands.

7.11   Arithmetic Operators

If you need to manipulate numbers within command procedures, you can use arithmetic operators to do so. For instance, you may need to add parameter values or divide the first parameter by the second. Table 7.3 lists the arithmetic operators.

Examine the following command procedure to see how the arithmetic operators are used in this example of computing averages. As you examine the example, notice also the use of the IF and GOTO commands:

Table 7.3 *Arithmetic Operators*

Operator	Result	Example
*	Multiplies two numbers	count=count*2
/	Divides two numbers	tally=count/4
+	Adds two numbers	sum=sum+1
–	Subtracts two numbers	diff=sum–1

```
$ ! av.com
$ !
$ ! action: compute arithmetic average
$ !
$ count = 1
$ sum = 0
$ while:
$ inquire term "term (enter positive integer, or 0 to stop)"
$ if term .eq. 0 then goto doorway
$ sum = sum + term
$ count = count + 1
$ goto while
$ doorway:
$ result = sum / count
$ write sys$output "count sum average"
$ write sys$output count, " ", sum, " ", result
$ exit
```

In this procedure, as long as you enter a nonzero value in response to the prompt *term (enter positive integer, or 0 to stop)*, a new value of SUM and COUNT will be computed and control will be transferred back to the WHILE label. If you enter a zero, control transfers to the line of this procedure labeled DOORWAY. This procedure has lots of variations that you might want to try.

7.12   Debugging Techniques

If a command procedure does not execute as you expected, you need to discover where in the procedure the error occurred. DCL offers a variety of tools that can be used in debugging a faulty command procedure. Table 7.4 lists a selection of these tools.

The SET VERIFY command is easy to use and helpful in tracing what happens during the execution of a command procedure. SET VERIFY displays each line of the procedure before it is executed so that you can see the

Table 7.4 *Debugging Tools*

Command	Result
SET VERIFY	Traces the execution of commands in the procedure
SET NOVERIFY	Turns off the verify mode
SHOW SYMBOL	Displays the values of local symbols P1 through P8 as well as any other symbols used in the procedure

line that generated the error. This command and its counterpart, SET
NOVERIFY, are used in the following context:

```
$ set verify
$ !
$ ! sequence of commands you want to trace
$ !
$ set noverify
```

For example, you could modify AV.COM, the command procedure that
computes averages, to trace the actions in the While loop of the procedure
(the changes to the file appear in bold):

```
$ ! av.com
$ ! version 1.1
$ !
$ ! action: compute arithmetic average
$ !
$ count = 1
$ sum = 0
$ set verify
$ while:
$    inquire term "term (enter positive integer, or 0 to stop)"
$    if term .eq. 0 then goto doorway
$    sum = sum + term
$    count = count + 1
$    goto while
$ doorway:
$    set noverify
$    result = sum / count
$    write sys$output "count sum average"
$    write sys$output count, " ", sum, " ", result
$ exit
```

You also could try using the SHOW SYMBOL command to display the symbol values of the symbols involved in the error.

7.13   Responding to Execution Errors

You can use the ON command to branch to an error-handling section of a
command procedure when an error occurs. For example, the following procedure, LEAVE.COM, automates purging and deletion of unneeded files (in
this case, of type .OBJ) when you log out:

```
$ ! leave.com
$ !
$ ! action: purge current directory and delete files of
```

```
$ !         type .obj
$ on error then. goto doorway
$ purge
$ delete/confirm *.obj;*
$ goto clean_exit
$ doorway:
$    write sys$output "Sorry, there are no files or type obj"
$    logout
$ clean_exit:
$    write sys$output "Purged, deleted files of type obj"
$    write sys$output "completed at: "
$    show time
$    logout
$ exit
```

When no files of type .OBJ exist, an error condition occurs. When the error occurs, the procedure displays a message and then logs out. Otherwise, the files are deleted, the procedure displays a message to that effect, and then the procedure logs out.

7.14   Commenting Techniques

In the design of command procedures, you should routinely use some fairly simple commenting techniques to clarify the actions of the procedures. Table 7.5 lists the types of comments.

Preconditions and postconditions are assertions that specify the required input and output for the command procedure. For example, you could change AV.COM so that it contained comments explaining the required parameters and the resulting output (the changes to the file appear in bold):

`$ ! ` **`filename:`** `av.com`

Table 7.5 *Types of Comments*

Type	Example
File specification	! **forever.com**
	! **version 1.0**
Preconditions (required input)	! **pre: p1 = file type**
Postconditions (required output)	! **post: print average value**
Action	! **action: purge specified**
	! **directory**

```
$ ! version 1.2
$ !
$ ! precondition:   0 or more positive integers
$ ! postcondition: (1) number of entries averaged
$ !                (2) sum of entries
$ !                (3) average entry value
$ !
$ ! action: compute arithmetic average
$ !
$ count = 1
$ sum = 0
$ set verify
$ while:
$ inquire term "term (enter positive integer, or 0 to stop)"
$ if term .eq. 0 then goto doorway
$ sum = sum + term
$ count = count + 1
$ goto while
$ doorway:
$ set noverify
$ result = sum / count
$ write sys$output "count sum average"
$ write sys$output count, " ", sum, " ", result
$ exit
```

Summary

Command procedures offer a means of simplifying the daily use of your system. This simplification starts with collecting commonly used groups of command lines that you find yourself having to enter repeatedly. Once you have a command procedure, it is simple to execute it:

$ @*command-procedure-specification*

Chief among the command procedures you will want to maintain and refine is your LOGIN.COM file. This command procedure makes it possible to customize your working environment. Thanks to your LOGIN.COM file, you have a means of tailoring your OpenVMS environment to your individual needs.

It also is helpful to become comfortable with the creation and use of logical names and symbols. With logical names, you can simplify the entry of complex file specifications. With symbols, you can simplify the entry of commands. For example, suppose your name is *Abbot* in the *Music* department. The Music department is listed in the directory ALLDEPTS, which is a directory of all departments. So, you can create the following logical name for your login directory:

```
$ define homeplate pack2:[alldepts.music.abbot]
```

Then, for any command procedure you have in your login directory, you can employ the HOMEPLATE logical name to specify the access path for these procedures. For instance, if you are in your OPENVMS subdirectory and want to list your LOGIN.COM file in your login directory, you would just type

```
$ type homeplate:login.com
```

You can experiment with assigning commonly used command lines to global symbols. For example,

```
$ showlog=="type homeplate:login.com"
```

The use of logical names and global symbols can become the basis for various refinements of your LOGIN.COM file. As a result, you should find that your use of your local system becomes easier and more enjoyable.

Tables 7.6 and 7.7 present the commands and important terms used in this chapter.

Table 7.6 *DCL Commands*

Command	Result
CLOSE	Closes a file
EXIT	Terminates the execution of a command procedure
GOTO	Directs the flow of execution to a label that identifies a block of commands
IF	Tests the value of an expression and executes a given command if the result of the expression is true
INQUIRE	Issues a prompt, reads the user's response from the terminal, and assigns it to a symbol
ON	Specifies an action to be performed if an error occurs
OPEN	Opens a file for reading or writing
READ	Reads a single record from a specified input file and assigns the contents of the record to a specified symbol name
RECALL	Displays previously entered commands so that you can reprocess them

Table 7.6 *DCL Commands (Continued)*

Command	Result
SET NOVERIFY	Inhibits the displaying of command and data lines in a procedure as the system reads the procedure (the default condition)
SET VERIFY	Causes the system to display each command or data line in a procedure as it reads the procedure
WRITE	Writes specified data to the output file indicated by the logical name

Table 7.7 *Important Terms*

Term	Definition
Command level	Equated with the input stream for DCL; it is at level 0 when you log in, and each subsequent execution of a command procedure changes the command level
Command procedure	File of commands
Global	Command language symbol that is accessible at all command levels
Label	Name assigned to a statement or group of statements
Literal	Character string enclosed in quotes or a number
Local	Command language symbol that is accessible only at the current command level and lower levels
Postcondition	Required output for a command procedure
Precondition	Required input for a command procedure
Symbol	Name representing a character string or an integer value

Exercises

1. When is your LOGIN.COM automatically executed?

2. Construct simple, complete command procedures to accomplish the following tasks, and give sample runs for each procedure:
   a. Delete, with confirmation, all your files of type .DAT, and list the remaining files in your current directory.

b. Delete, with confirmation, all your files of type .TXT, and list the remaining files in your current directory.

c. Produce a combination of (a) and (b).

3. One procedure can execute another. Write a command procedure called STEP, which calls a procedure called STEP2, which in turn calls a procedure called STEP3, which in turn calls a procedure called STEP4. Each time one of these procedures is executed, have it print the message *Hello, this is procedure name.*

4. Give an example of a command line that starts with @SHOWME (see Experiment 7.12) and does the following:

a. Has eight parameters, each of which is a pair of words.

b. Has one parameter with eight pairs of words.

c. Has one parameter with *Mozart's* full name.

5. Write a command procedure named GOV.COM that does the following:

a. Uses the local parameter P1 to determine whether to branch to your OPENVMS subdirectory or to any of the following subdirectories:

Subdirectory OPENVMS1 in OPENVMS

Subdirectory OPENVMS2 in OPENVMS

Subdirectory OPENVMS3 in OPENVMS

Subdirectory OPENVMS4 in OPENVMS

For example, if you type @GOV, you will branch to OPENVMS. If you type @GOV 2, you will branch to OPENVMS2 in OPEN-VMS, and so on.

b. Displays the name of the new subdirectory. Show the sample runs that result from typing each of the following:

```
$ @gov
$ @gov 2
$ @gov 1
$ @gov 3
```

6. Enhance the GOV.COM procedure created in Exercise 5 so that it uses P2 to decide whether or not to display a copy of the new subdirectory.

7. Create a logical symbol that makes it possible for you to execute the GOV.COM procedure from Exercise 5 from any of your directories. Show some sample runs.

8. Create a global symbol that makes it possible for you to execute the GOV.COM procedure from Exercise 5 by typing G, GO, or GOV to

change to your OPENVMS subdirectories. With this new symbol, for example, you should be able to change to your OPENVMS1 subdirectory by typing any of the following:

```
$ g 1
$ go 1
$ gov 1
```

Show some sample runs.

9. Incorporate the global symbol from Exercise 8 into your LOGIN.COM file and do the following:
   a. Give a listing of the new version of LOGIN.COM.
   b. Show sample runs to verify that the new version works correctly.

10. Write a command procedure named ERASE.COM that uses the P1 parameter to select all files of type P1 to purge. Show sample runs with the following:
    a. Files of type .OBJ.
    b. Files of type .DAT.

11. Enhance ERASE.COM from Exercise 10 so that it receives confirmation from you before files of type P1 are purged. Show some sample runs.

12. Enhance ERASE.COM so that it purges all the files in your current directory if P1 is null.

13. Create a global symbol that makes it possible to execute ERASE.COM by typing any of the following:

```
$ e parameter
$ er parameter
$ era parameter
$ eras parameter
$ erase parameter
```

Show some sample runs.

14. Incorporate the global symbol from Exercise 13 into your LOGIN.COM file and do the following:
    a. Give a listing of the new version of LOGIN.COM.
    b. Execute LOGIN.COM and then verify that the new global symbol works by doing the following:

    Create empty files AI.SKY;x, for $x = 1, ..., 10$.

    Create empty files BI.RED;x, for $x = 1, ..., 5$.

    Create empty files CI.TNT;x, for $x = 1,2$.

Purge files of type .SKY.

Purge files of type .RED.

Purge files of type .TNT.

15. Enhance ERASE.COM from Exercise 13 so that it uses parameters P1, P2, and P3 in the following ways:
    a. If P1 is null, it purges all files in your current directory and eliminates all but the most recent version of each file.
    b. If P1 is not null, it purges all files of type P1.
    c. If P2 is not null, it purges all files of type P2 as well as files of type P1.
    d. If P3 is not null, it purges all files of type P3 as well as files of types P1 and P2.

    Show sample runs of the new version of ERASE.COM by creating new versions of the files of type .SKY, .RED, and .TNT from Exercise 14.

16. (Debugging) Enhance the ERASE.COM file from Exercise 13 with error-checking command lines so that it does the following:
    a. Prints a *you need 2 parameters* error message and exits if P2 is not null and P1 is null.
    b. Prints a *you need 3 parameters* error message and exits if P3 is not null and either P1 or P2 is null.

    Show some sample runs.

Review Quiz

Indicate whether the following statements are true or false:

1. Any file of type .COM is a command procedure.

2. A command procedure containing only the following line cannot be executed:

   $!

3. A command procedure YES.COM can be executed by typing either *@YES* or *@YES.COM*.

4. A value is assigned to a global symbol with the = operator.

5. Assuming the symbol G*OPHER represents a command line, that command line can be entered by typing *G*.

6. Command procedures always have a minimum of nine local symbols.

7. If command procedure YES.COM is executed by typing *@YES*, then P1 of YES.COM is null when the execution of YES.COM begins.

   The next three statements refer to execution of the command procedure YES.COM using the following command line:

   ```
   $ @yes I think he said "Hello, Sam!" twice
   ```

8. Parameter P7 of YES.COM will be null.

9. Parameter P5 will be *HELLO,*.

10. Every parameter in YES.COM will not be null.

Further Reading

Pike, R., and B. W. Kernighan. "Program Design in the UNIX Environment." *AT&T Bell Laboratories Technical Journal* 63, no. 8, part 2 (October 1984): 1595–1605.

Digital Equipment Corporation, POB CS2008, Nashua, NH 03061:

Printed Documentation	*OpenVMS DCL Dictionary: A–M*
	OpenVMS DCL Dictionary: N–Z
	OpenVMS User's Manual
On-Line Documentation	OpenVMS On-Line Help Facility
	OpenVMS Bookreader
	http://www.openvms.digital.com

Appendix A

Reference Guide to Selected DCL Commands

APPEND   Appends one or more specified input files to the end of a specified output file.

Syntax:

```
append input-filespec[,...] output-filespec
```

Example:

```
$ append tool_box.com login.com
```

ASSIGN   Creates a logical name and assigns an equivalence string or a list of strings to the specified logical name.

Syntax:

```
assign equivalence-name[,...] logical-name[:]
```

Example:

```
$ assign test_data.lst sys$output
```

Command qualifiers:

/GROUP	Places the logical name in the group logical name table. Other users with the same UIC group number can access the logical name.
/PROCESS	Places the logical name in the process logical name table. If a logical name table is not specified with this command, the logical name will be placed in the process logical name table by default.
/USER_MODE	Logical names assigned with user mode are placed in the process logical name table and used during the execution of a single image.

BASIC (compiled)   Activates the DEC BASIC compiler.

Syntax:

```
basic [filespec[,...]]
```

If one or more file specifications are supplied, BASIC will compile the source file(s). If each source file specification is separated by commas, BASIC will compile each module separately and produce multiple object files.

Example:

```
$ basic sample1,sample2
```

If each source file specification is separated by a plus sign (+), BASIC will append the files and produce a single object module.

Example:

```
$ basic sample1+sample2
```

For further information, type the word help after activating the BASIC programming environment.

CLOSE   Closes a file that was opened for input or output with the open command.

Syntax:

```
close logical-name
```

Example:

```
$ close test_file
```

CONTINUE   Resumes execution of a DCL command, a program or a command procedure that was interrupted by pressing Ctrl/Y or Ctrl/C. This command also serves as the target command for an if or on command in a command procedure.

Syntax:

```
continue
```

Example 1:

```
$ run test_program
 Ctrl/y 
$ show users
      OpenVMS User Processes at 15-JAN-1998 19:55:11.84
   Total number of users = 14, number of processes = 24

Username  Interactive  Subprocess   Batch
AMALERICH      1
BPONEILL       1
EKNUTH         1
JDSIPPEL       1
JMUGGLI        2
 .
 .
 .

$ continue      (test_program execution continues)
```

Example: 2

```
$ on error then continue! Command procedure on error statement
```

COPY   Makes a copy of the specified input file(s) and stores the contents in the specified output file.

Syntax:

```
copy input-filespec[,...] output-filespec
```

Example 1:

```
$ copy login_backup.com login.com
```

Example 2:

```
$ copy test_data_3.dat,test_data_2.dat test_data_1.dat
```

CREATE   Creates a new sequential file that contains the typed input or commands entered at the DCL level. The command is terminated and the file closed after Ctrl/Z key press.

Syntax:

```
create filespec[,...]
```

Example:

```
$ create test.dat
13579
24680
12450
Ctrl/z
Exit
$
```

Command qualifier:

/PROTECTION=(*code*)   Defines the protection to be assigned to the file.

CREATE/DIRECTORY   Creates a new directory or subdirectory for cataloging files.

Syntax:

```
create/directory directory-specification[,...]
```

Example:

```
$ create/directory[.basic]
```

Command qualifier:

/PROTECTION=(*code*)   Defines the protection to be applied to the directory.

DEASSIGN   Removes a logical name assignment from the specified logical name table.

Syntax:

deassign `[logical-name[:]]`

Example:

$ **deassign sys$output**

Command qualifiers:

/GROUP	Specifies that the logical name is in the group logical name table.
/PROCESS	Specifies that the logical name is in the process logical name table.
/USER_MODE	Specifies that the logical name is in the process name table.

DEFINE   Creates a logical name and assigns an equivalence string or a list of strings to the specified logical name.

Syntax:

define `logical-name equivalence-string[,...]`

Example:

$ **define sys$output test.dat**

Command qualifiers:

/GROUP	Places the logical name in the group logical name table. Other users with the same UIC group number can access the logical name.
/PROCESS	Places the logical name in the process logical name table. If a logical name table is not specified with this command, the logical name will be placed in the process logical name table by default.
/USER_MODE	Logical names assigned with user mode are placed in the process logical name table and are used during the execution of a single image.

DEFINE/KEY   Assigns a set of attributes and an equivalence string to a specified key on the terminal keyboard.

Syntax:

define/key `key-name equivalence-string`

Example:

$ **define/key PF1 "show users"/terminate**

Command qualifiers:

/[NO]ECHO   Controls whether the equivalence string is displayed on the terminal.

/TERMINATE   Inserts carriage-return/line-feed characters after the specified key press. Similar to pressing Return after typing a command.

DELETE   Deletes one or more files from a user directory.

Syntax:

`delete` *filespec;version-number*[,...]

Example 1:

`$ delete test.dat;1`

Example 2:

`$ delete letter.txt;*`

DELETE/ENTRY   Deletes one or more plant or batch job entries from a specified queue.

Syntax:

`delete/entry`=*entry-number queue-name*[:]

Example:

`$ delete/entry=231 sys$print`

DELETE/KEY   Removes the key definition for a specified terminal key established using the DEFINE/KEY command.

Syntax:

`delete/key` [key-name]

Example:

`$ delete/key PF1`

DIRECTORY   Displays a list of files stored in a specified user directory and its corresponding information. If no file specification is given, information for the current directory will be displayed.

Syntax:

`directory` [*filespec*[,...]]

Example:

`$ directory [.basic]*.bas`

Command qualifiers:

/[NO]DATE   Displays the backup, creation, expiration, and modification dates for each specified file.

_____J Appendix A

/FULL   Displays all relevant information about a specified file.
/PROTECTION   Displays the file protection for the specified file.
/[NO]SIZE   Displays the file size in blocks used for the specified file.
/TOTAL   Suppresses the listing of all file information and only
                displays the trailing lines.

EXIT Terminates the processing of the current command procedure.

Syntax:

```
exit
```

Example:

```
$ show users
$ exit
```

GOTO Transfers control to a specified label statement within a DCL command procedure.

Syntax:

```
goto label
```

Example:

```
$ if p1 .eqs. "stop" then GOTO done
$ show users
$ done:
```

HELP Displays information on a specified topic (for example, DCL commands).

Syntax:

```
help [keyword]
```

Example:

```
$ help copy
```

IF Tests the value of an expression and executes the command following the THEN keyword if the test is true.

Syntax:

```
if test-expression then do-command
```

Example:

```
$ if p1 .neq. "stop" then goto fetch_nxt_num
```

INQUIRE Allows for interactive input from the terminal.

Syntax:

```
inquire symbol-name [prompt-string]
```

Example:

$ **inquire name "Enter your name"**

Command qualifier:

/[NO]PUNCTUATION   Controls whether a colon (:) and a space will be
                     displayed after the prompt message.

LINK   Activates the OpenVMS Linker to link one or more object modules
into a program image.

Syntax:

link *filespec*[,...]

Example:

$ **link random**

LOGOUT   Ends an interactive user session.

Syntax:

logout

Example:

$ **logout**

Command qualifiers:

/BRIEF   Displays the user name, date, and time.
/FULL   Displays a summary of accounting information.
/[NO]HANGUP   Controls whether the phone connected to your terminal
                will be hung up.

MAIL   Activates the OpenVMS Mail utility.

Syntax:

mail [*filespec*] [*recipient-name*]

Example:

$ **mail**

MERGE   Activates the OpenVMS Sort utility to combine from two to ten
similarly sorted files and creates a single output file.

Syntax:

merge *input-filespec-1,input-filespec-2*[,...] *output-filespec*

Example:

$ **merge test_1.dat,test_2.dat final.dat**

ON Defines the default courses of action when a command or program within a command procedure encounters an error condition or is interrupted by a Ctrl/Y.

Syntax:

on `condition` **then** `command`

Example:

`$` **on error then goto exit**

OPEN Opens a file for reading or writing.

Syntax:

open `logical-name[:]` `filespec`

Example:

`$` **open test_data final_1.dat**

PHONE Activates the OpenVMS Phone utility, which allows a user to communicate with other users during an interactive session.

Syntax:

phone `[phone-command]`

Example:

`$` **phone**

PRINT Sends one or more files to a particular print queue.

Syntax:

print `filespec[,...]`

Example:

`$` **print us_history.rpt**

Command qualifiers:

/[NO]NOTIFY	Controls whether a message will be displayed on your terminal once the file has finished printing.
/QUEUE=*queue-name*[:]	Places the file to be printed into a specified print queue.

PURGE Deletes all files located within a specified user directory except the highest numbered version(s).

Syntax:

purge `[filespec[,...]]`

Example:

`$` **purge**

Command qualifier:

/KEEP=*n*   Specifies the number of versions of the specified files to be retained in the directory.

RECALL   Displays up to the last 20 and 254 commands for reprocessing on OpenVMS VAX and OpenVMS Alpha, respectively.

Syntax:

recall [*command-qualifier*]

Example:

$ **recall show**

Command qualifier:

/ALL   Displays all the commands currently stored in the Recall buffer.

RENAME   Allows you to change the file specification of one or more files to a specified output file specification.

Syntax:

rename *input-filespec[,...] output-filespec*

Example:

$ **rename test.dat final.dat**

RUN   Activates a specified program image.

Syntax:

run *filespec*

Example:

$ **run square_roots**

SEARCH   Searches for a specified string or strings in one or more files and lists all lines containing occurrences of the strings.

Syntax:

search *filespec[,...]search-string[,...]*

Example:

$ **search resume.txt OPENVMS**

SET DEFAULT   Changes the default device or directory name for the current process.

Syntax:

set default *device-name[:][filespec]*

Example:

`$ `**`set default [.basic]`**

SET FILE   Modifies file characteristics.

Syntax:

`set file` *`filespec[,...]`*

Example:

`$ `**`set file test.dat`**

Command qualifiers:

/PROTECTION[=(*code*)]   Allows you to change or reset the protection for
one or more files.

/VERSION_LIMIT[=*n*]   Specifies the maximum number of file versions a
file can have.

SET PASSWORD   Allows for a password to be changed by the current user
of an account.

Syntax:

`set password`

Example:

```
$ set password
Old password: (typed characters will not be echoed)
New password: (typed characters will not be echoed)
Verification: (typed characters will not be echoed)
```

SET PROCESS   Changes the characteristics of the specified process. If no
process is specified, changes the characteristics of the current process.

Syntax:

`set process` *`[process-name]`*

Example:

`$ `**`set process`**

Command qualifier:

/NAME=*string*   Changes the name of the current process.

SET PROMPT   Allows the current user to change the default DCL prompt.

Syntax:

`set prompt``[=`*string*`]`

Example:

`$ `**`set prompt="Home>"`**

SET PROTECTION Changes the protection for a specified file or files.

Syntax:

`set protection[=(code)] filespec[,...]`

Example:

`$ set protection=(r:rwed) final.dat`

SET TERMINAL Changes the system's interpretation of the terminal characteristics.

Syntax:

`set terminal [device_name[:]]`

Example:

`$ set terminal/line_editing`

Command qualifiers:

/INSERT	Characters will be inserted when editing command lines.
/[NO]LINE_EDITING	Enables the advanced line-editing features for editing command lines.
/OVERSTRIKE	Characters will be overwritten when editing command lines.

SHOW DEFAULT Displays the current default device and directory names.

Syntax:

`show default`

Example:

`$ show default`

SHOW KEY Displays the key definition for a specified key.

Syntax:

`show key [key-name]`

Example:

`$ show key pf1`

SHOW LOGICAL Displays a logical name and its equivalence string or all logical names in one or more logical name tables.

Syntax:

`show logical [logical-name[:]]`

Example:

```
$ show logical sys$output
```

Command qualifiers:

/ALL   Displays all logical names in the specified logical name table.

/GROUP Displays the logical name in the group logical name table.

/PROCESS Displays the logical name in the process logical name table.

SHOW PROCESS Displays information about a process and any sub-process in the current process tree.

Syntax:

```
show process [process-name]
```

Example:

```
$ show process
```

SHOW PROTECTION Displays the current file protection that is applied to any new files created during the current interactive terminal session or batch job.

Syntax:

```
show protection
```

Example:

```
$ show protection
```

SHOW QUEUE Displays information about a specified print or batch queue.

Syntax:

```
show queue [queue-name]
```

Example:

```
$ show queue sys$print
```

SHOW QUOTA Displays the current disk quota that is authorized to the current user.

Syntax:

```
show quota
```

Example:

```
$ show quota
```

SHOW SYMBOL Displays the current value of a local or global symbol.

Syntax:

```
show symbol [symbol-name]
```

Example:

`$ show symbol my_basic`

Command qualifiers:

/ALL   Displays all symbols in the specified symbol table.
/GLOBAL   Displays only the symbols in the global symbol table.
/LOCAL   Displays only the symbols in the local symbol table.

SHOW SYSTEM   Displays a list of processes in the system and information about the status of each one.

Syntax:

`show system`

Example:

`$ show system`

SHOW TERMINAL   Displays the current terminal characteristics of a specified terminal.

Syntax:

`show terminal [`*device-name*`[:]]`

Example:

`$ show terminal`

SHOW TIME   Displays the current date and time.

Syntax:

`show [day]time`

Example:

`$ show time`

SHOW USERS   Displays information pertaining to the current interactive users.

Syntax:

`show users [`*username*`]`

Example:

`$ show users`

SORT   Activates the OpenVMS Sort utility to reorder the records in a file into a defined sequence and place them in a new file.

Syntax:

`sort `*input-filespec*`[,...] `*output-filespec*

Example:

`$ `**`sort temp.dat final.dat`**

SPAWN   Suspends the current process and creates a new process (sub-process).

Syntax:

spawn [*command-string*]

Example:

`$ `**`spawn phone`**

STOP/QUEUE/ENTRY   Stops the executing job on the specified batch queue.

Syntax:

stop/queue/entry=*entry-number queue-name*[:]

Example:

`$ `**`stop/queue/entry=1234 sys$batch`**

SUBMIT   Submits one or more command procedures to a specified batch job queue.

Syntax:

submit *filespec*

Example:

`$ `**`submit square_roots`**

Further Reading

Digital Equipment Corporation, POB CS2008, Nashua, NH 03061:

Printed Documentation	*OpenVMS DCL Dictionary: A–M*
	OpenVMS DCL Dictionary: N–Z
	OpenVMS User's Manual
On-Line Documentation	OpenVMS On-Line Help Facility
	OpenVMS Bookreader
	http://www.openvms.digital.com

Appendix B
File Protection

OpenVMS provides two file protection mechanisms for all system objects (files, directories, and devices): UIC (user identification code) and ACL (access control list).

B.1 UIC-Based Protection

Every OpenVMS system object has a UIC-based protection mask. You can see your own UIC by typing

```
$ show process
```

OpenVMS uses the UIC to identify users as well as groups of users. Table B.1 lists various forms of UICs. Every UIC has four levels of protection associated with it, as listed in Table B.2. Each protection level can be allowed or denied any of the types of access listed in Table B.3. For example, when you create a subdirectory, you can choose its protection as follows:

```
$ create/directory/protection=(s:rwed,o:rwed,g:re,w)
```

You can change the default UIC protection on your local system by inserting the following command line in your LOGIN.COM file:

```
$ set protection=(s:rwed,o:rwed,g,w)/default
```

Table B.1 *Sample UICs*

UIC	Interpretation
[100,6]	Group 100, member 6 (numeric form)
[MUSIC, MOZART]	Group MUSIC, member MOZART (alphanumeric)
[MOZART]	Group MUSIC, member MOZART is understood (alphanumeric)
[GROUP_100, YOU]	group_100, member you (alphanumeric)

Table B.2   *UIC Levels of Protection*

Level Name	Short Form	Scope
System	S	All system users
Owner	O	User UIC
Group	G	All users in the same group
World	W	All users

Table B.3   *Types of Access for Each UIC Protection Level*

Access Name	Short Form	Scope
Read	R	Allocate privilege to read from a file
Write	W	Allocate writing privilege
Execute	E	Allocate privilege to execute an image
Delete	D	Allocate privilege to delete a file

B.2   Access Control Lists

An access control list is associated with a system object. The SET FILE/ACL command makes it possible to establish an ACL for a system object. This command has the following syntax:

```
set file/acl [=(acl[,...])] filespec[,...]
```

Suppose, for example, you want users with the following UICs to have access to .com files in your OPENVMS.OPENVMS2 subdirectory:

UIC = [GROUP_2006, JSBACH]   (*not in your group*)
UIC = [WAMOZART]   (*in your group*)

Then you would type

```
$ set file/acl=(id=[group_206,jsbach],access=r+w+e+d)-
_$ /log/confirm[.openvms.openvms2]*.com
```

You can display the ACL for an object by typing

```
$ show acl [.openvms.openvms2]catch.com
```

Further Reading

Digital Equipment Corporation, POB CS2008, Nashua, NH 03061:

Printed Documentation   *OpenVMS DCL Dictionary: A–M*

 OpenVMS DCL Dictionary: N–Z

 OpenVMS Guide to System Security

 OpenVMS User's Guide

On-Line Documentation   OpenVMS On-Line Help Facility

 OpenVMS Bookreader

 http://www.openvms.digital.com

Appendix C
EDT Line Mode Commands

You can use line mode editing in EDT on any interactive terminal. This mode focuses on the line as the unit of text. Whenever you see the line mode asterisk prompt (*), you can type a line mode command.

Line mode commands use qualifiers and specifiers in addition to command words. Qualifiers, which modify the way EDT processes the command, always are optional. You must precede a qualifier with a slash (for example, /QUERY).

Specifiers tell EDT on which part of the text to operate. Optional specifiers are enclosed in square brackets (for example, [=*buffer*]). The main specifier is range, which references the line or lines affected by the command.

Table C.1 contains a brief description of the most commonly used line mode commands, along with their corresponding qualifiers and specifiers. The underlined letters in the line mode syntax statements in Table C.1 indicate the minimum allowable abbreviations for command words.

Table C.1 *Line Mode Commands*

Command	Description
CHANGE	Shifts EDT to keypad mode.
CLEAR *buffer*	Deletes the entire contents of the specified EDT buffer (text storage area) from your EDT session.
Ctrl/z	Causes EDT to exit from the keypad mode to the line mode editing. An asterisk prompt (*) will appear at the lower left margin of the terminal screen. To reenter the keypad mode, type C (for CHANGE) and press Return. The cursor will return to its former location in the text.
EXIT [/SAVE][*filespec*]	Ends the EDT editing session, saving a copy of the main buffer text in an external file. If you supply a file specification, EDT creates a file with that name and copies the contents of the main buffer into that file. A new version of an existing file is created only if the file is modified. The /SAVE command line qualifier tells EDT to save the journal file on exiting.
HELP [*topic*[*subtopic...*]]	Displays information on various EDT topics on your terminal. If you supply no topic, help gives information on how to use the EDT Help facility.
INCLUDE *filespec*[=*buffer*]	Copies the specified file into the current EDT session. If give no location specifiers, the copy is placed above the current line. *Buffer* represents the name of an EDT buffer where you want the external file stored. The equal sign (=) must appear before the buffer name.
QUIT[/SAVE]	Ends your EDT session without saving a copy of your editing work. The /SAVE qualifier saves only the journal file, not the edited file.
SET SCREEN *width*	Sets the maximum number of characters that EDT displays on a line of text.
SET WRAP *number*	Determines whether EDT wraps text being inserted in the keypad mode. Also determines the maximum line length for filling text. To remove word wrap, use the SET NOWRAP line mode command. The default is set nowrap.
SHOW BUFFER	Lists all buffers currently in use during your EDT session. Also lists the number lines in each buffer. An equal sign (=) indicates the current buffer. An asterisk (*) next to Main indicates that more lines are in the Main buffer, but EDT has not yet seen them.

Appendix D
Communicating with Remote Computers

An increasingly important aspect of using computers is the capability to communicate over open networks. OpenVMS systems support optional layered networking software products such as TCP/IP (transmission control protocol/internet protocol) that permit users to communicate with other computer systems in open, worldwide networks.

Each computer connected to a TCP/IP network is called a *host*. Each host has a unique name and address (or host name). The local host is the computer you are logged on to, and the remote host is the computer with which you are communicating.

This appendix provides a summary of several TCP/IP applications supported by OpenVMS. Because the command syntax can vary slightly among vendors and be unfamiliar to you, alternative command syntax was developed jointly with the TCP/IP vendors for OpenVMS. Table D.1 lists the commonly used TCP/IP applications and the commands that will be described in this appendix.

D.1   Host Names

Each computer system attached to a TCP/IP network is identified by a unique IP host name as well as a unique IP host address. TCP/IP supplies a mechanism for translating the host name to the appropriate host address.

The IP host name is a component of hierarchically arranged host names, called a *domain name* (somewhat like an address on a letter with location, classification, and country codes). The syntax of a domain name is

`[hostname.subdomain.]location-name.classification-type[.country-code]`

For example, a domain name might be TRUMPET.COMPUTING. SCHOOL.EDU and its corresponding IP address might translate to 103.180.5.5.

Table D.1   *Common TCP/IP Applications*

Operation	Standard Command	OpenVMS DCL Command
Remote terminal service	TELNET	SET HOST/TELNET
	RLOGIN	SET HOST/RLOGIN
Remote file access	FTP> GET	COPY/FTP
	FTP> PUT	
Remote directory listings	FTP> DIR	DIR/FTP

D.2   Remote Terminal Service

OpenVMS, via the TCP/IP application layer, enables you to log in to a remote host using your local terminal as though it were a terminal on the remote host. The two terminal applications available are

▶ TELNET service, which is the RFC standard virtual terminal interface

▶ RLOGIN utility, which is the Berkley standard virtual terminal interface

Both applications perform remote login operations, but in different ways. To access a remote host using one of these applications, you will need an account (user name and password) or, alternatively, use a public account.

D.2.1   Using the TELNET Service

TELNET can be used to establish a connection between your terminal connected to an OpenVMS computer and a remote host. The syntax used to invoke TELNET services is:

```
telnet [domain-name]
```

For example, to connect to a computer whose domain name is TRUMPET. COMPUTING.SCHOOL.EDU, you would type

```
$ telnet trumpet.computing.school.edu
Trying... Connected to TRUMPET.COMPUTING.SCHOOL.EDU
Username:
```

or, in place of the domain name you can use its IP address:

```
$ telnet
TELNET> connect 130.180.5.5
Trying... Connected to TRUMPET.COMPUTING.SCHOOL.EDU
Username:
```

You can end a TELNET session (close the connection) in one of the following ways. Log out at the remote host's system prompt

```
% logout
Connection closed by Foreign Host
TELNET> exit
$
```

or return to the TELNET prompt at the remote host's system prompt and disconnect the session. For example, to return to the local computer, hold down the Ctrl and Shift keys simultaneously and press the caret (^) key (which is shown on the 6 key), release the keys, then press the letter *c*. If successful, the following would be displayed on your terminal screen:

```
TELNET> disconnect
Connection closed
TELNET> exit
```

D.2.2 Using the RLOGIN Utility

RLOGIN is similar to TELNET, except support for the protocol is not as widespread and the protocol automatically authenticates the user instead of requesting both user name and password. The syntax used to invoke the RLOGIN utility is

```
rlogin [domain-name]
```

To connect to the remote host TRUMPET.COMPUTING.SCHOOL.EDU, type in the following command line:

```
$ rlogin trumpet.computing.school.edu
Password:
```

At the password prompt enter your password.

You can end a RLOGIN session (close the connection) in one of the following ways. Log out at the remote host's system prompt

```
% logout
Connection closed
$
```

or type the default escape characters, the tilde (~) followed by a period (.) at the remote host's system prompt

```
$ ~.
Connection closed
$
```

The escape characters will not display on the terminal screen until after the period has been typed.

D.3   Remote File Access with FTP

FTP (file transfer protocol) is a simple way to move files across a TCP/IP network. The ftp command invokes a utility that permits the user to transfer files between local and remote hosts that do not necessarily support the same file systems (for example, between OpenVMS and UNIX hosts).

D.3.1   Starting an FTP Session

Typing either can start an FTP session

```
$ ftp
FTP> wuarchive.wustl.edu
```

or

```
$ ftp wuarchive.wustl.edu
```

Normally, the user executing the ftp command must have a user name and password on the remote host. Some systems (similar to the previous example) use the anonymous FTP service, which accepts a user name of anonymous and no password (anonymous account passwords typically are the users electronic mail address):

```
Connection opened (Assuming 8-bit connections)
<wuarchive.wustl.edu FTP server (Version wu-2.4.2-academ[BETA-15](1)
Tue Oct 14 12:20:29 CDT 1997) ready.
Username: anonymous
```

The remote host will prompt you for a password:

```
<Guest login ok, send your complete e-mail address as password.
Password:
```

D.3.2   Navigating Remote Host Directories

Before transferring files to or from a remote host, it is useful to get a listing of files and directories located on the remote host. To do so, you would type

```
WUARCHIVE.WUSTL.EDU>dir

<Opening ASCII mode data connection for /bin/ls.
total 25
drwxr-xr-x   17 0         0      512 Dec 19 10:59 .
drwxr-xr-x   17 0         0      512 Dec 19 10:59 ..
lrwxrwxrwx    1 0         1        7 Jan 14 21:13 bin -> usr/bin
drwxr-xr-x   10 0         0      512 Feb 29  1996 decus
dr-xr-xr-x    2 0         1      512 Aug  6 10:37 dev
drwxr-xr-x   22 0         0      512 Oct 31  1996 doc
drwxr-xr-x    6 0         0      512 Feb 29  1996 edu
```

```
drwxr-xr-x    3 0        1      512 Nov  8 09:57 etc
drwxr-xr-x    8 0        0      512 Jan 16 18:35 graphics
drwxr-xr-x    7 0      200      512 Jan 16 08:52 info
drwxr-xr-x   12 0        0      512 Jan 15 17:55 languages
drwx------    2 0        0     8192 Jan 13 12:52 lost+found
drwxr-xr-x    6 0        0      512 Jan 15 23:21 multimedia
drwxr-xr-x   23 0        0      512 Jan 15 23:56 packages
drwxr-xr-x    2 0        1      512 Nov 19 18:43 pub
drwxr-xr-x   18 0        0      512 Jan 15 17:51 systems
drwxr-xr-x   17 0      203      512 Jan 15 07:17 usenet
drwxr-xr-x    4 0        1      512 Nov 16 22:26 usr
<Transfer complete.
```

The appearance of the directory listing will depend on the type of system that you are connected to.

To move to a different directory location use the CD command followed by the name of the subdirectory. For example, you might type the following:

```
WUARCHIVE.WUSTL.EDU>cd pub
```

Typing *CD* ... will move you from the then current directory back up one level.

D.3.3 ASCII Files versus Binary Files

Keep in mind when transferring files that different operating systems store text files in different manners. Most important, the character or characters used to denote the end of a line vary. If a file is transferred via ASCII mode, the file you requested would be converted to the appropriate format for the local host you are logged onto. Generally, binary mode should be used for nontext files. When you begin an FTP session the mode can be selected with the commands

```
WUARCHIVE.WUSTL.EDU> binary
```

or

```
WUARCHIVE.WUSTL.EDU> ascii
```

D.3.4 Transferring Files Between Computers

To get a copy of a file from the remote host, use the command

```
WUARCHIVE.WUSTL.EDU> get filename
```

Similarly, to put a copy of a file onto the remote host, use

```
WUARCHIVE.WUSTL.EDU> put filename
```

Sometimes it may be desirable to save a file under a different name. Commands of the form

```
WUARCHIVE.WUSTL.EDU> get old_filename new_filename
WUARCHIVE.WUSTL.EDU> put old_filename new_filename
```

will transfer the file *old_filename,* giving it the name *new_filename.*

You can use wildcard specifications such as *.TXT or README.* to transfer all files matching a certain pattern. However, you must use the MPUT and MPUT commands to do this.

D.3.5 Ending a FTP session

When you have completed transferring files, you can end your FTP session by typing *quit,* as seen in the following example:

```
WUARCHIVE.WUSTL.EDU>quit
Goodbye.
$
```

Further Reading

Digital Equipment Corporation, POB CS2008, Nashua, NH 03061:

Printed Documentation	*OpenVMS DCL Dictionary: A–M*
	OpenVMS DCL Dictionary: N–Z
	TCP/IP Networking on OpenVMS Systems
On-Line Documentation	OpenVMS On-Line Help Facility
	OpenVMS Bookreader
	http://www.openvms.digital.com

Appendix E
Program Development on OpenVMS Systems

OpenVMS provides a common programming environment that permits the development of mixed-language application programs and portable programs, as well as application programs with distributed functions that run in client/server environments.

The software applications that you develop under the OpenVMS operating system involve building and modifying source code modules and compiling, linking, and executing the resulting program images (or executables). The components of an application program typically consist of a main program, shared libraries, functional routines, and a user interface.

The aim of this appendix is to point out the bare essentials needed to compile and run a program written in a programming language such as Pascal.

E.1   Software Development Tools

OpenVMS software tools that can aid you in the development of these applications include

▶ Language compilers, interpreters, and assemblers

▶ Linkers and debuggers

▶ Text processors and other program development utilities

▶ Callable system routines such as run-time routines, system services, and other utility routines

▶ Record management services (RMS) routines and utilities

Table E.1 lists several of the software tools that are available in the OpenVMS environment.

Table E.1 *Development Software Tools*

Type	Tools
Text processors	DEC text processing utility (DECTPU)
	Extensible versatile editor (EVE)
	EDT editor
Programming utilities	Linker
	OpenVMS debugger
Other development utilities	Command definition utility
	Librarian utility
	Message utility
Callable system routines	Run-time library routines
	System services
	Utility routines
	Record management services (RMS) routines and utilities

E.2   Creating Program Source Files

The first step is to create (or modify) a program source file utilizing one of the OpenVMS text-processing utilities such as EVE or EDT. For example, to begin the creation of a Pascal program, SAMPLE.PAS, you might type

```
(*
This is a sample Pascal program to print a message.
*)
program sample (output);
begin
     writeln ('Hello, world!');
end.
Ctrl/z
Exit
$
```

E.3   Generating Files the Computer Can Understand

Next, you need to compile your source file. A compiler is a program that translates a source file into machine-readable form. In a OpenVMS programming environment, a compiler typically produces a machine-readable file with an .obj file type. For example, to compile the sample program SAMPLE. PAS, you would type

```
$ pascal sample
```

If the source file compiled correctly, the directory will have a SAMPLE.OBJ entry.

E.4   Creating an Executable Program

After a program source file is created, it must be compiled or assembled into object modules (.OBJ) by a language processor and then linked. The Open-VMS Linker binds the object modules into an image that can be executed under the OpenVMS operating system.

The linker is a program that does a variety of things needed to prepare an executable version of a program. It resolves references you might have made to internal and external procedures as well as performing various housekeeping tasks needed to install the executable version in physical memory. For example, to use the linker to link the sample program, you would type

```
$ link sample
```

Now a SAMPLE.EXE file is listed in the directory.

E.5   Running the New Program

The last step is to execute the file. For example, to execute the sample program, you would type

```
$ run sample
Hello, world!
```

If you get stuck and you are not sure how to use any of the compilers on your system, enter the HELP command followed by the programming language name. Help about that compiler appears. For example you might type

```
$ help pascal
```

Other language compilers, interpreters, and assemblers supported in the OpenVMS VAX and OpenVMS Alpha programming environments are listed in Table E.2.

Table E.2 *Supported OpenVMS Languages*

Language	Characteristics
DEC Ada	Conforms to ANSI and MIL-STD standards
	Has Ada validation
VAX BASIC	Can be used as a compiler or interpreter
	Supported by OpenVMS debugger
	Full reentrant code
DEC BASIC for OpenVMS Alpha	Optimizing compiler
	Compatible with VAX BASIC
	No interpretive environment
VAX C	Full implementation
	OpenVMS performance enhanced features
DEC C for OpenVMS Alpha	ISO/ANSI-standard compliant
	Supports 64-bit virtual addressing
DEC C++	Class libraries
	Run-time library
	Debug support
	Facilities object-oriented program design
DEC COBOL	ANSI-standard compliant
	Enhancements to screen-handling, file-sharing, report-writing facilities
DEC FORTRAN for OpenVMS VAX	Supports ANSI-standard FORTRAN-77
	Conforms to FIPS standards
	Optimization compiler
DEC FORTRAN for OpenVMS Alpha	Supports standard FORTRAN-77
	Support for DEC FORTRAN for OpenVMS VAX extensions
VAX MACRO	Supported on VAX computers running under the OpenVMS operating system
	Supports large instruction set

Table E.2 *Supported OpenVMS Languages (Continued)*

Language	Characteristics
MACRO-32 Compiler	Available on OpenVMS Alpha systems
	Used for porting existing VAX MACRO code to an Alpha system
MACRO-64 Assembler	Available on OpenVMS Alpha systems
	RISC assembly language
DEC Pascal	Supports ANSI-standard Pascal
	Supports enhanced character instruction sets and OpenVMS virtual memory

E.6   Bug Clinic: Detecting Programming Errors

Each of the compilers supplied by Digital provides debugging facilities as well as helpful, verbose, contextual error messages. For example, with the SAMPLE.PAS file, you might have typed the following *incorrect* version of the program:

```
(*
This is a sample Pascal program (with a bug!).
*)
program buggy (output);
begin
    writeln (Hello, world!');
end.
```

This version of SAMPLE.PAS (called BUGGY.PAS) has a missing apostrophe. To find bugs, you can compile the source file with the /LIST qualifier. For example, you could compile BUGGY.PAS by typing

```
$ pascal/list buggy

        writeln (Hello, world!');
.................^
%PASCAL-E-UNDECLID, Undeclared identifier HELLO
at line number 6 in file PACK2:[YOURGROUP.YOU]BUGGY.PAS;1

        writeln (Hello, world!');
........................^
%PASCAL-E-UNDECLID, Undeclared identifier WORLD
at line number 6 in file PACK2:[YOURGROUP.YOU]BUGGY.PAS;1
```

```
        writeln (Hello, world!');
.........................^
%PASCAL-E-SYNASCII, Illegal ASCII character
at line number 6 in file PACK2:[YOURGROUP.YOU]BUGGY.PAS;1

        writeln (Hello, world!');
.................................^
%PASCAL-E-QUOBEFEOL, Quoted string not terminated before end
of line
at line number 6 in file PACK2:[YOURGROUP.YOU]BUGGY.PAS;1

        writeln (Hello, world!');
............................^
%PASCAL-E-SYNSEMMODI, Syntax: ";", "::" , "^", "." or "["
expected
at line number 6 in file PACK2:[YOURGROUP.YOU]BUGGY.PAS;1
%PASCAL-E-ENDDIAGS, PASCAL completed with 5 diagnostics
$
```

BUGGY.LIS appears in the current directory. This file cross-references the
machine code, virtual memory addresses, and your assembly language source
text. It also provides the symbol table for any labels used in the program. In
addition, it shows how the compiled program (the .OBJ version) has been
organized. To see this, you would type

```
$ type buggy.lis
BUGGY               Source Code Listing        18-JAN-1998 14:4
5:13    DEC Pascal V5.2-19                      Page   1
01                                              17-JAN-1998 23:3
6:57    PACK2:[YOURGROUP.YOU]BUGGY.PAS;1
IDC-PL-SL
  C  0  0    1 (*
  C  0  0    2 This is a sample Pascal program (with a bug!).
  C  0  0    3 *)
     0  0    4 program buggy (output);
     0  0    5 begin
     0  1    6         writeln (Hello, world!');
                      ..................1......2....34..5
%PASCAL-E-UNDECLID, (1) Undeclared identifier HELLO

%PASCAL-E-UNDECLID, (2) Undeclared identifier WORLD

%PASCAL-E-SYNASCII, (3) Illegal ASCII character

%PASCAL-E-SYNSEMMODI, (4) Syntax: ";", "::" , "^", "." or "[" expected

%PASCAL-E-QUOBEFEOL, (5) Quoted string not terminated before end of line

     0  0             7 end.
 ..
  .
  .
  .
```

You can use the /DEBUG qualifier to invoke a debugger program. For example, you could type

```
$ pascal/debug buggy.pas
```

The /DEBUG qualifier invokes the debugger after program execution has been interrupted by either a Ctrl/Y or Ctrl/C. For more information about /DEBUG, type

```
$ help debug
```

References

Peters, J. F. *The Art of Assembly Language Programming VAX-11.* Englewood Cliffs, N.J.: Prentice-Hall, 1985.

Peters, J. F. *Pascal with Program Design.* New York: Holt, Rinehart, and Winston, 1986.

Digital Equipment Corporation, POB CS2008, Nashua, NH 03061:

Printed Documentation	*OpenVMS DCL Dictionary: A–M*
	OpenVMS DCL Dictionary: N–Z
	OpenVMS Debugger Manual (V6.1 and V7.0)
	OpenVMS Linker Utility Manual
	OpenVMS Programming Environment Manual
	OpenVMS Software Overview
On-Line Documentation	OpenVMS On-Line Help Facility
	OpenVMS Bookreader
	http://www.openvms.digital.com

Appendix F
Character Sets

Table F.1 *ASCII Character Set*

Char	Dec	Octal	Hex	Char	Dec	Octal	Hex	Char	Dec	Octal	Hex
Nul	0	0	0	+	43	53	2B	V	86	126	56
^A	1	1	1	,	44	54	2C	W	87	127	57
^B	2	2	2	-	45	55	2D	X	88	130	58
^C	3	3	3	.	46	56	2E	Y	89	131	59
^D	4	4	4	/	47	57	2F	Z	90	132	5A
^E	5	5	5	0	48	60	30	[	91	133	5B
^F	6	6	6	1	49	61	31	\	92	134	5C
bell	7	7	7	2	50	62	32	]	93	135	5D
bksp	8	10	8	3	51	63	33	^	94	136	5E
tab	9	11	9	4	52	64	34	_	95	137	5F
lnfeed	10	12	A	5	53	65	35	`	96	140	60
vtab	11	13	B	6	54	66	36	a	97	141	61
ff	12	14	C	7	55	67	37	b	98	142	62
cr	13	15	D	8	56	70	38	c	99	143	63
^N	14	16	E	9	57	71	39	d	100	144	64
^O	15	17	F	:	58	72	3A	e	101	145	65
^P	16	20	10	;	59	73	3B	f	102	146	66
^Q	17	21	11	<	60	74	3C	g	103	147	67
^R	18	22	12	=	61	75	3D	h	104	150	68

Table F.1   *ASCII Character Set (Continued)*

Char	Dec	Octal	Hex	Char	Dec	Octal	Hex	Char	Dec	Octal	Hex
^S	19	23	13	>	62	76	3E	i	105	151	69
^T	20	24	14	?	63	77	3F	j	106	152	6A
^U	21	25	15	@	64	100	40	k	107	153	6B
^V	22	26	16	A	65	101	41	l	108	154	6C
^W	23	27	17	B	66	102	42	m	109	155	6D
^X	24	30	18	C	67	103	43	n	110	156	6E
^Y	25	31	19	D	68	104	44	o	111	157	6F
^Z	26	32	1A	E	69	105	45	p	112	160	70
ESC	27	33	1B	F	70	106	46	q	113	161	71
FS	28	34	1C	G	71	107	47	r	114	162	72
GS	29	35	1D	H	72	110	48	s	115	163	73
RS	30	36	1E	I	73	111	49	t	116	164	74
US	31	37	1F	J	74	112	4A	u	117	165	75
space	32	40	20	K	75	113	4B	v	118	166	76
!	33	41	21	L	76	114	4C	w	119	167	77
"	34	42	22	M	77	115	4D	x	120	170	78
#	35	43	23	N	78	116	4E	y	121	171	79
$	36	44	24	O	79	117	4F	z	122	172	7A
%	37	45	25	P	80	120	50	{	123	173	7B
&	38	46	26	Q	81	121	51			124	174	7C
'	39	47	27	R	82	122	52	}	125	175	7D
(	40	50	28	S	83	123	53	~	126	176	7E
)	41	51	29	T	84	124	54	del	127	177	7F
*	42	52	2A	U	85	125	55				

Table F.2 *DCL Character Set*

Symbol	Symbol Name	Meaning
@	At sign	Execute procedure command.
:	Colon	Device name delimiter in a file specification. A double colon (::) is used as a node name delimiter.
/	Slash	Qualifier prefix.
+	Plus sign	Parameter separator or parameter concatenator with some commands. Also, can be used as a string concatenation operator, unary plus sign, and addition operator in a numeric expression.
,	Comma	Parameter or argument list separator.
-	Hyphen	Command continuation character. Also, can be used as a string reduction operator, unary minus sign, subtraction operator in numeric expressions, and directory searching wildcard character.
( )	Parentheses	Argument list delimiter. Used to indicate the order of operations in a numeric expression.
[ ]	Square brackets	Directory name delimiters in a file specification. Equivalent to angle brackets.
< >	Angle brackets	Directory name delimiters in a file specification. Equivalent to square brackets.
?	Question mark	Help character.
&	Ampersand	Execution-time substitution operator. Normally a reserved special character.
\	Backslash	Reserved special character.
=	Equal sign	Separates a qualifier name from its argument. Used as an assignment statement when defining symbols.
^	Circumflex (Caret)	Reserved special character.
#	Number sign	Reserved special character.
'	Apostrophe	Substitution operator.
.	Period	Subdirectory delimiter. Used as a file type and version number delimiter in file specifications.
;	Semicolon	Version number delimiter in a file specification.
%	Percent sign	Wildcard character in a file specification.
!	Exclamation point	Comment character.
"	Quotation mark	Literal string delimiter.
$	Dollar sign	Default DCL command prompt. Used in DCL command procedures as a start-of-command-line designator.

Appendix G
ANSI Mode Control Sequences

This appendix describes each control sequence recognized by a VT200 or VT100 terminal in ANSI mode. Many of the sequences described in this appendix conform to the basic format, as specified by the ANSI X3.64 standard.

G.1   Syntax for Control Sequences

The syntax for control sequences is

ESC [*Ps/Pn* F

ESC [is the lead-in sequence as specified by the ANSI standard. Sometimes it is referred to as the *control sequence indicator. Ps* refers to a selective parameter; *Pn* refers to a numeric parameter. Some sequences use selective parameters, and others use numeric parameters, the two never are used together. If the *Ps* or *Pn* value is not specified, the default value is assumed. *F* is the termination character of the sequence. It specifies the function to be performed. This character varies with each function.

G.2   Define the Scrolling Region

The command syntax is

ESC [*x;y* **r**

This command is used to set the top and bottom lines of the screen-scrolling region. The lines on the screen are numbered 1 through 24. The first numeric parameter, *x,* sets the top boundary. The second numeric parameter, *y,* sets the bottom boundary of the scrolling region. The default values are the entire screen (that is, *x* = 1 and *y* = 24).

G.3   Move a Single Character

The command syntax is

ESC [*Pn* **F**

By using a single control sequence, the cursor can be moved any number of increments up, down, right, or left. The numeric parameter specifies how many increments the cursor is to move; the default value is 1. The value of the termination character (F) determines the direction of movement, as specified in Table G.1.

G.4   Absolute Cursor Positioning

The command syntax is

ESC [*x;y* **H**

or

ESC [*x;y* **f**

Either of these control sequences can be used for positioning the cursor on an absolute basis. These sequences will position the cursor to the line specified by x and the column specified by y. The default value for both x and y is 1.

G.5   Index

The command syntax is

ESC D

This sequence causes the cursor to move down one position. If the cursor is positioned on the bottom line of the screen or the bottom of the screen scrolling region, the contents of the screen or scrolling region will scroll up one line.

Table G.1 *Cursor Control Commands*

Command Name	F Value	Control Sequence
Cursor up	A	**ESC [** *Pn* **A**
Cursor down	B	**ESC [** *Pn* **B**
Cursor right	C	**ESC [** *Pn* **C**
Cursor left	D	**ESC [** *Pn* **D**

G.6 Reverse Index

The command syntax is

ESC M

This sequence causes the cursor to move up one position. If the cursor is positioned on the top of the screen or the top of the scrolling region, the contents of the screen or scrolling region will scroll down one line.

G.7 Next Line

The command syntax is

ESC E

This sequence causes the cursor to move to the beginning of the next line. If the cursor is positioned on the bottom line of the screen or the bottom of the screen scrolling region, the contents of the screen or scrolling region will scroll up one line.

G.8 Erasure Commands

The command syntax is

ESC [Ps F

The same control sequence format is used for all erasure commands. The termination character, (F), determines whether erasure will occur on a line or screen basis. The selective parameter, (Ps), determines the portion of the line or screen to be erased, as seen in Table G.2. In all cases, erasure commands do not cause the cursor to move.

Table G.2 *Erasure Commands*

Command Name	F Value	Ps Value	Control Sequence
From the cursor to the end of the line	K	0, or none	**ESC [0 K**
From the beginning of the line to the cursor	K	1	**ESC [1 K**
The entire line containing the cursor	K	2	**ESC [2 K**
From the cursor to the end of the screen	J	0, or none	**ESC [0 J**
From the beginning of the screen to the cursor	J	1	**ESC [1 J**
The entire screen	J	2	ESC [2 J

G.9   Change the Line to Single Height and Single Width

The command syntax is

ESC #5

This command will cause all characters displayed on the line marked by the cursor to be single height and single width.

G.10   Change the Line to Single Height and Double Width

The command syntax is

ESC #6

This command cause all characters displayed on the line marked by the cursor to be single height and double width. If the line previously was single height and single width, all characters from the middle of the line to the end of the line are lost. The cursor remains at the same character position unless the character position is lost, in which case, the cursor is moved to the right margin.

G.11   Change the Line to Double Height and Double Width

The command syntax is

ESC #3

and

ESC #4

These two commands are used as a pair, on adjacent lines, from double-height and double-width characters. The same character must be sent to the same column of both lines to form each character. If the line previously was single height and single width, all characters from the middle of the line to the end of the line are lost. The cursor remains at the same character position unless the character position is lost, in which case, the cursor is moved to the right margin.

G.12   Video Attribute Commands

Data on the screen can be displayed in any combination of the following video attributes: high intensity, underline, blink, or reverse video.

The attributes are cumulative. Data received will be displayed according to all the attributes enabled. The control sequence format for enabling video attributes is

ESC `[Ps;Ps;...Psm`

where *Ps;Ps; . . . Ps* is the parameter string defining which video attributes to enable. If multiple video attributes are to be enabled with one control sequence, use a semicolon to separate each selective parameter in the sequence. Table G.3 summarizes all the video attributes and their associated selective parameters.

Table G.3 *Video Attribute Commands*

Attribute	Selective Parameter	Control Sequence
Attributes OFF	0 (default)	**ESC [M**
High intensity	1	**ESC [1M**
Underline	4	**ESC [4M**
Blink	5	**ESC [5M**
Reverse video	7	**ESC [7M**

Appendix H
DECTPU Programming Language

DECTPU programming language can be viewed as the most basic component of DECTPU. To access the features of DECTPU, you can use the EVE editor or write a program in the DECTPU language and then use the utility to compile and execute the program. A program written in DECTPU can be as simple as a single statement or as complex as the section file that implements EVE.

The block-structured DECTPU language is easy to learn and use. DECTPU language features include a large number of data types, relational operators, error interception, looping and case statements, and built-in procedures that simplify development or extension of an editor or application. Comments are indicated with a single comment character, an exclamation point (!), so that you can document your procedures easily. There also are capabilities for debugging procedures with user-written debugging programs.

DECTPU runs on the OpenVMS VAX and OpenVMS Alpha operating systems and supports screen-oriented editing on the VT400-, VT300-, VT200-, and VT100-series terminals, as well as on other video display terminals that respond to ANSI control functions.

This appendix discusses some of the basic components of the DECTPU language. To learn more about the DECTPU language refer to the reference material listed at the end of the appendix.

H.1   DECTPU Features

DECTPU aids application and system programmers in developing tools that manipulate text. Special features that DECTPU provides are

▶ Multiple buffers, windows, and subprocesses

▶ Keystroke and buffer-change journaling

▶ Text processing in batch mode

- ▶ Insert and overstrike text entry
- ▶ Free or bound cursor motion
- ▶ Learn sequences
- ▶ Pattern matching
- ▶ Key definition
- ▶ Procedural language
- ▶ Callable interface

H.2   Data Types

The DECTPU language has an extensive set of data types. A data type is a group of elements that *belong together*. The elements are formed in the same way and treated consistently. A variable's data type determines the operations that can be performed on it.

You can use data types to interpret the meaning of the contents of a variable. Unlike many languages, DECTPU language has no declarative statement to enforce which data type is assigned to a variable. A variable in DECTPU assumes a data type when it is used in an assignment statement. For example, the following statement assigns a string type to the variable *this_var*:

```
this_var:='Can be any string of characters';
```

Table H.1 lists those keywords that represent the DECTPU data types.

H.3   Language Declarations and Statements

A DECTPU program can consist of a sequence of declarations and statements. These declarations and statements control the action performed in a procedure or a program. Table H.2 describes the reserved words that are the language elements that when combined properly make up the declarations and statements of DECTPU.

H.4   Lexical Elements

DECTPU programs are composed of lexical elements. A lexical element may be an individual character, such as an arithmetic operator, or a group of characters, such as an identifier. Table H.3 describes the available DECTPU lexical elements.

Table H.1 *Data Types*

Type	Definition
ARRAY	A structure for storing and manipulating a group of elements
BUFFER	A work space for manipulating text
INTEGER	DECTPU performs only integer arithmetic
KEYWORD	Reserved words that have special meaning to the DECTPU compiler
LEARN	A collection of DECTPU keystrokes for later use
MARKER	A reference in a buffer
PATTERN	A structure used when searching for text in a buffer
PROCESS	Built-in procedure that returns a value of the process data type
PROGRAM	The compiled form of a sequence of DECTPU procedures and executable statements
RANGE	Contains all the text between (and including) two markers
STRING	Used to represent character data. Use double quotations ("") or single quotations (' ') as the delimiter for a string
UNSPECIFIED	The initial value of a variable after it has been compiled
WIDGET	DECWindows version of DECTPU provides the widget data type to support DECWindows widgets
WINDOW	The portion of the screen that displays as much of the text buffer as will fit in the screen area

H.5   Case Sensitivity of Characters

The DECTPU compiler does not distinguish between uppercase and lowercase characters except when they appear as part of a quoted string. For example, the word EDITOR has the same meaning when written in any of the following ways:

```
EDITOR
EditOR
editor
```

The following quoted strings, however, represent different values:

```
"XYZ"
"xyz"
```

Table H.2 *Declaration and Statements*

Type	Reserved Word
Module declaration	MODULE, IDENT, ENDMODULE
Procedure declaration	PROCEDURE, ENDPROCEDURE
Repetitive statement	LOOP, EXITIF, ENDLOOP
Conditional statement	IF, THEN, ELSE, ENDIF
Case statement	CASE, FROM, TO, INRANGE, OUTRANGE, ENDCASE
Error statement	ON_ERROR, ENDON_ERROR
Return statement	RETURN
Abort statement	ABORT
Miscellaneous declarations	EQUIVALENCE, LOCAL, CONSTANT, VARIABLE

H.6   Creating DECTPU Programs

When writing a DECTPU program, keep the following pointers in mind:

▶ A program can be a single executable statement or a collection of executable statements.

▶ You can use executable statements either within procedures or outside procedures. You must place all procedure declarations before any executable statements that are not in procedures.

▶ You can enter DECTPU statements from within EVE by using the EVE command TPU.

H.7   Program Syntax

You can write your own procedures that combine DECTPU language statements and calls and DECTPU built-in procedures. DECTPU procedures can return values and can be recursive.

The rules for writing DECTPU programs are simple. When writing a procedure, use the following guidelines:

▶ Begin each procedure with the word *PROCEDURE*, followed by the procedure name of your choice.

▶ End each procedure with the word *ENDPROCEDURE*.

Table H.3 *Lexical Elements*

Element	Definition
Character set	Use the /CHARACTER_SET qualifier to specify the character set that you want DECTPU to use when first invoked. Those character sets that can be used are DEC Multinational Character Set, ISO_LATIN1 Character Set, General or TPU$CHARACTER_SET (refer to the DCL HELP topic for this logical name).
Identifiers	Used to name programs, procedures, keywords, and variables. They can be a combination of alphabetic characters, digits, dollar signs, and underscores and can not be any more than 132 characters long. No spaces or symbols can be used.
Variables	Storage locations that hold values. There are two types, global and local.
Constants	Can be integers, strings, or keywords that consist of one or more characters.
Operators	Refer to Table H.4 for list of DECTPU operators.
Expressions	Can be a constant, variable, procedure, or any combination of the three. Expressions frequently are used within DECTPU conditional language statements.
Reserved words	Defined by DECTPU and have a special meaning for the compiler. DECTPU reserved words can be divided into the following categories: keywords, built-in procedure names, predefined constants, and declarations and statements.
Lexical keywords	Lexical keywords can be split into two groups, conditional compilation and radix of numeric constants. Conditional compilation lexical keywords are used in a manner similar to ordinary IF/THEN/ELSE/ENDIF statements. Radix of numeric constants are constants specified as binary, octal, hexadecimal, and decimal.

▶ Place a semicolon after each statement or built-in call that is followed by another statement or call. Otherwise, the semicolon is not necessary.

▶ All procedure declarations that are not part of a procedure declaration must be placed before any executable statements.

The syntax for a DECTPU program might be

```
PROCEDURE
  .
  .
  .
ENDPROCEDURE
```

```
PROCEDURE;
.

.

.
ENDPROCEDURE;
.

.

.
PROCEDURE
.

.

.
ENDPROCEDURE;
statement 1;
statement 2;
.

.

.
statement n;
```

H.8   Simple versus Complex DECTPU Programs

A DECTPU program can be classified as either simple or complex. A simple program could be a single executable statement, such as

```
! This program consists of a single DECTPU built-in procedure.
show(summary)
```

DECTPU programs are classified as complex programs if they contain several executable statements. Avoid the following programming practices when writing complex DECTPU programs:

▶ Creating large procedures

▶ Creating large numbers of procedures

▶ Including a large number of executable statements that are not within procedures

These practices, if carried to extremes, can cause the parser stack to overflow.

An example of a complex program might be,

```
!EDT2-Return Key
!
PROCEDURE edt2$return
local left_margin;
left_margin: = get_info (current_buffer, "left_margin");
split_line;
if mark    (none = end_of (current_buffer))
```

```
then
   move_vertical (-1);
endif;
edt$indent_line_to (left_margin);
ENDPROCEDURE;
```

The source files that implement the EVE editor are additional examples of a complex DECTPU program. The EVE source code files are located at

Table H.4 *Operators*

Type	Symbol	Function
Arithmetic	+	Addition, unary plus
	−	Subtraction, unary minus
	?	Multiplication
	/	Division
String	+	String concatenation
	−	String reduction
	*	String replication
Relational	<>	Not equal to
	=	Equal to
	<	Less than
	<=	Less than or equal to
	>	Greater than
	>=	Greater than or equal to
Pattern			Pattern alternation
	@	Partial pattern assignment
	+	Pattern concatenation
	&	Pattern linkage
Logical	AND	Boolean AND
	NOT	Boolean NOT
	OR	Boolean OR
	XOR	Boolean OR

SYS$EXAMPLES:EVE$*.*. You can examine these files to learn the programming techniques that were used to create EVE.

H.9   Compiling DECTPU Programs

Before compiling programs in DECTPU, enable the display of informational messages to help you locate errors. EVE automatically enables the display of informational messages for you when you use the EXTEND EVE command. For more information on displaying messages, see the description of the SET (INFORMATIONAL) built-in procedure in the *DEC Text Processing Utility Reference Manual.*

The DECTPU compiler numbers the lines of code it compiles. The line numbers begin with 1. For a string, all DECTPU statements are considered to be on line 1. For a range, line 1 is the first line of the range, regardless of where in the buffer the range begins. Buffers are numbered starting at the first line. When a compilation error occurs, DECTPU tells you the approximate line number where the error occurred. To move to the line that caused the error, use the POSITION (integer) built-in procedure.

In EVE, you can use the LINE command. For example, the command LINE 42 moves the editing point and the cursor to line 42. To see DECTPU messages while in EVE, use the BUFFER MESSAGES command. To return to the original buffer or buffer of your choice, use the BUFFER *name-of-buffer* command.

There are two ways to compile a program in DECTPU: on the command line of EVE or in a DECTPU buffer.

H.9.1   Compiling on the EVE Command Line

You can compile a simple DECTPU program by entering it on the EVE command line. For example, if you use the TPU command and then enter the SHOW (SUMMARY) statement, DECTPU compiles and executes the program associated with the SHOW (SUMMARY) statement.

H.9.2   Compiling in a DECTPU Buffer

DECTPU programs usually are compiled by entering DECTPU procedures and statements in a buffer and then compiling the buffer. If you are using EVE, you can enter the following program

```
!
!
!EDT2—Return Key
```

```
!
PROCEDURE edt2$return
local left_margin;
left_margin: = get_info (current_buffer, "left_margin");
split_line;
if mark      (none = end_of (current_buffer)
then
    move_vertical (-1);
endif;
edt$indent_line_to (left_margin);
ENDPROCEDURE;
```

in a buffer and compile the buffer by using the TPU command and entering the following statement after the prompt:

compile (current_buffer);

If no error messages are issued while you compile the *current buffer,* you can invoke it with the name *edt2$return,* using the following statement:

execute (edt2$return);

DECTPU first compiles and then executes the buffer, range, or string if used as a parameter for the EXECUTE built-in procedure.

H.10   Debugging DECTPU Programs

To debug DECTPU programs, you can write your own debugger in the DECTPU language or use the DECTPU debugger provided in TPU$DEBUG.TPU. If an error occurs, you may find it helpful to display error line numbers by using SET (LINE_NUMBER, ON). It also may be beneficial to display those procedures called when an error occurs by using SET (TRACEBACK, ON). Refer to the reference section found in this appendix for further information on debugging DECTPU programs.

H.11   Additional DECTPU Program Examples

The following two procedures are additional examples of using the DECTPU language.

H.11.1   Example 1

```
!
!
!EDT2-Capitalize String
!
```

```
!
! Capitalize a string-like change_case (string, capital)
! would be. Ignore leading punctuation, so things like "Hi"
! and (foo) can be capitalized.
!
! Parameters
!
!     cap_stringstring to be capitalized-input/output
PROCEDURE edt2$capitalize_string (cap_string)
local initial_letter,      ! initial substring ending at
      ! first letter
      initial_index,       ! Loop index used in search for
          ! first letter
      cap_string_length,   ! Length of cap_string parameter
      rest_of_string;      ! Remainder of cap_string after
          ! initial_letter
initial_index := 1;
cap_string_length := length (cap_string);
loop
     initial_letter := substr (cap_string, 1, initial_index);
     exitif initial_index = cap_string_length;
     exitif index (edt$x_not_alphabetic,
         substr (cap_string, initial_index, 1)) = 0;
     initial_index := initial_index + 1
endloop;
rest_of_string := substr (cap_string, initial_index + 1,
     cap_string_length);
change_case (initial_letter, upper);
change_case (rest_of_string, lower);
cap_string := initial_letter + rest_of_string;
ENDPROCEDURE;
```

H.11.2 Example 2

```
!
!
! EDT2 - Set Status Line
!
!
PRODECURE edt2$set_status_line
local model_string,
      left_margin,
      right_margin,
      wrap_string,
      margin_string,
      direction_string;
if   (current_buffer = dcl_buffer) or
     (current_buffer = paste_buffer)
then
```

```
                this_filespec :=
                    get_info (current_buffer, "name") + "Buffer";
                set (status_line, current_window, reverse,
                this_filespec);
                return;
        else
                this_filespec :=
                    get_info (current_buffer, "output_file");
                if    this_filespec = 0
                then
                      this_filespec := edt$empty;
                endif;
                this_filespec := "File: " + this_filespec;
        endif;
        if    length (this_filespec) > 43
        then
                this_buffer_label := substr (this_filespec, 1, 43);
        else
                this_buffer_label := this_filespec +
                    substr (edt$x_extra_spaces, 1,43 - length
                                              (this_filespec));
        endif;
        if    get_info (current_buffer, "mode") = INSERT
        then
                mode_string := | INS |";
        else
                mode_string := " | Ovstr |";
        endif;
                !
                ! Find out if the user is in Overstrike or Insert Mode.
                !
        if    (current_window = top_window) or
              (current_window = main_window)
        then
                if    edt$x_first_window_wordwrap <> 0
        then
                      wrap_string := " Wrap |";
                else
                      wrap_string := " No Wrap |";
                endif
                if    edt$x_secd_window_wordwrap <> 0
                then
                      wrap-string := " Wrap |";
                else
                      wrap_string := " NoWrap |";
                endif;
        endif;
        if    get_info (current_buffer, "direction") = REVERSE
        then
```

```
        direction_string := " Rev | ";
else
        direction_string := "Fwd | ";
endif;
    !
    ! Find out if the user is moving up or down the screen.
    !
left_margin := str (get_info (current_buffer,
"left_margin"));
right_margin := str (get_info (current_buffer,
"right_margin"));
margin_string := "M[" + left_margin + ","
    + right_margin + "]";
    !
    ! Find out what the current margins settings are.
    !
set (status_line, current_window, reverse,
    this_buffer_label + mode_string + wrap_string +
        direction_string + margin_string;
    !
    ! Print out status line on screen for the associated
    ! window.
    !
ENDPROCEDURE;
```

References

Digital Equipment Corporation, POB CS2008, Nashua, NH 03061:

Printed Documentation   *DEC Text Processing Utility Reference Manual*
                             Guide to the DEC Text Processing Utility
                             OpenVMS Software Overview

On-Line Documentation   OpenVMS On-Line Help Facility
                             OpenVMS Bookreader
                             http://www.openvms.digital.com

Index

Other Books from Digital Press

Introduction to OpenVMS, Fifth Edition by Lesley Ogilvie Rice
November 1998   300pp   pb   1-55558-194-3

OpenVMS and the Internet by Terence P. Sherlock
December 1998   400pp   pb   1-55558-196-X

OpenVMS Alpha Internals: Scheduling and Process Control by Ruth E. Goldenberg
1997   672pp   pb   1-55558-156-0

OpenVMS Operating System Concepts, Second Edition by David Miller
1997   550pp   pb   1-55558-157-9

OpenVMS Performance Management, Second Edition by Joginder Sethi
September 1998   300pp   pb   1-55558-206-0

OpenVMS System Management Guide by Lawrence Baldwin
1995   416pp   pb   1-55558-143-9

UNIX for OpenVMS Users, Second Edition by Philip Bourne
September 1998   450pp   pb   1-55558-155-2

Writing Real Programs in DCL, Second Edition by Paul Anagnostopoulos
November 1998   500pp   pb   1-55558-191-9

. . . .

Feel free to visit our web site at: http://www.bh.com/digitalpress

These books are available from all good bookstores or in case of difficulty call:
1-800-366-2665 in the U.S. or +44-1865-310366 in Europe.

E-MAIL MAILING LIST

An e-mail mailing list giving information on latest releases, special promotions, offers and other news relating to Digital Press titles is available. To subscribe, send an e-mail message to majordomo@world.std.com.
Include in message body (not in subject line): subscribe digital-press